"How often have you had the opportunity to follow a scholar and thinker's transformation from academic psychologist and laboratory researcher to psychoanalyst? Never, I wager. But that fascinating thread of development is just the beginning of what you will find here. Neil Skolnick uses the theme of temporality to examine the development of his own substantial contributions to the field, offering introductions that contextualize each chapter in psychoanalytic history. In the process he gives us a compelling account of the development of relational psychoanalysis. If you want to grasp the relational turn, follow the thread of Skolnick's work. He has been there for all of it."

Donnel Stern, Ph.D., William Alanson White Institute and NYU Postdoctoral Program in Psychotherapy and Psychoanalysis

"In this scholarly, lucid and compelling volume, Neil Skolnick takes on a range of topics that he creatively links to the overarching theme of time. This fascinating theme has rarely been explored from a relational psychoanalytic perspective. Yet time silently shapes much of our experience within and outside the analytic encounter. Skolnick enacts something of time's complex effect by tracing the evolution of his own professional thinking across the broad sweep of his career, from his beginnings as a doctoral research candidate. He leaves us in the present, where he muses about the limits of relational theory. En route, Skolnick moves across a range of conceptual dimensions and clinical issues. He challenges and re-sculpts existing psychoanalytic wisdom about several issues. One chapter, for example, offers a new take on Fairbairn by proposing the existence of an unconscious good object, something of an oxymoron in traditional Fairbairnian thinking. In a chapter on the use of the couch, Skolnick again challenges our traditional understanding by arguing against a perspective linking the couch tightly with 'true' analysis.

Skolnick's broad and measured book is thick with personal, clinical and theoretical reflections that push the reader to think outside the box. It invites the reader 'in' and invites us to theorize hard and question hard. A pleasure to have a new book from such a creative clinician and thinker."

Joyce Slochower, Ph.D., NYU Postdoctoral Program in Psychoanalysis and Psychotherapy

"Neil Skolnick's *Relational Psychoanalysis and Temporality* is really several fascinating books in one. Written in an accessible, scholarly yet unburdened way, Skolnick takes an essential axis in psychoanalytic theory, temporality, and weaves it through the fabric of clinical work and the evolution of contemporary psychoanalytic theory. Skolnick offers a rich understanding of the relationship between patient and analyst's internal objects and the unique intersubjective field. Finally, readers will also discover a sophisticated historical view of the history of ideas and concepts developed within the relational tradition. It is an imaginative journey filled with appreciation and criticism of relational theory, inspiring questions about our next turns in psychoanalytic theory."

Steven H. Cooper, Ph.D., Associate Professor
in Psychiatry, Harvard Medical School

Relational Psychoanalysis and Temporality

In *Relational Psychoanalysis and Temporality*, Neil J. Skolnick takes us on a journey that traces his personal evolution from a graduate student through to his career as a relational psychoanalyst. Skolnick uniquely shares his publications and presentations that span his professional career, weaving in issues around temporality and relational psychoanalysis.

Accessible and deeply thought-provoking, this book explores the many ways our lives are pervaded and shaped by time, and how it infuses the problems that psychoanalysts work with in the consulting room. Skolnick begins each chapter with an introduction, contextualizing the papers in his own evolution as a relational analyst as well as in the broader evolution of the relational conceit in the psychoanalytic field. Following an incisive description of the realities and mysteries of time, he highlights how psychoanalysts have applied several temporal phenomena to the psychoanalytic process. The papers and presentations address an assortment of time-worn psychoanalytic issues as they have become redefined, reconfigured and re-contextualized by the application of a relational psychoanalytic perspective. It purports to chart the changes in the field and the author's practice as, like many psychoanalysts, Skolnick explains his shifted perspective from classical to ego psychological, to relational psychoanalysis across the trajectory of his career. Finally, the author struggles to understand the contributions of time to the process of change in psychoanalytic thought and practice. This book also provides a fascinating guide to how our lives are contextualized in the invisibilities of time, illuminating the most frequent ways time influences psychoanalytic thinking and practice.

Relational Psychoanalysis and Temporality will be of immense interest to psychoanalysts, psychoanalytic psychotherapists and therapists of all persuasions in their practice and training. It should also be of interest to philosophers, historians and scholars of psychoanalysis who have a general interest in studying the role of psychoanalysis in influencing contemporary trends of Western thought.

Neil J. Skolnick, Ph.D., is currently an Associate Clinical Professor at the NYU Postdoctoral Program in Psychoanalysis and Psychoanalytic Psychotherapy. He was previously an Associate Professor of Psychology at the Ferkauf Graduate School of Psychology, Yeshiva University. He currently is also a faculty member and supervisor at the National Institute for the Psychotherapies (NIP) and its affiliates, the Institute for the Psychoanalytic Study of Subjectivity (IPSS) and the National Training Program (NTP). He is faculty and supervisor at the Westchester Center for the Study of Psychoanalysis and Psychotherapy (WCSPP). He maintains a private practice in psychoanalysis and supervision in Manhattan.

RELATIONAL PERSPECTIVES BOOK SERIES

LEWIS ARON, ADRIENNE HARRIS,
STEVEN KUCHUCK & EYAL ROZMARIN
Series Editors

The Relational Perspectives Book Series (RPBS) publishes books that grow out of or contribute to the relational tradition in contemporary psychoanalysis. The term *relational psychoanalysis* was first used by Greenberg and Mitchell[1] to bridge the traditions of interpersonal relations, as developed within interpersonal psychoanalysis and object relations, as developed within contemporary British theory. But, under the seminal work of the late Stephen A. Mitchell, the term *relational psychoanalysis* grew and began to accrue to itself many other influences and developments. Various tributaries—interpersonal psychoanalysis, object relations theory, self psychology, empirical infancy research, and elements of contemporary Freudian and Kleinian thought—flow into this tradition, which understands relational configurations between self and others, both real and fantasied, as the primary subject of psychoanalytic investigation.

We refer to the relational tradition, rather than to a relational school, to highlight that we are identifying a trend, a tendency within contemporary psychoanalysis, not a more formally organized or coherent school or system of beliefs. Our use of the term *relational* signifies a dimension of theory and practice that has become salient across the wide spectrum of contemporary psychoanalysis. Now under the editorial supervision of Lewis Aron, Adrienne Harris, Steven Kuchuck and Eyal Rozmarin, the Relational Perspectives Book Series originated in 1990 under the editorial eye of the late Stephen A. Mitchell. Mitchell was the most prolific and influential of the originators of the relational tradition. Committed to dialogue among psychoanalysts, he abhorred the authoritarianism that dictated adherence to a rigid set of beliefs or technical restrictions. He championed open discussion, comparative and integrative approaches, and promoted new voices across the generations.

Included in the Relational Perspectives Book Series are authors and works that come from within the relational tradition, extend and develop that tradition, as well as works that critique relational approaches or compare and contrast it with alternative points of view. The series includes our most distinguished senior psychoanalysts, along with younger contributors who bring fresh vision. A full list of titles in this series is available at https://www.routledge.com/mentalhealth/series/LEARPBS.

1 Greenberg, J. & Mitchell, S. (1983). *Object relations in psychoanalytic theory*. Cambridge, MA: Harvard University Press.

Relational Psychoanalysis and Temporality

Time Out of Mind

Neil J. Skolnick

LONDON AND NEW YORK

First published 2020
by Routledge
2 Park Square, Milton Park, Abingdon, Oxon OX14 4RN

and by Routledge
52 Vanderbilt Avenue, New York, NY 10017

Routledge is an imprint of the Taylor & Francis Group, an informa business

© 2020 Neil J. Skolnick

The right of Neil J. Skolnick to be identified as author of this work
has been asserted by him in accordance with sections 77 and 78 of
the Copyright, Designs and Patents Act 1988.

All rights reserved. No part of this book may be reprinted or
reproduced or utilised in any form or by any electronic, mechanical,
or other means, now known or hereafter invented, including
photocopying and recording, or in any information storage or
retrieval system, without permission in writing from the publishers.

Trademark notice: Product or corporate names may be trademarks
or registered trademarks, and are used only for identification and
explanation without intent to infringe.

British Library Cataloguing-in-Publication Data
A catalogue record for this book is available from the British Library

Library of Congress Cataloguing-in-Publication Data
Names: Skolnick, Neil J., author.
Title: Relational psychoanalysis and temporality : time out of mind /
    Neil J. Skolnick.
Description: Abingdon, Oxon ; New York, NY : Routledge, 2019. |
    Includes bibliographical references and index.
Identifiers: LCCN 2019013065 (print) | LCCN 2019017602 (ebook)
    | ISBN 9780429281075 (Master eBook) | ISBN 9780367236595
    (hardback) | ISBN 9780367236601 (pbk.)
Subjects: LCSH: Time—Psychological aspects. | Object relations
    (Psychoanalysis) | Interpersonal relations. | Psychoanalysis.
Classification: LCC BF468 (ebook) | LCC BF468 .S54 2019 (print) |
    DDC 153.7/53—dc23
LC record available at https://lccn.loc.gov/2019013065

ISBN: 978-0-367-23659-5 (hbk)
ISBN: 978-0-367-23660-1 (pbk)
ISBN: 978-0-429-28107-5 (ebk)

Typeset in Times New Roman
by Swales & Willis Ltd, Exeter, Devon, UK

DEDICATION

This book is lovingly dedicated to my wife, Karen, and my two daughters, Kate and Amelia. You have all been, each in your own delightful and unique way, my muse.

Contents

	Acknowledgments	xi
	Foreword	xiii
	NANCY MCWILLIAMS	
	Introduction	1
	NEIL J. SKOLNICK	
1	Time out of mind: 2017	9
	NEIL J. SKOLNICK	
2	Vertical transmission of acquired ulcer susceptibility in the rat	
	Introduction	40
	Article: 1980	49
	NEIL J. SKOLNICK, SIGURD H. ACKERMAN, MYRON A. HOFER AND HERBERT WEINER	
3	Secrets in clinical work: A relational point of view	
	Introduction	56
	Article: 1992	61
	NEIL J. SKOLNICK AND JODY MESSLER DAVIES	
4	The good, the bad and the ambivalent: Fairbairn's difficulty locating the good object in the endopsychic structure	
	Introduction	84
	Article: 1998	92
	NEIL J. SKOLNICK	

x   Contents

5   What's a good object to do? A Fairbairnian perspective
    Introduction   112
    Article: 2018   118
    NEIL J. SKOLNICK

6   Termination in psychoanalysis: It's about time
    Introduction   143
    Article: 2010   149
    NEIL J. SKOLNICK

7   Resilience across the lifespan: A confluence of narratives
    Introduction   170
    Article: 2011   177
    NEIL J. SKOLNICK

8   Rethinking the use of the couch: A relational perspective
    Introduction   197
    Article: 2015   202
    NEIL J. SKOLNICK

9   Relational psychoanalysis: An assessment at this time   226
    NEIL J. SKOLNICK

    Index   243

Acknowledgments

I gratefully acknowledge the following people, each of whom has contributed at one time or another to my ability and efforts in creating this book:

Lewis Aron and Adrienne Harris, and their associates, Steven Kuchuck and Eyal Rozmarin, for including this volume in the Relational Perspectives Book Series.

Jill Salberg for encouraging me to turn my ideas, papers and presentations into this book.

My co-authors, editors and co-editors throughout my career, all of whom have made contributions to various papers included in this volume, including Sigurd Ackerman, Neil Altman, George Cicala, Graham Clarke, Jody Messler Davies, Don Grief, Myron Hofer, Ruth Livingston, David Scharff, Paul Stepansky, Susan Warshaw, Herbert Weiner and Marvin Zuckerman.

All those who read portions of this book and provided me with invaluable feedback: Susan Baskin, Michael Garrett, Karen Goldberg and Nancy McWilliams. Also, Jim Fosshage, Kenneth Frank and Dennis Shulman, members of my peer writing group, provided helpful feedback on several of the original versions of the papers appearing in the book.

All my teachers, supervisors, supervisees, students and study group members, far too numerous to mention, with whom I have been fortunate enough to have had contact. You have all enriched my life-long quest for learning and provided me with knowledge of what I did not know.

I would like to call out special mention to one study group in particular that I have been running for about 30 years. The members of this group have come and gone, so I am listing the current members as representatives of them all. They are Leslie Goldstein, Katie Hall, Steven Spitz, Mimi Spiro, Kate Washton and Suzanne Weisman.

I extend my appreciation to the following publishers for allowing me to use previously published papers: Taylor & Francis, The Analytic Press, Routledge, and the American Association for the Advancement of Science (AAAS).

Last but not least, Sabe Basescu, my analyst, who helped me immeasurably to heal and grow.

Foreword

Nancy McWilliams

It is a privilege to introduce readers to Neil Skolnick's meditations on time and mind. In this absorbing volume, the author not only presents his writings chronologically, as is conventional, but also reflects on them in ways that evoke the mysteries of chronology itself. He makes explicit the temporal backdrop of psychological theorizing; periodically, the background becomes the foreground. He invites our attention to coexisting, shifting, then-is-now psychic experiences of time (*Kairos*) as well as to the inexorable march of unrecoverable, linear, mortal time (*Chronos*). His opening essay on time illuminates this organizing construct, highlighting nuances and paradoxes that are both obvious and invisible.

This book is the offering of a seeker, a man who has thought deeply about core human questions throughout a long, generative career. As such, it asks us to accompany him through lived and remembered time on what he would never be so presumptuous as to call, but which I cannot resist framing as, a version of the classic hero's quest: his journey to becoming a relational psychoanalyst of his own definition and individual expression.

Not everyone's personal journey is book-worthy. This one is. It begins – surprisingly for a psychoanalytic excursion – in the psychology laboratory, with rats. Who knew that Neil Skolnick was the first researcher to demonstrate, using an animal model, the intergenerational transmission of separation trauma? Using rigorous experimental methodology, he and his colleagues showed in 1980 that not only does premature separation from caregivers damage young mammals, it damages their eventual offspring as well. The research design itself is a fascinating interweaving of creativity with *Chronos*.

My own prior ignorance of this paradigm-upending study, ignorance I assume is shared by most of my psychoanalytic colleagues, suggests that xiv Foreword

Skolnick's research was simply too radical – its findings too unthinkable – for its time in intellectual history. At a point when genetic investigations had not yet modulated Darwinian orthodoxy, the scientific community was evidently not ready to embrace results that supported a distinctly Lamarckian position. Currently, we know enough about epigenesis to start explaining phenomena which, if viewed only through a Darwinian lens, would have been utterly unaccountable. If this book makes no other impact, I hope it finally affords proper credit to the author's precocious scientific achievement.

Readers should attend not just to the content of these articles, but the process, the evolution of a scholar and a movement over several decades, that they reveal. In the essays, we are invited into the mind of a creative thinker who, over time, becomes not only knowledgeable but also wise. A colleague of mine once noted that we all begin as principalists: We construct our clinical interventions according to the tenets of our chosen or received theory. With experience, we gradually become consequentialists; that is, we make therapeutic choices based on our accumulated subjective understandings of what is, to the best of our knowledge, likely to be their impact on each person we try to help. In Skolnick's early papers, we see him repeatedly in dialogue with his object-relational and ego-psychological forebears (most notably Fairbairn, whom he has studied and written about in great depth), subjecting the principles they had derived from their psychoanalytic era to the clinical challenges of a later time. Although unfailingly respectful toward those who came before him, his critiques are incisive.

In the later essays, Skolnick is less carefully deferential, less concerned with whether the psychoanalytic elders will excommunicate him for heresy, more confident in simply saying how things seem to him. This is another journey most analysts make in some form: We begin with the sense that we must reassure the parental generation that we haven't gone completely off the rails, and then we gradually develop trust in our own clinical experience and instincts, eventually realizing that *we* are now the parental generation. Another trick of time.

With this account of the struggles of one searching intellect toward the deepest levels of emotional honesty, we are privy to an intimate story of the birth and maturation of the relational movement. If Skolnick's community of analytic peers had not been able to articulate their own clinical sensibilities – inspiring one another to increasingly egalitarian, nondefensive, intellectually robust engagement with their psychoanalytic predecessors – Freud's beloved movement may have fragmented into isolated sects or dribbled into obscurity.

As a scholarly discipline, psychoanalysis has always straddled the territory between natural science and hermeneutics, between being a collection of empirically verifiable findings and being a wisdom tradition like those of the great religious and philosophical movements.

Although Skolnick's writing goes back and forth between those areas and has much to say from each perspective, I will focus here on the clinical wisdom side. Whereas scientific literatures build on consensually acknowledged facts and theories, wisdom literatures engage with meaning, value, ambiguity and complexity. They evolve out of deep engagement, reflection, tolerance of paradox, and concern for the welfare of the current human community and the generation to come. They tend more toward hypothesis-generation and integration of knowledge than toward hypothesis-testing and explication of definitive facts. They teach via metaphor, ritual, parable.

Progress over time in psychoanalysis requires experiential immersion as much as intellectual competence. It calls for disciplined devotion to exploring areas in self and other that are often ugly and always incompletely understood. Skolnick's case examples attest to this radical and demanding commitment: They are recounted forthrightly, in all their density, with no evasion of the author's emotional participation. These genuinely two-person vignettes arrest us and sometimes surprise us. This is clinical writing at its most real, its most wise.

There is a small empirical literature on wisdom (e.g., Sternberg, 2003; Baltes, Glück and Kunzmann, 2002), explicating its difference from simple data collection and hypothesis-testing and emphasizing its value-laden quality and communal purpose. But over millennia, great thinkers have tried to articulate the nature of wisdom, and they have usually been a lot pithier than psychologists. Aeschylus opined that it comes from suffering; Sophocles ascribed wisdom to openness to learning without fearing loss of dignity. Confucius emphasized "knowing what we don't know." As the Judeo-Christian texts were finding the origins of wisdom in humility, the Buddha urged us to "Wear your ego like a loose-fitting garment." Jimi Hendrix, of all people, captured it

xvi Foreword

in the way most relevant to psychoanalysis: "Knowledge speaks, but wisdom listens."

Above all else, wisdom requires what this book keeps circling back to: Time. A few years ago, Cynthia Baum-Baicker (e.g., 2012) did in-depth interviews with 18 psychoanalytic elders viewed by their professional community as notably wise. She found that these diverse analysts, then in their seventies, eighties and nineties, spontaneously mentioned certain common themes: Openness to experience, capacity to tolerate uncertainty and paradox, sensitivity to complexity, respect for conventional rules coexisting with a willingness to challenge them, and a sense of balance between immersion in experience and critical reflection. Skolnick's writing is replete with these elements from the beginning, but as his thinking matures, they are more and more evident. An interesting challenge to our profession inferable from this book is that by the time one's own generation attains its hard-won version of wisdom, the next generation is ready to dismantle it. In fact, they need to do so to make it their own.

In that light, I found Skolnick's reflections toward the end of this volume particularly astute. His pleas to relational colleagues for less co-construction, more attention to validity and more lucidity seem worthy to me. They are especially important coming from a pioneering insider in the relational movement. His recommendation that we re-engage with psychoanalytic theories that are currently out of fashion (another area in which he challenges our subservience to *Chronos*) is a central concern of mine as well. But probably most important, he suggests that we now presumably wise elders distinguish ourselves from a more authoritarian psychoanalytic generation by not "eating our young." The next wave of analytic thinkers will have to deconstruct our psychoanalysis and build their theoretical edifice from bricks like these.

I urge readers not to skip over the introductions to the various papers collected here. They are not simply *pro forma* overviews. In many edited books, such essays amount to boring exegeses on the theme of "And then I got interested in another topic." In this volume, Skolnick contextualizes each paper, giving us a sense of what he was dealing with at the time he wrote it: Intellectually, professionally and personally. He often mentions what he would say differently if he were engaging with his topic at this temporal moment. His voice is authentic, passionate, curious and slightly self-disparaging; this collection is not an exercise in self-congratulation. The book is written in lively prose that is itself profoundly relational: It insists on having a conversation with its readers. I have learned a great deal from this conversation with Neil Skolnick. You will, too.

Nancy McWilliams Visiting Full Professor
Rutgers Graduate School of Applied and
Professional Psychology

References

Baltes, P.B., Glück, J. and Kunzmann, U. (2002). Wisdom: Its structure and function in regulating successful lifespan development. In C.R. Snyder and S.J. Lopez (eds.), *Handbook of Positive Psychology* (pp. 327–347). New York: Oxford University Press.

Baum-Baicker, C. (2012). Clinical wisdom in psychoanalysis and psychodynamic psychotherapy: A philosophical and qualitative analysis. *The Journal of Clinical Ethics*, 23(1): 13–27.

Sternberg, R.J. (2003). Creative thinking in the classroom. *Scandinavian Journal of Educational Research*, 47: 325–338.

Introduction

Neil J. Skolnick

On a recent op-ed page in the *New York Times* (December 25, 2018), a woman recounts her yearly rendezvous with Christmas ornaments. She remarks that as she looks at the ornaments she is reminded of the 25 years she has inhabited her house and that she becomes connected with who she has been, and who everyone she loves has been, for the last two dozen years. Her time extends even further back, before she lived in the house, when she gazes at the unpacked Christmas ornaments. Beholding the ornaments, time also extends into the vague outlines of her future. She finally realizes that her decorations are a reminder of time eternal, a space where past, present and future exist simultaneously, a space she repeatedly enters at, and only at, Christmastime

The author of the above op-ed conveys well what has always captivated and fascinated me about time. Time frames our existence and our non-existence. It can extend indefinitely into the future and endlessly into the past. It exists everywhere and nowhere at one and the same, well, time. As our seasonal decorator above reminds us, we can exist in the past, present and future simultaneously. And despite its acknowledged importance to us, in both our most quotidian existence and in our most cherished rituals, most of us would be hard-pressed to clearly define what time actually is.

We play endlessly with time. We kill time, fill time, waste time, need time, fritter it away or utilize it efficiently. It can move at a rapid clip or painstakingly slow. We can have nothing but time or we can run out of it.

This book aims to accomplish three tasks. First, it is a compendium of my previous published papers and presentations. It is, then, a partial record of what I've done with my time over the past 30 years. And for the purposes of my first aim in publishing this book, the papers are presented in their own right, to present my ideas, the way I think, practice, and write, all separate from the issue of shifting to a relational perspective or issues of time. I've garnered a lot of experience and knowledge in 30 years and I present these papers hopefully to inform, and maybe even inspire, psychoanalysts at all levels of experience as they set out to achieve satisfaction in this consistently challenging, always changing, endlessly impossible, but remarkably gratifying (sorry professor Freud) lifetime pursuit. And, by the by, if they help a patient along the way, so much the better. Also, I feel compelled to add, I have never once, in over 30 years of practice, been hesitant to wake up and go to work.

Except for the first paper, in which I present the research I conducted for my doctoral dissertation, the papers by and large address an assortment of time-worn psychoanalytic issues as they have become redefined, reconfigured and re-contextualized by the application of a relational psychoanalytic perspective. These concepts and constructs I write about no longer invoke the meta-psychological drives of classical Freudian psychoanalysis as the building blocks of their substance and meaning. Instead, they are reconsidered from the perspective of relational configurations. The drives are not ignored, but rather, figure and ground have been reversed. Instead of relationships obtaining their shape and meaning from the demands of the drives, the drives obtain their shape and meaning, secondarily, through the configurations of relationships.

One of my goals in writing this book was to chart the changes, over time, as I, like many psychoanalysts, shifted our perspective from classical to relational psychoanalysis, across the trajectory of my career. As I reviewed my writings contextualized by this time of great foment, I realized that I was also struggling to understand the contributions of time to the process of change that had taken place in me and, more importantly, in our discipline; change that has brought us to the moment where a basic paradigmatic shift has occurred in our theory and technique. A lion's share of the shift is well documented, and more or less considered mainstream thought today. But it wasn't always this way. I will note briefly that, today, as a whole, relational analysts tend to subscribe to relative truths and not absolute truths. Though there is also room to entertain the existence of absolute truths, they are given lesser status in the process. Toward this end we construct narrative truths. We tend to eschew categorical descriptions. We focus on objects (both internal and external) as people seeking relationships (object relations and interpersonal theorists) or self-cohesion (self-psychologists). Our primary motivations are seen as rooted in establishing

Introduction 3

and maintaining connections, both within ourselves and with others, not drive reduction. Our theories tend to be, but not always, cast in two-person, not one-person, paradigms Clinically, intersubjectivity is explored, not just subjectivity. We see ourselves less as blank screens and more as active participants. We talk more, though still tolerate silence, but do not necessarily regard silence as resistance, and we place less emphasis on fantasy. I consider downplaying the importance of fantasy a mistake (more on a critique of these changes in Chapter 9).

The second task of the book is an attempt to chart the evolution of relational theory both in the discipline in general and in my own evolution as a relational psychoanalyst. The shift to a relational model has required major shifts in theory and technique, all which have occurred over a period of time. Through an examination of my papers and presentations I have attempted to highlight my own struggles, as well as the struggles of relational psychoanalysts in general, to abandon anachronistic models, in whole or in part, of human psychological functioning and embrace a new paradigm within which to describe what we do and how we do it. After 40 years of living with theoretical and technical revisions we have begun to seriously evaluate the advantages and disadvantages of relational contributions at a more mature, experience-tested level. With the passage of time, and the increased acceptance of relational thinking in the mainstream, we are freer to be more critical than we were earlier on in its inception when gaining acceptance was a major focus. I point to two recent volumes that have garnered critiques of relational theory from prominent relational psychoanalysts: *De-Idealizing Relational Theory: A Critique from Within* and *Decentering Relational Theory: A Comparative Critique*. Both compendiums are edited by Lewis Aron, Sue Grand and Joyce Slochower and published by Routledge. To my knowledge they represent the largest collection of critiques from within the relational fold, rather than from opposing psychoanalytic schools.

Looking to the past, I cut my psychoanalytic teeth at an auspicious time in the history of psychoanalytic thought, during the advent of relational theory onto the scene. It was an exciting and heady time at the NYU Postdoctoral Program in Psychoanalysis and Psychoanalytic Psychotherapy, where relational psychoanalysis as a school of thought was arguably hatched. A group of faculty, graduates and candidates came together to discuss and debate relational theory. The group, rapidly reaching a critical mass, petitioned the program and successfully instituted a

4 Neil J. Skolnick

new relational training track[1] under Susan Warshaw, its first director. I became one of the initial faculty members on the new relational track, which, at a later time I co-directed, first with Muriel Dimen and subsequently with Nina Thomas. Additional members of the original faculty included: Neil Altman, Lewis Aron, Tony Bass, Beatrice Beebe, Jessica Benjamin, Philip Bromberg, Jody Messler Davies, Muriel Dimen, James Fosshage, Bernie Friedland, Emmanuel Ghent, Virginia Goldner, Ruth Gruenthal, Adrienne Harris, Frank Lachmann, Stephen Mitchell, Doris Silverman, Joyce Slochower and Susan Warshaw. As Jody Messler Davies has pointed out, we all were immigrants from the other tracks at NYU: the Freudian, interpersonal/humanistic and unaligned tracks.

In this volume, through the use of my presentations and papers, presented in chronological order, I first set out to trace the evolution of changes in relational thinking since the inception of the concept "relational" into our psychoanalytic lexicon, around the mid-1970s. On the way, I realized how much of my pursuit and the pursuits of psychoanalysis were similarly tied up with the meanings of time. I became extremely curious about time and the more I followed my curiosity, the more curious I became. I realized I was not alone and discovered that, in fact, there are psychoanalysts who consider time to be the very essence of the entire endeavor. And so the third aim in publishing this book was to place the advent and evolution of relational concepts squarely in the phenomena of temporality and time.

Each chapter in this compendium is preceded by an introduction that locates the paper's place in the evolution of relational theory. The chapter introductions also, when relevant, expound upon the relevance of the paper to issues of temporality. I also discuss my struggles as I evolved from basic science researcher to an interpersonal psychoanalyst and finally to a relational psychoanalyst. The conceit of the book ultimately evolved into a synthesis of: the content of my papers, the evolution of the study of relational psychoanalysis, the evolution of my own relational orientation, and the relationship of all of the above to issues of temporality and time.

The first paper, "Time out of mind," I do not present with an introduction. In some sense it provides, in addition to this Introduction, another introduction to a sub-theme of this book, that of *time*. The chapter captures my interest in, and fascination with, time as a dimension of our physical and psychological landscape. It serves to contextualize all the papers in the book, integrate them, and at times, synthesize them into heuristic suggestions.

The second paper, "Vertical transmission of acquired ulcer susceptibility in the rat," returns the reader to 1980 and to my dissertation research. It was, in essence, an epigenetic study, though the issue of epigenetics had not yet been either named or identified as part of the wide ranging scope of epigenetic studies that exists today. The study of epigenetic phenomena has had an immeasurable effect on the study of heredity. Briefly stated, epigenetic phenomena posit that environmental experiences during the lifespan of a living organism can affect the transmission of traits into the next generation. Darwin quite adamantly insisted that environmental events cannot alter the structure of DNA therefor precluding an event's effect on subsequent generations. He posited that only the very rare occurrence of random mutations of DNA material plus the subsequent survival value of the mutations could propel the alterations of a trait, such as susceptibility to a disease process or response to a trauma, obtained during the life of an organism into subsequent generations. While epigenetic research continues to support Darwin's idea that genetic material is extremely difficult to alter, its central tenet is that environmental events can bring about change that affects the *expression* of genetic material in subsequent generations.

Prior to my study, it had been shown that environmental events in the form of medications could alter traits in one generation and affect a number of subsequent untreated generations. For example, a single subdiabetic dose of alloxan, administered to either a male or female rat before mating, had been associated with abnormal glucose tolerance in their untreated progeny (Spergel, Levy and Goldner, 1971). My research demonstrated that a susceptibility to ulcer disease, acquired by premature separation of rat pups from their mothers, was transferred to a subsequent generation of rats, who had been separated from their mothers at the normal time. To my knowledge, my dissertation research was the first report of an altered susceptibility to a particular disease, acquired by an environmental manipulation, as opposed to a chemical manipulation, during postnatal development in one generation, that was transmitted to offspring in the next.

At the time, we could not attribute the phenomenon to any known process. Since then, with the advent of the study of epigenetic effects, we can now speculate that early maternal separation induced an alteration in the expression of genetic material in the next. Similar to an *après coup*, whereby an event such as a trauma, can have one meaning at the time of the trauma and a different meaning at a later date, the results of my dissertation study can now be attributed to explanations that were unknown at the time of the study. The vicissitudes of temporality altered the context and meanings of my research. I heretofore considered the results an interesting but somewhat irrelevant scientific anomaly. I can now, in light of the accumulation of findings from epigenetic studies, present the results of my study with both a newfound pride and an expanded significance.

Chapter 3, "Secrets in clinical work: A relational point of view," which I wrote with Jody Messler Davies, was significant for a number of reasons. Jody, coming to the relational track at NYU Postdoc from an allegiance to the Freudian track, and I, coming from the interpersonal/humanistic track, came together and wrote about secrets from a relational perspective. It was our first attempt to commit our ideas about relational theorizing to the printed page. We redefined secrets from a relational sensibility. The classical model had put great explanatory value on the function of secrets to defend against the revelation of sexual or aggressive content. We defined several different types of secrets, the classification of which was based on the relational role of a secret in promoting or hindering connections to others. While clearly proffering a definition of a secret from a set of assumptions (relational), orthogonal to drive theory assumptions, we were also careful not to dismiss classical interpretations. Thus, we cautiously promoted that either approach was as valid and useful as the other rather than any suggestion the two were mutually exclusive. These days with the mainstream acceptance of relational theories, my guess is we would not feel the need to be quite so cautious and could refer to relational ideas as accepted knowledge. We would not need to establish their divergent validity from classical theory, nor point to classical sensibilities as separate but equal.

In Chapter 4, "The good, the bad and the ambivalent," I lift Fairbairn by his own petard. Sounding a lot like him, I challenge his most controversial idea, that there are no bad objects in the unconscious. In an exceedingly Fairbairnian, dense, theoretical treatise, I argue that he made a temporal mistake when he came to the conclusion, misguided in my opinion, that the unconscious is devoid of bad objects. In essence, I argue that his argument makes sense during and from a paranoid/schizoid psychic organization, a time in development when splitting defenses are in ascendance, but is no longer a viable conclusion during the depressive position organization of the psyche when ambivalence and a sense of historicity have entered the developmental scene. My writing this paper was for me, in part, an Oedipal moment and in part, a Bar Mitzvah ceremony. I was in the business of taking on the mantle of an adult psychoanalyst. Was my argument correct? While I still think it was, that wasn't the only issue I was addressing ...

In the next three chapters, "What's a good object to do? A Fairbairnian perspective"; "Termination in psychoanalysis: It's about time"; and "Resilience across the life span: A confluence of narratives," I consider several issues which arise in our work, reframed primarily from a relational psychoanalytic perspective but also with a measure of focus on temporal issues. In "What's a good object to do?" I consider the role of the therapist from both Fairbairn and Klein's theories. Fairbairn (1952) emphasized that the analyst provides a new experience for a patient, which the patient internalizes through a process of dynamic identification (Skolnick, 2006). He also repeatedly underlined the importance of accepting a patient's love (Fairbairn, 1952). I invoke (Klein, 1964, 1975) to emphasize the importance of distinguishing the phenomenology of the paranoid/schizoid and depressive positions in order to provide a more attuned empathic response for each.

Chapter 8, "Rethinking the use of the couch: A relational perspective" provides a historical overview of the use of the "couch ritual" from its inception with Freud to the present. Widely considered the sine qua non of the entire psychoanalytic endeavor, I consider conservative and radical critiques of its use as well as potential for its misuse. I conclude by extolling its virtues in some situations while at the same time being of the sentiment that it is by no means necessary for a psychoanalytic treatment. I do encourage analysts of all stripes to experiment with placing patients on and off the couch during the course of a psychoanalysis.

In Chapter 9, "Relational psychoanalysis: An assessment at this time," I present a critique of the relational school of thought at this point of its evolution, when it has established itself as a major school of psychoanalytic theory and practice. There have been a growing number of critiques of relational psychoanalytic perspectives to date. Reaching its middle age allows us to consider its usefulness from a more mature, time-tested vantage point, both as a theory and as a treatment modality. Not wanting to be repetitive with much that has already been written, I provide several of my own criticisms, from more or less major criticisms to minor pet peeves.

Of importance, I reiterate what Susan Warshaw and I maintained in the introduction to our 1992 compendium of relational authors, *Relational Perspectives in Psychoanalysis*. In essence we noted that there is no one integrated relational theory. Relational psychoanalysts hale from many diverse camps, from object relational, self-psychological, interpersonal, intersubjective, infant research, field theory, neurobiological approaches, neo-Kleinian schools, and others. The situation remains somewhat the same today. While relational psychoanalysts have more clearly delineated some of the important similarities and differences amongst the different schools, each offering a relational perspective, both theoretically and clinically, we have yet to produce a unified relational theory. While that was arguably the hope back then, a more unified theory has not materialized. That's not necessarily a bad thing. It is what it is, a group of diverse psychoanalytic approaches that have rejected Freud's meta-psychological drives as the ultimate explanatory bottom line in human development, motivation and psychopathology, and replaced them with human relationships, at the center of the relational psychoanalytic *raison d'etre*.

Note

1 The NYU postdoctoral program is comprised, almost since its inception in the 1960s, of several training tracks. Prior to the addition of the relational track, there were three tracks: the Freudian track, the interpersonal/humanistic track and the unaligned track. Candidates are not expected or required to align with a track, but the training faculty are each members of a single designated track.

References

Aron, L., Grand, S. and Slochower, J. (2018a). *De-Idealizing Relational Theory: A Critique from Within*. New York and London: Routledge.

Aron, L., Grand, S. and Slochower, J. (2018b). *Decentering Relational Theory: A Comparative Critique*. New York and London: Routledge.

Fairbairn, W.R.D. (1952). *An Object Relations Theory of the Personality*. New York: Basic Books.

Klein, M. (1964). *Contributions to Psychoanalysis: 1921–1945*. New York: McGraw-Hill.

Klein, M. (1975). *Envy and Gratitude and Other Works: 1946–1963*. New York: McGraw-Hill.

Skolnick, N.J. (2006). What's a good object to do? Psychoanalytic Dialogues, 16: 1–28.

Skolnick, N.J. and Warshaw, S.C. (1992). *Relational Perspectives in Psychoanalysis*. New Jersey: The Analytic Press.

Spergel, G., Levy, L.J. and Goldner, M.G. (1971). Glucose intolerance in the progeny of rats treated with single subdiabetogenic dose of alloxan. *Metabolism, 20*: 401–413.

Chapter 1

Time out of mind[1]
2017

Neil J. Skolnick

> Time . . . thou ceaseless lacky to eternity.
>
> William Shakespeare, *The Rape of Lucrece*
>
> We've got nothing but time.
>
> Susan Baskin, writer

Held up by some to be the fourth dimension, time remains one of existential reality's most intriguing and elusive concepts. It is tasteless, colorless and lacks a corporeal form, yet it pervades the very fabric of our lives. It contextualizes our life narrative, moment-to-moment, year-to-year and generation-to-generation. Eva Hoffman (2009), in a neat little essay exclaims, "It is one of the fascinations of time that it is both the most intangible of entities and the most inexorable" (p. 14) and she boldly goes on to declare that:

> In a sense time has been reality's last unconquered frontier . . . The time revolution is taking place not in the interplanetary sphere but within our daily lives, perceptions, even bodies, and with enormous repercussions for social relations, forms of experience and, indeed, for our very understanding of what it means to be human.
>
> (p. 15)

We can never actually see time, we must infer it from movement – the hands moving on a clock or the sun moving across the sky, or the changing height of a child as he or she moves through time. Aristotle (in *Physics*, 1941) argues that time and change or movements are inextricably intertwined. Meissner (2007) understands Aristotle as maintaining that we experience time and elapse of time only when we perceive some movement from before to after – that is movement experienced externally via sense experience (again hands moving on a clock) or internally introspectively (experiencing oneself aging). Theoretical physicists, charting the universe from the smallest atomic particle to the unimaginable expanse of large spaces and forces, are mystified by time and are ubiquitous in their not being able to explain it particularly well because, unlike every other process in the physical world, time, as we know it, cannot be reversed. It relentlessly travels on a one-way ticket, which physicists refer to as the "arrow of time." Interestingly, Stephen Hawking (1988) actually postulates three arrows of time (thermodynamic, psychological and cosmological).[2]

Time's nature has also baffled poets, philosophers and physicists, and the quotidian experience of train conductors, chefs and anyone rushing to a meeting since, well, time immemorial. Witness the facile ways we speak of time, without ever fully comprehending what time is all about: We can be ahead of time or behind time; we can live in the best of times and the worst of times. While we tend to divide time into past, present and future, many students of time note that the present moment of time is impossible to experience because by the time we do, it has passed. Einstein's relative model of time boldly considers past, present and future to be illusions. We can make time, kill time, save time, waste time, and I could go on but I would use up all your time. Implicit in the way we structure our professional practice, time is money and existentially, in no time, we are out of time.

"Time is of the essence in psychoanalysis," wrote the psychoanalyst William Meissner (2007). In this chapter I will attempt to demonstrate how time silently pervades and influences not only the very essence of everyday life, but also the entire endeavor of psychoanalysis, both consciously and unconsciously. Far from exhaustive, I hope to demonstrate its pervasive presence and influence on the multiple fabrics and meanings of our lives, not only in our work as psychoanalysts, but also in our everyday existence. Broadly speaking objective time can be linear, propelling us directly through past, present and future, but subjectively determined time can be balletic as it twists and turns and dances and pirouettes through inner worlds with the facility and mystery of an Olympic figure skater. Our perceptions travel back and forth through time resulting in dizzying experiences whereby the past influences present perceptions and present events can have marked effects on our memories of the past. And if that were not confusing enough, future expectations can influence both present experiences and past memories. Circumstances such as anniversaries or traumas can stop time or speed it up. I will attempt to describe several issues in which time overlaps with psychoanalytic explorations, including how we develop a sense of time, the effects of psychopathology on our perceptions of time, and interventions I have found useful with patients whose rigid, distorted subjective experience of time can be deleterious to their functioning.

In my brief exploration of the literature on the nature of time, I was directed through realms of philosophy, art, music, Einsteinian and Newtonian physics, aging, development, and most pertinent to this presentation, the psychoanalytic process. Andre Green (2009) notes that Freud, "never brought together his diverse conceptions of time into a single presentation. Thus, he left us with a mosaic of temporal mechanisms without conceptual unification" (p. 1). By and large psychoanalytic writers have not ventured prodigiously into speculating about issues of time in our work or the experiences of our patients. This is changing. A contemporary psychoanalyst, Dana Birksted-Breen (2016), makes the claim that, "Issues concerning time are at the basis of psychoanalytic theory, of the analytic setting and of the clinical phenomena we encounter. They also underlie important technical and theoretical differences in psychoanalytical approaches, implicitly or explicitly" (p. 139). I believe she is signaling an increased interest being directed toward the issue of time by contemporary psychoanalysts.

Hans Loewald wrote extensively and creatively about time, though, as Seligman (2018) notes, his heuristic 1980 essay on time has been largely and unfortunately ignored. Loewald boldly conjectured that psychic structures, which typically assume a spatial metaphor, are better described as temporal in nature. He is not talking about objective tick-tock time, but refers rather to psychic time, what the ancient Greeks referred to as *Kairos* time, and the active relationship between the modes of time, past, present and future. For example, he speaks of the ego as a structure that organizes times past and brings them into the present:

> The remarkable fact is that in mental life the past, that is psychic past, is not in the (objective) past but is active now as past, and that the psychic present acts on the psychic past. The psychic past and the psychic present are represented in psychic systems, agencies or structures, as Freud has variously called them, which are actual and active in the objective present of mental life.
>
> (p. 45)

12   Neil J. Skolnick

Likewise, Loewald defines the superego as organizing future time (e.g., the consequences of our actions) also bringing them into the present. He states:

> The superego functions from the viewpoint of a future ego, from the standpoint of the ego's future that is to be reached, is being reached, is being failed or abandoned by the ego. Parental authorities, as internalized in the agency of the superego, are related to the child as representatives of a future and of demands, hopes, and misgivings, or despair, which pertain to an envisioned future of the child.
>
> (p. 46)

Ultimately, he "points to the importance of time as being the inner fiber of what we call psychical" (p. 52).

Mitchell (1992) was influenced by Loewald when he considered reformulating psychic structures as organized by temporal considerations rather than by spatial metaphors. He invokes Ogden's consideration of Kleinian positions as being dialectical in nature in order to make an argument for considering our shifting experiences on a temporal plane (before, now and after) rather than a spatial plane (surface and deep). Ogden considered Klein's positions as each defining and negating each other, rather than representing a primitive or advanced psychic organization. Likewise, Mitchell conjectures: "Again, it is a mistake to think of one form of experience as more basic or deeper, because they are not layered in space; rather they shift back an forth as forms of self-organization over time" (p. 18).

Most students of time have developed various ways of classifying types of time. Categorizing time might actually present us with an easier task than actually defining any singular essence of time. We might have to settle for that. Moreover, I can state with some degree of certainty that while there are many definitions and classifications of time, coming from a range of disciplines, there is a consensus that most theorists will concur that one dimension of time exists as a real, true, tick-tock linear phenomena. The ancient Greeks referred to this time as *Chronos*, distinguishing it from the previously mentioned *Kairos*. Corresponding to something akin to Bion's concept of O, this is Newton's absolute time. It is an immutable reality that exists separately from our perceptions of it and the meanings we give it. It travels inexorably in one direction that as far as our most current state of knowledge has it, cannot be reversed. In contrast to Newton's model of absolute time, Einstein concocted a drastically different model of objective time, one referred to as relative time, which, by contrast, is not absolute or fixed. Like *Chronos* time, the perception and measurement of relative time is objective but the measurement of it depends on our distance from where it is recorded as well as our speed from the point in space where it is being measured (Isaacson, 2008). It is a malleable time, one that can be altered and re-contextualized, but nonetheless is still measurable by objective measures, and not subjective perceptions.

In psychoanalysis we also make distinctions between types of time. For example, Modell (1990) utilized the previously mentioned terms used by the ancient Greeks to distinguish between absolute and non-linear time, *Chronos* and *Kairos*, respectively. Stern expands the definition of *Chronos*, or objective time, as the "kind of time (that) lies outside the realm of human experience . . . it leads inexorably from birth to death; it is linear, irrevocable, and without human meaning" (Stern, 2012, p. 56). This is what I refer to as tick-tock time; it is the time that paradoxically cradles and contextualizes all of life while at the same time it stalks, torments and tyrannizes us with the eventual demise of life. By contrast, *Kairos*, as Modell (1990) uses it, corresponds to our subjective sense of time. While it might be tempting to equate *Kairos* time with Einstein's relative time that would actually be a mistake. Einstein's relative time, while malleable, is determined not by vicissitudes in human subjectivity, but rather by variations in its measurement. In contrast, *Kairos* is not measured objectively. It is non-linear, imbued with human meaning, and, to quote Stern (2012), "can turn back on itself in ways that allow meanings to change and grow" (p. 56). To put this another way, *Chronos* time includes both Newton's objective time and Einstein's relative time, both of which can be reliably measured, but not *Kairos* time, which is subjectively determined.

Freud ventured into the realm of *Kairos* time when he postulated the timelessness of the unconscious, and by extension, dreams. For him, primary process, the wellspring of human subjectivity and meaning, is not rooted in the one-way linearity of objective time. It has no starting or ending point of reference. It playfully moves forward and backward in time, wreaking havoc with objective reality and meaning-making as the past, present and future influence each other in decidedly non-linear fashion creating such phenomena as *nachträglichkeit* and *après coup* with the alluring impenetrability of a Salvador Dali painting. *Kairos* is the time of dream imagery that we can employ in attempting to understand where our patients live.

Recently there has been a resurgence of interest in dreaming, more broadly and metaphorically defined than Freud (Ogden, 2016; Parsons, 2009; Bion, 1962, and others). Parsons, a British psychoanalyst (2009), defines "living in time," taken from a chapter in Winnicott's *Playing and Reality* (1971), not as the area where our experience is lived, but rather, as the time and place in which we become truly alive. Moreover, he proffers, "I want to put forward the idea that to be fully and creatively alive means living at a point of intersection between time and timelessness" (p. 37). As with Ogden (2016), no longer is dreaming confined to sleeping states. Instead, another distinction is forged in our categorizing different types of time. Parsons again, "To describe a dream belongs to the temporality of daily life, but the experience of dreaming lies outside of this ordinary temporality" (p. 38). Primarily because of a dream's direct connection to the unconscious, controls and defensiveness give way to unstructured timelessness, a form of time without the linearity, directionality, predictability and causality of tick-tock time. In the intersection of time and timelessness, the analyst is made privy to the engine room of the patient's aliveness. Here it becomes not only important to decipher the meaning of a dream, but more importantly, it is a place and time to experience, with a patient, the expanded corners of their individual idioms, those creative places where they feel truly and wholly alive. I have always felt that when a patient dutifully attempts to interpret the meaning of a dream there is a shortchanging of another type of experience that can be located more from the patient's associating to the experience of the dream. It is here where I encourage the patient to freely wander, an unstructured venturing into the intersection between time and timelessness. Here is where the patient may come truly alive.

From the contemporary psychoanalytic school of Field Theory, Baranger and Baranger (2008) have also focused on temporality in their work. As they put it:

> The temporal aspect of the (analytic) field is nothing like the time experienced in everyday situations. The time of the analysis is simultaneously a present, a past, and a future. It is this temporal ambiguity, the mixture of present past and future, that permits patients not only to become aware of their history but also to modify it retroactively . . . take them on again with new meaning.
>
> (p. 80)

An important contribution to the overlap of relationality, temporality and development has been made by the developmental psychoanalyst, Stephen Seligman, in a recently published book, *Relationships in Development: Infancy, Intersubjectivity, and Attachment* (2018). In a beautifully written chapter, "Coming to life in time," he expounds upon the life-affirming responsiveness, often non-verbal and bodily, of the mother with her baby that contributes to a child's expectations of a lively, efficacious future. He also discusses its opposite, the deadening, futile truncating of a forward moving temporality that can be engendered by a non-responsive mother. He refers to these problematic organizations of a sense of time (past, present and future) as "disorders of temporality." He distinguishes two broad types of temporal disorders: "Disorders of Simultaneity" when the past and present become melded together and "Disorders of Subsequency" – a profound sense of futility felt as things will never change. "Disorders of Simultaneity" is in essence the stuff of trauma. During "Disorders of Subsequency," the unprocessed past overshadows and truncates a fully alive experience of the present.

Nachträglichkeit,[3] loosely translated as deferred action, and *après coup or afterwardness* (Birksted-Breen, 2003) are two expressions used to denote a similar process by which the meaning of a past event is obtained temporally after its occurrence by a retrospective analysis of the forces that were operating at the time of a memory's occurrence. Fonagy (1992) notes that the actual memories that surface in an analysis are not as important as the procedural memory that organize and influence the surfaced memories. Stern (2012) extends this idea such that the meaning of a surfacing memory is to be found in the here and now co-construction of the memory by the intersubjective mélange of the interacting analyst and patient. This would be the non-linear balletic time I referred to earlier. Our perceptions travel back and forth through time, influencing our objective and subjective realities in powerful ways.

We have come to take as a given that historic events, especially trauma, can both stop time and influence our perceptions of the present and future time. Moreover, current events, again, particularly traumas, can influence and alter our perceptions and memories of past time.

Parsons (2014) privileges not only the past's influence on the present but notes that the future also can have a marked effect on the present and, likewise, the present can have a marked effect on the future. He refers to this phenomenon as *avant-coup* and claims it is bi-directional. In one direction, what he refers to as the future counterpart of *après coup*, the future can be affected by the present. As he states, "future experience takes on a richer potential because its range of possibility can be constantly imagined afresh from the present" (p. 20). Likewise, the present can be influenced by the future. In his words, "present experience acquires a greater range of possibility by being re-imagined from the standpoint of a future that has not yet taken form" (p. 20). Parsons also encourages analysts to help their patients live at the intersection of time and timelessness.

I actually do not prioritize any of the above specific processes above the other, per se, or direction of influence, in understanding my patients' experience. Recognizing that influential direction can time-travel from present to past or past to present, or present to future, that it may be co-constructed or only constructed by one of the intersubjective pair, convinces me that none of our means of constructing past, present or future realities is mutually exclusive of the others. Furthermore, it is probably the case that all dimensions of time – past, present and future – always infuse the others to some extent and that any attempt to denude any dimension from the others will result in an experience of an interpretation, say, that is flatter, less alive and less meaningful. Furthermore, temporal truths are not fixed, but instead, they can change in time (i.e., what was true yesterday may no longer be true from today's perspective). In my work with patients I keep searching for what resonates as true for the patient's experience, regardless of the source of the memory, the influences upon it or the temporal truth it expresses.

In a recent paper, I wrote about contemporary relational perspectives on termination (Skolnick, 2010). I came across a bifurcation of the concept of time similar to but not exactly parallel to *Chronos* and *Kairos*. Bollas (1989) invokes Winnicott and makes a distinction between *Somatic* time and *Object* time. *Somatic* time is rooted in timelessness, and is provided by the solipsistically created subject mother who, by accommodating to the infant's cycle of needs and satisfactions, protects the child from the ultimate demands of real or *Object* time. Then, as the mother gradually fails the infant's omnipotent desires, she becomes a real object for the child, and teaches the child about real *Object* time. As he or she struggles to negotiate the gap between the mother's absence and presence, the child gradually and angrily relinquishes a hold on somatic time and increasingly internalizes a sense of real time.

This classification of time into *Somatic* and *Object* closely parallels Winnicott's developmental progression from object relating to object usage. Somatic time belongs to the universe of object relating, it's a flexible time that in large part serves to shield the child from the demands of real, objective time. It's a temporal equivalent of a parent comforting a child with proclamations of, "Everything will be OK." It's the language of fairy tales, "A long time ago in a land far, far away," or the comforting words used when discussing death with a child, "It's such a long time from now you don't have to even think about it." Or the open-ended times of bliss when feeding at the breast as an infant, or becoming lost in ecstatic sex as an adult. And likewise, when confronted with real objective time, as in when the child must relinquish the timelessness of object relating for the groundedness of object usage, transferring to objective time can evoke rage and destruction.

I think of somatic time and object time existing dialectically and in tension with each other. Moreover, termination reckons with both senses of time. That we need to end a psychoanalysis evokes issues of real, object time, clock-ticking time. A death/loss model of termination is one which deals with the realities of object time, the clock running out of ticks.

When we leave our door open for future contact, we are evoking issues of maternal somatic time, which also continues to exist in the internal world of the adult. In this case, time does not become limited to the length of the episode of therapy. Instead, the possibility existing for future contact with the analyst can ease the stresses of the running out of object time. Like the workings of an hourglass, once the sand runs out, the hourglass can be flipped over, restarting the flow of time.

Traditionally, termination meant the end of the analytic relationship period. Goodbye, have a good life. Gradually, throughout my career, I started responding to the end of the treatment more as a moment in somatic time by leaving open the possibility of future therapeutic contact. I did not neglect object time, in that the therapy would end and a termination date would be set and honored with a termination process. Yes, the end of treatment can *resemble* a death. But not to overstate the obvious, unless one of the treatment pair dies, no one has actually died in real time and that is a fact of the termination as well. To leave open the possibility of future contact places an obvious but important limit on the traditional death/mourning/ grieving model of termination. To end a period of analytic work with the offer of an open door in the future takes the termination out of the realm of the finite. The message given is no longer,

> You must now learn to accept the limitations of our relationship, and the gratifications it potentially offers, because it is permanently finished. You will be able to have continued contact with me as I exist in your internal world, but you must relinquish all other wishes for it to be otherwise.

In contrast, by leaving the door open for future contact, termination becomes a moment in somatic time. We now are saying to a patient,

> Our relationship is over for the time being and we will be separating. Yes, the therapy and termination process has involved the loss of pieces of yourself and pieces of us, but it has also provided new ways and possibilities of being – new ways of being that have been obtained partially through our relationship. The relationship is over for now, but do know that I am available for your use in the future.

This crucial change in message pertaining to termination parallels a basic sea-change that has come about in the shift to a relational psychoanalysis. A one-person model asks the analysand to relinquish any attachments to the analyst rooted in the solipsism of one's closed internal world with all its attendant infantile wishes. The analyst's role has been essentially to evoke the past connections in the internal world, elucidate them and render them vestigial. The clock starts ticking from the moment the analysis begins. There will be a fixed amount of energy rearranged in a linear, fixed amount of time. While there is plenty of time to explore, contemplate, act out, enact and identify with the analyst, time is of the essence! It's over when it's over and hopefully the analysand will hit the road moving forward by virtue of giving up old ways of being and with new, more adaptive ways of being firmly entrenched within the psyche to assure durability over time. The analysand must accept the limits of time, make those changes, relinquish hurtful, self-destructive connections, mourn their loss and move on. It is a closed-system, energic model of psychoanalysis, which asks the patient to go back in time in order to move forward.

A two-person relational model, while not eschewing the past, invites the patient to connect in the present time in order to create an alternative narrative in the future, and then move forward. The new narrative does not assume a fixed amount of energy or linear directionality. The treatment dyad is freer to move backward and forward in time. Both older and newer ways of being and connecting are tried on, accepted and/or discarded. As I stated elsewhere (Skolnick, 2006) the hope is that the patient will, in the therapy, interact with a good object in the form of the analyst and then carry the interactions into their lives following termination. The relinquish-*or*-not sensibility of an older one-person model is replaced by a relinquish-*and*-not tension of a newer relational model of treatment. It is assumed that the older maladaptive ways of being will not evaporate, but they will continue to live in tension with the newer ways of being. In that the older self states and self/other interactions are not necessarily given up, but rather added to, there is less emphasis on mourning a "dead" subjectively created analyst. The analyst, as new object, is allowed to survive. In that he or she survives, the analyst is available to interact with the patient at a time in the future. Future contacts are not mourned, as they are in a classical model, but welcomed as a possibility in a relational model.

Eva Hoffman, whom I noted earlier, is a contemporary memoirist and critic. In her book, labeled appropriately, *Time*, she briefly describes two additional categories in which time lives. These types of time are rooted in the movement of time. One, "the arrow of time", I have referred to earlier as the unidirectional movement of tick-tock time. It stresses "the singularity of each event as it occurs, one unrepeatable time, in the temporal continuum . . . and encourages notions of development and sometimes progress" (Hoffman, 2009, p. 123). Hoffman distinguishes the arrow of time from "cylindrical time" or "cyclical time," as she sometimes refers to it. "In the cyclical vision of temporality, events are not so much unique manifestations of singular historical moments as archetypes of larger historical or mythic patterns" (p. 123). This is the type of time we utilize in psychoanalysis to mark psychic patterns and make associations between an event at time 1 and an event at time 2, 3 and so on, often in order to parse character truths in a patient's narrative. One aspect of arrow and cylindrical time that is particularly noteworthy is that as time speeds up in our fast-moving, ever-changing world, it has become increasingly difficult to identify events. Events are typically an artificial grouping of temporally related phenomena. Think of the Iron Age, or adolescence, two periods of time whose temporal boundaries are not as

20 Neil J. Skolnick

clear-cut as they might appear. When exactly does adolescence start – 8? 10? Or 13? And when does it end? 21? 25? Or 30? Think of our world as we have come to live in it during Trump time. Crises appear weekly, if not daily. The order and meaning of events can come and go so rapidly, sometimes as rapidly as between the first sentence Trump makes in a speech and the last, that we lose, in a dizzying pace, the definition of an event let alone its connection to other events, so that it can become impossible to use either the arrow of time or cylindrical time. We begin to feel unhinged from any temporal sense of time. Are voting rights legal today? Do we still recognize the Iran Treaty? Or not? Events are increasingly experienced as ephemeral. Temporal chaos is the new normal.

Developmental considerations in the acquisition of a sense of time

In one of the more comprehensive books exploring the intersection of psychoanalysis and time, William Meissner (2007) reflects generally on the development of our sense of time:

> The development of the sense of time is ... a lifelong process that varies according to the complexities and variability of individual subjective experience and the organization and functioning of the personal self-system ... that reflects basic biological as well as personal, cultural, and social influences.
>
> (p. 19)

He further states that according to Piaget (1969), "the baby's first inklings of time are somatically connected, deriving from the natural rhythms of sleep, feedings and elimination." These rhythms and patterns are closely related to Winnicott's concept of "going on being." Furthermore, Meissner states, "The subjective time sense is not a given of human experience but undergoes a process of development extending from the earliest experiences of life" (p. 19).

From another perspective, Freud, as has been frequently noted, proclaimed that the first ego is a body ego. I would add, in light of the ideas put forward in this discussion, that the development of the body ego is accompanied by a close second, a temporal ego. A nascent developing sense of time provides a context for, as well as a determining role in, the development of self. Just as skin provides for the boundaries, possibilities and limits of our ego, time provides the containing structure that also provides for the boundaries, possibilities and limits of a developing self. Within the context of the everyday mother–infant relationship, exposure to the rhythms of real and subjective time provides for the earliest organizations, structures, rhythms and continuity of self in time.

From the perspective of object relations, Hartocollis (1974) noted that the notion of time is the result of the integration of two general areas of psychological development – the perception of spatial relationships and the development of primitive motivational states organized around relationships with others. He claims that a appreciation of the concept of time is predicated on the development of consciousness and he further notes:

> For the consciousness of time to grow, it is necessary to acquire the consciousness of two elementary aspects of physical reality: the consciousness of movement, i.e., the awareness that objects about oneself move or change; and the consciousness of objects as unique, continuous, relatively stable.
>
> (p. 243)

Or as William James (1890) said, "Awareness of change is ... the condition on which our perception of time's flow depends" (p. 620).

When further considering the literature concerning the child's development of a sense of time, it rapidly became obvious that a manifold appreciation of time sense is cultivated primarily in experiential gaps. Regardless of the theoretical perspective, psychoanalysts tend to envision the acquisition of a sense of time as cultivated in the gap between the activation of a motivational requirement and the satisfactory – or not – provision of its supplies. The motivational requirements that bookend the gap between arousal and satisfaction are usually defined by the theoretical orientation of the analyst.

So, for example, a drive theorist would consider the time between an arousal of a biological need and its satisfaction to be a crucial determinant of an internal sense of the passage of time. Likewise, an object relations analyst would look to the gap between arousal and provision of a need by an object, and a self psychologist would look to the gap between the arousal of a self need and its provision by a self object.

Priel (1997) advances a relational perspective on this model by contrasting real time with a subjective construction of the mother–infant interactions. Priel states:

> A different perspective on the sense and concept of time can be envisioned, not as pertaining to an isolated perceiving mind (Freud's model), but as a mutually construed organizational principle characteristic of mother–infant interactional patterns . . . The sense of time can be better understood as the unfolding of basic meanings related to identity and differentiation, continuity and change, in the context of infant caregiver interactional patterns.
>
> (p. 435)

Steve Seligman (personal communication), evoking Winnicott, has been exploring the disruption of temporality in the infant that occurs at the nexus of the unresponsive object and the spontaneous gesture of intentionality. He locates the infant's development of his or her sense of living in the flux of time in the intersubjective space of gesture and response. An unresponsive object can produce not only emotional deadness, but a truncated experience of a life existing in time.

If the gaps I just enumerated are appropriately attuned to the child's developing needs and capacities, chances are the child will be able to establish a subjective sense of time more closely aligned to, or clearly differentiated from, the constraints of real objective time. Trouble can develop if the parent is not attuned to the needs of the child and provides the wrong satisfactions at the wrong time. A patient of mine wept as she remembered waiting what seemed to her to be hopelessly endless hours, for her divorced father to pick her up for weekly visitations. On many occasions he failed to show. Then, in order to deny the intense pain of his abandonment, she would make excuses for him and developed a sense of time that masochistically contained a wide range of acceptable contingencies, with a wide range of sadistic men who rarely respected her temporal needs. They either would never be on time, or not show up at all.

The experience of time, of course, changes throughout the life cycle and is strongly associated with the specific challenges of each of life's seasons. Calvin Colarusso, a child psychiatrist, has carefully and sensitively chronicled these seasons, from childhood through old age, and their accompanying demands. Time does not allow an extensive examination of

Colarusso's pioneering studies. Ah, there it is again, *Chronos* time, now acting as a harbinger of limitation. But also as a segue into the next section of this paper which I have labeled:

Time and the frame: adventures in *Chronos*

Can't bring back time. Like holding water in your hand.

James Joyce, *Ulysses*

A somatic, timeless and malleable perception of time pervades the mysteriously flowing process of an analysis. Less intriguing perhaps, but of crucial importance nonetheless, is the provision of a contained objective time that sets the contours of the analytic process, what we typically refer to as the frame. For most psychoanalysts, creating and maintaining a reliable and reasonably flexible temporal frame for the treatment setting provides the process with secure boundaries. It functions as a crucial prerequisite to the facilitation of a safe bounded environment in which the loopy and looping time travel of an analysis can take place. The consistent time and timing of the session defines the space of the analytic process. The session flows linearly in time with a beginning, middle and end. It also flows cyclically from the same time or number of times from week to week. The setting of the frame is the stuff of *Chronos*, the objective, real, model of linear, finite time which, paradoxically is required so the analytic pair can feel safe enough to enter the world of *Kairos* or somatic time, a time which is unbounded, sometimes boundless, and can turn back on itself, backward and forward in time in the search for narrative, meaning and an expanded sense of self. Winnicott (1965) compared the structure and regularity of the frame to the ministrations of a good-enough mother. In the same way that the predictability and ritual that a mother provides for her child allows that child to safely express, explore and extend its developing self, the provision of a consistent frame of time and space in analysis provides a patient with similar regularity, ritual and safety.

This safety is a requisite for the child's growing sense that life is an ongoing life-affirming process that does not yield to the annihilation anxieties and pressures that the child must negotiate. In order to develop their own separate, independent sense of self a child needs the consistency of good-enough *Chronos* mothering to feel safe and assured in the continuity and predictability of life, in the conviction that all is not chaos or dissolution, in the belief that life will go on. A child can then safely expect that when they wake up from sleep, the skin they inhabit will be exactly where they left it at the time they fell asleep. The child has experience with the regular rhythms of their life crucial for the development of a regulated sense of self existing in the current of time.

Similarly, we expect our patients to commit to and respect the mutually agreed-upon frame we establish. We expect them to come regularly, on time, and to withstand the anxieties that attend the beginning and end of sessions. But of course, we know that some patients are not necessarily cooperative or appreciative of the frame we establish. They challenge it in myriad ways. They come consistently late or early or contact us at times other than those times we reserve for them. I was taught to listen for resistance, anger or oppositional attitudes being expressed in the infractions against the time frame.

While that might indeed be the case at times, for some patients, I have come to appreciate another major contributor to a disrespect of real time. It's been my experience that some patients who consistently mangle the timing of sessions struggle with a particularly insidious narcissistic impairment. From the perspective of this discussion, they are locked in *Kairos* or *Somatic* time unable to relinquish it to *Chronos* or *Object* time. Raised by excessively controlling self-interested parents who are especially unattuned to the regulatory needs of their children, or by parents who provide no *Chronos* limits, these patients have great difficulty being able to relinquish omnipotent control of their solipsistic creation of the external world. They have difficulty transcending what Winnicott referred to as object relating, the creation of others to fill their narcissistic needs, and traversing the rage-filled space required to reach a stage of object usage, the acceptance of an integrated loving but humanly imperfect other existing in real time. Relevant to this discussion, when faced with the limitations of real, objective time, time that we all need to surrender to, time that they cannot omnipotently control, they are flooded with both rage and powerful annihilation anxiety, two sides of the same coin. Their protests against the real constraints of time take many forms. Consistently coming late to sessions or ignoring the constraints of biological clocks for reproduction are two such protests. There is often an unacknowledged sense of grandiosity and superiority accompanying the disrespect for time that goes something like,

Time limits are for the mass of other lesser people than me to heed. I am superior to them, I exist outside and above time, and therefore am not wedded to a clock as much as those less fortunate souls. I can have control over time and operate outside of its limitations. For me, time is endless.

It's a pyrrhic victory, of course. Living above time is really living in a deadened world of no time and the frequent feeling of narcissistically disordered patients that life is passing them by actually comes to pass, often with tragic results of empty, unaccomplished lives devoid of mature relationships or personal achievements. What the analyst needs to uncover, appreciate and address is the enormous fear, rage and pain of the crippling annihilation anxiety that accompanies the prospect of relinquishing an omnipotent control over time. To be empathic to their pain is typically a challenge because their arrogance and grandiosity, not to mention their lateness and abuse of our time, often work at cross purposes with our desire to be empathic. One sign to the analyst that treatment is working is the development of a sense of urgency in the patient.

I have on occasion colluded with a patient's mangling of tick-tock time. In what I now see as a mutual enactment, I remained blind to my patient's perpetual lateness. Just below my conscious awareness I realized my patient's lateness served me just fine. It provided me with a welcomed break in the midst of a busy day. We were in cahoots for a stolen wink.

One such patient, Gloria, was a bright, intelligent and successful real estate broker who consistently came to our sessions late, sometimes by minutes and sometimes by 35 minutes. Despite her stated desire to marry and have a child, she was near deaf to the tick tocking of her biological timepiece. She was not involved in any attempt to locate a partner. Her mother was a highly successful, controlling and competitive woman who had been a rebel throughout her own life, priding herself on her non-conformity to the norms of society. This extended to her childrearing in which she provided few limits, including treating her young children as adults and, for example, allowing them to attend her frequent drug-infused orgies. Her mother's desire to rebel blinded her to her children's need for regularity, ritual, stimulus reduction and consistency. Gloria, because of her mother's inability to provide consistent attention to her developmental needs, clung to the world of somatic time and never completely relinquished it to the structures of object time.

Years of interpretations, typically in the range of my accusations of her hostile resistance, yielded no change whatsoever. Her lateness continued and instead of addressing it, I gradually came to accept it and, by way of a mutual enactment, enjoy it. Clearly several shifts had to happen in both of us before progress was made. First, and foremost, I needed to wake up and recognize my role in the mutual enactment, an enactment designed to deny the imperative of adhering to *Chronos* tick-tock time. I liked my breaks. I anticipated them as time to read my emails. But what was her enactment designed to do for her? I realized the iron grip that her illusory, omnipotent control had on time was not a hostile resistance to the surfacing of unconscious material or conflict. I came to realize the abject terror and rage she had at the prospect of relinquishing her omnipotence over her private *Kairos* time and the accompanying terror of yielding to the constraints of *Chronos*. Instead of insisting that she was being angry and oppositional, I needed to become empathic for her fear and terror engendered by her well-meaning but inattentive mother whose issues blinded her from the necessity of providing sufficient protection and regulation for her daughter. As we entered this territory Gloria alternately became enraged, disappointed and depressed. Ultimately, she inconsistently though inexorably achieved a measure of peace with living within the world of real time, and in the nick of time, she managed to give birth to her daughter. It was a surprise to neither of us when, at our final session, we presented each other with gifts. With loving and knowing smiles, I gave her a book about time – and she handed me a clock.

Another consequence of a refusal to acknowledge the constraints of *Chronos*, of real tick-tock time, is an intractable denial of aging and death. I have been working with a talented 60-something playwright with some measure of notoriety who suffered significant physical and mental abuse from a tyrannical father and a sweet but ineffectual mother who turned a blind eye to her husband's abuse of her children, despite being abused by him herself. Nick, my patient, was married young to a similarly wounded woman, Roberta. Nick and Roberta had enough strengths between them that enabled them to create and inhabit a supportive symbiotic cocoon that, while somewhat isolated, enabled them to preserve a long-term successful marriage. Their love was fueled by sadomasochistic dynamics but was nevertheless persistent. It worked for them. In her early fifties Roberta contracted cancer, followed several years later by relapse, which were both successfully treated with surgery and chemotherapy. Then, in her early sixties, she was stricken by acute leukemia. Apparently, acute leukemia, always quick acting and fatal, is suspected of being an iatrogenic consequence of the chemotherapy used to cure other cancers. Hanging onto every shred of hope the doctors offered, they submitted to all treatments, including those that were highly experimental. I'm not certain how much the doctors were honest with them about the very slim chances she had of survival, but they clung to each scrap of hope as if they were passengers on the *Titanic* desperately unconvinced that it was sinking even as it rose vertically and inexorably slipped into the ocean.

A week or so before she succumbed, they were given information that unequivocally signaled the end was imminent. When I empathically communicated it was time to prepare for her death, Nick went into a rage and informed me that I didn't get it, that she was going to live. She would be cured and the two of them would be walking out of the hospital any day now and returning to their life. He was adamantly certain of the fact. When, ultimately, she did die, he absolutely could not process it almost to the point of delusion. He could not conceive or picture that she was dead. She returned to him for a number of months in both real dreams and daydreams and he fully was prepared for the joyous reunion he would experience when the footsteps he imagined in the hallway were hers returning to embrace him and assure him she had not indeed passed away. After a number of months, his experience changed markedly. While he still could be reduced to profound sobbing within seconds of encountering a chair she sat in or a sweater she wore, he focused more and more on his own aging and the limited number of years left for him to live. His mourning had morphed into terror and rage at his own mortality, which he had never considered to be, as it is for all of us, his ultimate fate. He fully expected, as he repeatedly stated with honest surprise, that he and she would live forever, that their lives were magical and slotted for immortality. And when he finally began to realize that his life had limited time, and his rage subsided, he began to plan for his future and how to construct his life now that she was gone. In a very condensed period of time Nick went through a developmental leap most of us struggle with for a lifetime, relinquishing his omnipotent hold over time and accepting the inevitability of *Chronos* time and death, even his.

Time after time: adventures in *Kairos* time

> Alice: How long is forever?
> White Rabbit: Sometimes just one second.
>
> Lewis Carroll

By coincidence, just as I was invited to present this paper, I had the good fortune to have a number of former patients, some of whom I had not seen for as many as 30 years, return to treatment. What a fortuitous, and I must say, timely, occurrence! It presented me with a fabulous opportunity to observe, first-hand, some of the effects of time on my patients, on me and on our relationship. And of course, there was this paper to write ... Overnight my consulting room became a study in *Kairos*. Time rapidly became dizzyingly airborne, shuttling back and forth in multiple directions, being created, recreated and altered even as we spoke. How had I constructed and held on to memories of my patients who at the same time constructed and held on to memories of me? Now all memories were about to be affected by our mutual reconstruction of what had already become reconstructed over time. How had the intervening years affected my memories of them and their memories of me. What did we remember? What was forgotten? What memories were lost, changed and how were they altered and how did they morph into what? It became an exercise in temporal Rashomon on steroids!

Fortunately, and to set the stage, these were mostly patients toward whom I felt positively, my feelings ranging from neutral, to fond to avuncular, to loving. My work with them ranged from tumultuous, to rocky, to frustrating, to satisfying and extremely rewarding. And while I certainly would not claim success in a number of my other patients, these were all patients about whom I could point to some measure of success in treatment.

In a broad stroke, what stood out in particular was that my familiarity with each of them has remained similar to the day they left treatment. It has been like running into a long lost friend when you immediately kick into a familiar and comfortable gear together, collapsing all intervening time. Life did go on, in some predictable and of course unpredictable ways and contributed to changes in all of us. But even with those whom I had had no contact for *many* years, as much as our appearances had succumbed to the contributions of age, and as much as there were new facets to our personalities, our emotional familiarity and experience with each other remained markedly similar and true to my memory. For me, this bespeaks the continuity of not only character, but of intersubjectively created memory. Paradoxically, while psychoanalysis purports to promote change it also assures for continuity. I have had an uncanny experience with each of my returning patients, both physically and psychologically, that has remained exactly the same, locked in time. Despite the life circumstances and changes we all have experienced, a unique essence of our relationship remained. I recognized them and they recognized me, as if no time had elapsed. Whatever co-construction of our experience we created, the intersubjective reality of each other and of our relationship with each other, in manifest ways had not been altered. This has, for me, provided yet another testament to the continuity of the self and the dyad.

Similarly, it was surprising that the uncanny ways in which my perceptions of the ambiance as well as the emotional atmosphere in the room, different for each patient, came flooding back. My memories of the details of the bits and pieces of their lives, while not immediately present, began cascading through my mind with escalating rapidity. To my relief, the more I remembered, the more I remembered.

But that has not been the whole story. As I have noted before, some of the memories and perceptions have been altered. Many of these returnees profess to my having said such and such and that it had a profound effect on them. In my mind, not only do I not have even a trace of saying such and such, I know that the words comprising such and such would never have come out of my mouth. But there are two aspects to this phenomenon. One is that the memory absolutely does not ring true for me. It feels false, emanating from the subjectivity of the patient. But also, the overwhelming majority of the occurrences in which they retained something I never said have been infused with idealization. I am not hearing, "You said such and such and I have always been angry about that." All of these false memories purportedly have had a profoundly positive effect on them.

In my attempt to understand this phenomenon I find myself resorting to clichés. But there is always truth embedded in a cliché. I present the idea that internalized hope might indeed reign eternal, a version of "time heals all wounds." These idealized remnants of our interaction that were internalized and survived the years have continued to shade and create memories of the past. While the content of the specific memories might not fit the reality, the idealizing and life-affirming processes that were identified with during the treatment have continued to function as positive organizational forces shaping their internal worlds. Perhaps functioning as good objects for our patients during treatment enables them to internalize and identify with a positive, hopeful and life-affirming organizational dynamic that contributes to the healing process and to the continued integration of their internal worlds.

Of course, this was a biased sample, made of people who had relatively helpful experiences in therapy. Those patients who ended therapy with decidedly lesser feelings toward me probably would never come into treatment with me again 30 years hence.

These dynamic identifications have been further cemented and enhanced during whatever mourning process took place after the therapy ended. Others might have it that the goodness of the analyst is idealized defensively to guard against the difficult feelings of anger, disappointment and loss that are evoked during the termination process. While not mutually exclusive alternatives, my emphasis is not on the content of the analyst's deeds and words, but on the dynamic psychic organization of the affirmation of life that is internalized during the analysis. This creates new shades of goodness that remain relatively stable through time. But that is a longer discussion we might continue when we have more – time.

My patients have also informed me about harboring continued anger about the disappointing things I did and said during our work together. By and large, as opposed to the fictional positive memories, these less-than-enthused memories have rung true to my memory. So perhaps bad real internalized objects never disappear, they are just countered by an increased ability to organize interpersonal and intersubjective memories in life-affirming ways. As I often tell my patients when I am asked if they will always feel the rage, bitterness, anger, disappointments, envious and toxic feelings they struggle with, they don't go away but the volume can be turned way down. Now I would add that more satisfactory approaches to life might be amped up and become more default.

In this light I would like to describe an interesting experience I've had with one patient. He is a successful man who actually stalked me at times during our work over 25 years ago. Without getting too detailed about the case, we had come to the idea that he suffered from deficits in object permanence brought about by an indifferent and self-absorbed mother. His stalking had been going on for years prior to our work together when he would obsessively track anyone in his life, male or female, who he thought might provide him with the attention, recognition and consistent love he so desperately craved. Most important was his overwhelming feeling that he and others would have no memory trace of each other. Out of sight, out of mind, permanently. Since leaving treatment, he married, moved up the ladder in his career and successfully raised two children. He had also stopped his obsessive stalking and was not as plagued by fears of him or others disappearing. He came back into treatment to work on issues of aging and retirement.

Years before, he had been a difficult, challenging and provocative patient. The treatment ended prematurely when he was transferred out of state. He left therapy as challenging and confrontational as when he entered.

As we meet again now, the memories of our relationship come flowing back for both of us. This time, however, the provocative edge is gone and we are able to talk about the trying aspects of our previous work, even with humor at times. His remembering the occasions when I became overtly angry with him is concordantly matched by my memories of his provocations and taunts. This time, however, we talk, this time we do not engage in the impossible enactments that riddled our previous contact. He does not become provocative and I do not become frustrated and angry. In fact, it is clear that there is a growing affection we have for each other that is transforming our previous memories of stormy interactions. We both now cast a compassionate, tolerant and empathic shadow on those two characters who had engaged in constant dueling. Sometime between then and now, his memories of our stormy engagement became detoxified. He is now able to tell me that even when the tension increased between us, he felt both calmed by my demeanor and great relief when my moments of anger did not remain eternal and rapidly passed.

So what happened? I would like to propose that *nachträglichkeit* can exert a positive dynamic. Relevant to the issue of time, the loving and tolerant aspects of our relationship that we internalized during our previous engagement, now acted retrospectively to reorganize the difficult memories into more tolerable, positive remembrances. Typically, we speak of *nachträglichkeit* as the expression of traumatizing forces influencing our perceptions at a time subsequent to the actual events. In this case my memories of the difficult interactions between me and my patient were softened considerably in the intervening years. Actually, as I thought about him, what came to mind was a dim recollection that even when I was hating him years before, it was always with an asterisk signaling feelings of great affection that I did not understand at the time and rapidly pushed out of my mind. Through time, and by virtue of my own evolved development and maturity, I can recognize my willingness to entertain more compassionate, even loving, feelings in me toward him that I was unable to process at the time because of my own identifications with some of his less-than-noble attributes like envy and greed. These are conflict-ridden affects that I had not yet analyzed in myself sufficiently 30 years ago. Likewise, I find myself feeling more capable of sustained empathy and compassion for his experience back then. We have, in essence, altered our perceptions and memories of our past selves and the memory of our past relationship that existed 25 years ago via the action of a positive *nachträglichkeit*, which has detoxified, through time, and mutual evolution, our feelings for each other. Absence, indeed, has made our hearts grow fonder.

I recently started working with Jeremy, a man now in his sixties who also returned to therapy with me after a 25-year hiatus. When I first started working with him around 1985 he entered therapy concerned about his relationships with women and his stalled career as a writer. He had had aspirations to write novels since high school and to date had not been successful in finishing a single book. He was a very intense narcissistically scarred man who wore his insecurities on his bombastic, overwhelming interpersonal demeanor, in many respects not unlike his recently deceased father. He actually did not need to try to exaggerate his talents because in truth he was extremely bright and talented. His talents stood on their own needing no boost from his pomposity, which in actuality turned people off and detracted from his well-honed gifts and talent as a novelist.

Briefly, he grew up in a small western city to the wealthiest family in town. His father made his wealth in the business world. His mother was not a shrinking violet. She was a "lady who lunched" and was actively involved with charities and civic affairs. Both parents were equally and highly critical of Jeremy. They were also equally negligent of him as they focused their energies toward his institutionalized, severely developmentally impaired older brother. While unstated, it was clear to Jeremy that his purpose in life was to compensate for his impaired brother and rescue his parents from their shame. Their hanging their wounded selves on his successes was meant more to compensate for his impaired brother than for him to own and embrace. To quickly sum up our work together, Jeremy formed a good working relationship with me. He overcame his inhibitions with both women and writing. He married and managed to grind out and publish a couple of short stories for which he achieved a modicum of recognition.

When he re-presented for therapy in the present time, our memories of our previous work have been fairly veridical up to a point; then they dramatically diverge. What I remember next was that his attitude toward me underwent a sudden and drastic shift. He entered a session feeling markedly glum and saddened, if not depressed. When I made a rather brief and innocuous statement meant to be empathic with his mood, the exact nature of which has unfortunately succumbed to my imperfect memory, he went into a rage at me, shouting loudly that what I said was not what he needed to hear and I had not helped him one whit throughout our work together. Shortly thereafter, after cancelling several consecutive sessions, he quit therapy and never returned to say goodbye. Despite my attempts to make contact, that was the last I heard from him. His disappearance, feeling more like an evaporation, left me futilely clapping with one interpretive hand as I tried to understand what had happened. I was left with only unsatisfactory conjecture.

That was my memory of the experience. So, as he entered therapy in the present time I eagerly awaited the opportunity, after all this time, to hopefully gain a better understanding of what had happened. Silly me. Once again time and its conspiratorial relationship with my unconscious had played one of its endless tricks on me. Imagine my confusion when he told me he had no memory of having left in anger. Not only does he not remember the enraged manner in which he terminated therapy, he can't imagine ever having been angry with me. What has set in instead is an inexorable idealization of me as the therapist who saved his life. He has returned for a repeat performance. Once again, he is feeling blocked in his work. This time he is coming after having achieved major recognition and acclaim for the novels he has written since we last saw each other.

I imagine as I work with all my returnees, I will be further enlightened and surprised by the ways in which we have been altered by the magical mystery tour that time has cast upon our selves. Past, present and future will continue to challenge our organization of memory in unpredictable ways as it thumbs its noses at real tick-tock time. Whoever or whatever forces created the universe were spot on when they invented real, objective tick-tock time, but we have certainly messed it up with the advent of our subjective, boundless and un-tethered-by-reality time.

Restarting time

Before ending I would like to speak to an experimental clinical technique I have begun to develop derived from my experience working with patients who are either stuck in a paranoid/schizoid state or even in a depressive episode. I have written elsewhere (Skolnick, 2006, 2014) about the importance of the analyst honing a deep empathy for the experience of unintegrated psychic states, states that have not achieved the depressive level of psychic organization according to Klein. Other clinicians as well have described the phenomenology of experience in a paranoid/schizoid psychic organization (Ogden, 1990; Bromberg, 2011). I would also hold up Meissner (2007) who writes about the confluence of time and psychic experience in this group.

Most analysts have witnessed the experience of our patients stuck in a paranoid/schizoid position. Their subjective sense of time is organized in a decidedly different manner than someone occupying a more integrated depressive position. Paradoxically, the sense of time in this state is both stuck in the moment, and eternal. The experience of time grinds to a halt, it becomes in essence timeless and endless. What is felt at the moment has always felt exactly the same, will always feel the same and it has and will always feel immutable. Moreover, the paranoid/schizoid experience is rooted in unintegrated, part object organization. In part object worlds, affects are uncommonly powerful, without significant modulation. The experience of self and other is not symbolic. A patient in this state does not think you are an asshole, they know you are an asshole. And of particular significance, the experience of each paranoid/schizoid state exists as a separate universe unto itself. The states do not talk to each other, nor do they talk to psychic states organized into more integrated structures. A patient I saw resided in such an organization for long periods of time. I wish to focus here not on the etiology of her inner world organization, but rather on its phenomenology with special emphasis on its relationship to her sense of time. For the purposes of this discussion I am concerned with form, not content.

My patient, Cherize, lived on a reverse day/night schedule. The reversal allowed her basic withdrawn, schizoid terror of relationship to manifest in a world where time could be structured to minimize meaningful contact with others. Generally, her demeanor was dreamy and distant. She could, though, in a split second enter a paranoid/schizoid organization in which I was for her bizarrely idealized. She would proclaim, "All your words are golden. I hang my existence on your every word. They and you are perfect." Again, she did not think I was golden, she knew I was golden. It was not her subjective opinion, for her it was the objective truth. Lest I let this get to my head, her sentiments about me could and would change mid-sentence, more rapidly than a shark seeking and devouring its prey. Without warning she could proceed to excoriate me, loudly, proclaiming me to be the worst example of the lowest worm who barely deserved to be alive. Working herself into a frenzy, which at times left me shaking, she could fly out of the room slamming the door while damning everything on my side of it. The next day, she would return, cool and calm as if nothing had occurred. When I questioned her about the previous day's explosion, she would, lightly and without contrition, declare she had no idea what had gotten into her. It made no sense to her now. Her two states had not communicated with each other.

Time, for Cherize, was sequestered under her omnipotent control. Only rarely could she either recognize or attempt to relinquish control. Indeed, the abuse and traumas she suffered as a child had been exceptionally severe. We do not have the time to perform a psychological autopsy on them all, but I will refer to just one episode to highlight the severity of abuse that forced her to feel unsafe in any time structure other than her own. When she was an adolescent, her father organized international conferences for an organization he administered, comprised of world-renowned delegates. At these conventions she was delegated the job, by her father, of making herself available sexually to any delegate who so desired. I bring her up to illustrate the devastation wrought on her sense of time by severe trauma. But again, for the purposes of this discussion, I am not concerned with etiology, I am concerned with the form of her sense of time.

When Cherize experienced me as a monster, it was not just a momentary blip. Climbing into her experience, it was clear to me that for her I had always been and would always be, a seething monster eager to do her harm. The good me was no longer, nor had it ever been on the stage. With Cherize, as well as other patients who could enter a paranoid/schizoid sense of timelessness frequently, I have resorted to a cognitive intervention that bypasses an analytic understanding. The goal is not to understand the meaning of the state. To present understanding and empathy can of course be enormously helpful in negotiating the pain of a paranoid/schizoid experience of timelessness. Understanding can also promote a modulation of mood and communication between dissociated time states. I will only start my intervention, however when the patient is in a calmer more integrated place. Otherwise she/they have no way of processing it.

What I say to Cherize, and other patients who have entered similar timeless holes, is something like, "When you are so actively in hate with someone [me, yourself, whoever] you are in a 'state'." People tend to easily understand being in states, a colloquial version of our multiple state theories. I continue:

> When you are in a "state" try to plant a grain of a thought in the back of your mind. It probably will make absolutely no sense to you at the time but put it there anyway. The grain of thought is that you will not always feel this way. It is just how you are feeling at the moment, and while it will make no sense to you at the time, again, try to just put it there. In time you will go back to a better place where there's room to feel a range of feelings and your "state" will end. Again, it won't seem possible when you are in the "state," but time will pass and you will feel differently, more like you usually feel, when you're not in that hateful "state."

What I am attempting to replicate are the ministrations of a good-enough mother when her child needs help modulating his or her moods. Futhermore, I am helping the patient to enter a different organizational state and achieve a more adaptive, flexible sense of time which is neither eternal nor stuck in time, without movement. Imagine the frustrated child denouncing his parent with a decisive, "I hate you!" If an insecure parent cannot tolerate her child's rage she might respond with a slap and some version of, "No! I hate you! Don't ever say that. If you ever say that to me again you will be punished. You're a rotten child!" For this child, threatened by such a confusing rupture of connection, time has indeed stopped. Now it might feel like the parent will hate them forever. Contrast that with the more secure parent who responds with some version of, in essence, "You hate me now but see how you feel later," or even with some version of harried annoyance (we can't always be perfect), "It hurts Daddy's feelings when you say that, but after a nap you might feel differently." These interventions stress the integration of loving and hating feelings, and the modulations brought about by the passage of time. They help the child understand and accept the difficulties and the joys of being human. Similarly, therapists can help a patient understand and utilize time/state related phenomena to modulate, negotiate and integrate the storms and disruptions that arise in therapy and interrupt an ongoing sense of self and relationship.

Notes

1 A previous version of this paper was presented at the Chicago Center for Psychoanalysis, Chicago, IL. October, 2017.
2 To explore the contemporary arguments about the philosophical and scientific nature of time is beyond the purview of this book. For an excellent summary I refer the reader to Chapter 1 of Meissner (2007).
3 See Birksted-Breen (2016, pp. 139–157), for a complete exegesis of the origin of the term '*nachträglichkeit*' and the confusion created by its different translations in French and English, and its different uses by Freud and Lacan, who preferred the French '*après coup*'.

References

Aristotle. (1941). *Physics*. In R. McKeon (ed.), *The Basic Works of Aristotle* (pp. 213–394). New York: Random House.

Baranger, M. and Baranger, W. (2008). The analytic situation as a dynamic field. *International Journal of Psycho-Analysis*, 89: 795–826.

Bion, W. (1962). *Learing from Experience*. London: Heinemann. [Reprinted in *Seven Servants*. New York: Aronson, 1977.]

Birksted-Breen, D. (2003). Time and the après-coup. *The International Journal of Psychoanalysis*, 84: 1501–1515.

Birksted-Breen, D. (2016). *The Work of Psychoanalysis: Sexuality, Time and the Psychoanalytic Mind*. London: Routledge.

Bollas, C. (1989). *The Shadow of the Object: Psychoanalysis of the Unthought Known*. New York: Columbia University Press.

Bromberg, P.M. (2011). *The Shadow of the Tsunami: And the Growth of the Relational Mind*. New York: Routledge.

Carroll, Lewis. (2019). *Alice's Adventures in Wonderland*. Urbana: Project Gutenberg. Retrieved March 10, 2019, from www.Gutenberg.org/ebooks/19033.

Fonagy, P. (1992). The theory and practice of resilience. *Journal of Child Psychology and Psychiatry*, 35(2): 231–257.

Green, A. (2009). From the ignorance of time to the murder of time: From the murder of time to the misrecognition of temporality in psychoanalysis.

In L.G. Fiorini and J. Canestri (eds.), *The Experience of Time: Psychoanalytic Perspectives* (pp. 1–21). London: Karnac.

Hartocollis, P. (1974). Origin of time: A reconstruction of the ontogenetic development of the sense of time based on object-relations theory. *Psychiatric Quarterly*, 43: 243–261.

Hawking, S. (1988). *A Brief History of Time*. New York: Bantam Books.

Hoffman, E. (2009). *Time*. New York: Picador.

Isaacson, W. (2008). *Einstein: His Life and His Universe*. New York: Simon & Schuster.

James, W. (1890). *The Principles of Psychology*. New York: Henry Holt and Company.

Joyce, J. (2018). *Ulysses*. Urbana: Project Gutenberg. Retrieved August 1, 2008, from www.Gutenberg.org/ebooks/etext4300.

Loewald, H.W. (1980). *Papers on Psychoanalysis*. New Haven: Yale University Press.

Meissner, W.M. (2007). *Time, Self, and Psychoanalysis*. New York: Jason Aronson.

Mitchell, S. (1992). True selves, false selves and the ambiguity of authenticity. In N.J. Skolnick and S.C. Warshaw (Eds.), *Relational Perspectives in Psychoanalysis*. New York: The Analytic Press.

Modell, A.H. (1990). *Other Times, Other Realities*. Cambridge, MA: Harvard University Press.

Ogden, T.H. (1990). *The Matrix of the Mind*. Northvale: Jason Aronson.

Ogden, T.H. (2016). *Reclaiming Unlived Life*. London: Routledge.

Parsons, M. (2009). Why did Orpheus look back? In L.G. Fiorini and J. Canestri (eds.), *The Experience of Time: Psychoanalytic Perspectives* (pp. 35–45). London: Karnac.

Parsons, M. (2014). *Living Psychoanalysis: From Theory to Experience*. London: Routledge.

Piaget, J. (1969). *The Child's Conception of Time*. New York: Ballantine Books.

Priel, B. (1997). Time and self. *Psychoanalytic Dialogues*, 7: 431–451.

Seligman, S. (2018). *Relationships in Development: Infancy, Intersubjectivity, and Attchment*. London: Routledge.

Shakespeare, William. (2019). *The Rape of Lucrece*. Urbana: Project Gutenberg. Collins Edition. Retrieved October 1998 from www.Gutenberg.org/ebooks/etext1505.

Skolnick, N.J. (2006) What's a good object to do? *Psychoanalytic Dialogues*, 16: 1–29.

Skolnick, N.J. (2010). Termination in psychoanalysis: It's about time. In J. Salberg (Ed.), *Good Enough Endings* (pp. 223–241). New York: Routledge.

Skolnick, N.J. (2014). The analyst as good object: A Fairbairnian perspective. In G.S. Clarke and D.E. Scharff (eds.), *Fairbairn and the Object Relations Tradition* (pp. 249–263). London: Karnac.

Stern, D. (2012). Witnessing across time: Accessing the present from the past and the past from the present. *Psychoanalytic Quarterly*, 81: 53–81.

Winnicott, D.W. (1965). *The Maturational Processes and the Facilitating Environment*. New York: IUP.

Winnicott, D.W. (1971). *Playing and Reality*. London: Tavistock.

Chapter 2

Vertical transmission of acquired ulcer susceptibility in the rat

Introduction

This article is the published version of my doctoral dissertation research. It appeared in *Science* in 1980. While the study is designed to contribute a measure of validity to a psychoanalytically derived model of the pathogenesis of ulcer disease, it stands far afield from relational psychoanalysis in a number of significant ways. Not the least, it was a study designed to explore an animal model of ulcer susceptibility in rats. It stood squarely in the realm of examining a psycho-soma interaction in which a somatic process was influenced by an environmental disruption. Moreover, it was psychoanalytically inspired by a model of a disease process that postulated the susceptibility to an illness (gastrointestinal lesions) in rats was induced by a maternal disruption early in the life of an animal. Rats prematurely separated from their mothers developed a predisposition to ulcer disease so that they developed stomach lesions when stressed as adults. Rats separated from their mothers at the normal time developed significantly fewer stomach lesions when stressed as adults.

This phenomenon had been demonstrated in animal studies prior to my dissertation (Erdösová, Flandera, Krecek and Wiener, 1967; Ackerman, Hofer and Weiner, 1975). Through the use of animal models, it had been shown that events occurring early during the lifespan of an animal could create a heightened susceptibility to a disease pathogenesis later in life. In this way, the predictions of these animal studies are based on a model of pathogenesis similar to that of psychoanalytic theory, which predicates adult psychological disruption with disruptions in early development.

Of interest to the study of time, taken together, these studies illustrate a model of disease pathogenesis that includes a long gap between the acquisition of disease susceptibility and its manifestation at a later time in the lifespan. There are a number of disease processes that include gaps of time between the acquisition of the disease and its overt clinical manifestation (e.g., venereal disease) or inherited illness that might manifest not at birth but at a future time in the lifespan (e.g., Huntington's Chorea). What is new is that some disease processes are induced by an early environment event, rather than an infection, which manifests as a disease at a later time in life.

With more stunning implications, it has also been demonstrated that events incurring early in the life of an animal not only result in a disease process onset in later life, but whatever patho-genetic changes that are induced by the early events have been shown to cross a generational boundary and result in a disease onset in subsequent generations of animals not exposed to the environmental event. For example, a single sub-diabetic dose of alloxin, administered to either a male or female rat before mating, has been associated with abnormal glucose tolerance in their untreated progeny. The degree of glucose intolerance increased progressively over seven successive generations not exposed to the alloxin (Spergel, Levy and Goldner, 1971). In my doctoral dissertation study, in contrast to Spergel et al., the results were the first example that I know of where susceptibility to a disease induced in the parent generation by an environmental manipulation, rather than by the introduction of a drug (Skolnick, Ackerman, Hofer and Weiner, 1980), resulted in a susceptibility to a disease in the offspring, who had not experienced the environmental event.

Rats born to mothers who had been separated early from their mothers were allowed to grow to reproductive age and produce offspring. The offspring were not separated early but were weaned at the normal time. These normally weaned rats born to mothers who had been separated early demonstrated significantly more ulcers when stressed as adults than normally weaned rats born to normally weaned mothers and stressed as adults. The acquired susceptibility to ulcer disease had crossed a generational boundary to a subsequent generation.

These results go to the heart of the historic feud between the French naturalist Jean-Baptiste Lamarck and Charles Darwin. For Darwin, the evolution of life forms is driven by the occurrence of rare genetic variation combined with natural selection. Some randomly obtained variations bestow the animals with an increased chance of survival and reproduction in their natural habitat. By contrast, for Lamarck, evolution of life is driven by variation and the accumulation of small gradual changes. Considered by Darwin to be "veritable rubbish," Lamarck's theory postulated the existence of the inheritance of acquired characteristics. For example, for Lamarck, giraffes obtained their long necks by stretching to eat leaves from tall trees and the elongated necks were then passed on to future generations (Rosenfeld and Ziff, 2018).

Lamarck could not explain the mechanism of the process. A clue was provided by the discovery of the molecular structure of DNA, and its role in reproduction, but alas, it was strongly considered resolved dogma that the structure of DNA could not be altered in any way by the environment or a person's way of life. The transfer of characteristics to the next generation, it was known, could be altered but only by the rarest of genetic mutations, and, it was commonly thought, never by alterations in the environment during the course of an animal's lifespan.

During the last 20 years or so, the study of epigenetics has ushered in a growing literature that supports nothing less than a paradigmatic shift in the science of heredity. My dissertation provided one of the first studies to demonstrate the effects of an environmental event on the traits of a subsequent generation of animals not exposed to the environmental event. Epigenetic theories hold that acquired traits can be transferred to a subsequent generation without any alteration to DNA. The transfer of the trait acquired by an environmental event appears to be the result of an alteration in the mechanisms involved in the expression of the genetic makeup in the subsequent generation. It was necessary, then, to investigate whether environmentally induced disease susceptibility could be transferred vertically, which is exactly what was demonstrated by this study.

Moreover, in an attempt to understand the mechanism of the vertical transmission, I designed a cross-fostering experiment to tease out whether the transmission of the susceptibility was the consequence of a prenatal or postnatal process. Was something altered in the prenatal environment of the rat pups to increase their susceptibility to stressed induced ulcers? Or alternatively, did the mother rats (themselves separated from their mothers early) provide altered maternal behavior for their rat pups, which in turn increased their ulcer susceptibility.

The results demonstrated unequivocally that the increased susceptibility to stress induced ulcers was transmitted to the offspring of early separated mothers in utero, despite the finding that the early separated mothers were indeed behaviorally different mothers than normally separated mothers. Moreover, these results pointed to the probability that the mechanism for the transfer of the ulcer susceptibility was of an epigenetic process. The mothers who had been subjected to early maternal separation provided a prenatal environment for their future offspring that was altered in such a way as to affect the expression of their genetic material and increase ulcer susceptibility in the offspring.

The study of epigenetic phenomena has burgeoned since I first reported my dissertation results. The studies are too numerous to mention for the purposes of this book. I will only mention a few of note. An article published in *Science* in 2017 reported that a certain roundworm (C. elegans), when exposed to an ambient temperature change, would begin to glow. Furthermore, the induced glowing continued to appear in 14 subsequent generations that were not exposed to the temperature change (Klosin Casas, Hidalgo-Carcedo, Vavouri and Lehner, 2017).

While there have been many animal studies demonstrating epigenetic phenomena, there have been comparably fewer reports of such epigenetic changes in humans. The presence of epigenetic phenomena in humans has remained steeped in controversy. For a number of reasons these studies are infinitely more difficult to design. Inherited effects in humans are difficult to measure due to the long generational times and the ensuing difficulty planning for and maintaining longitudinal records. There are, nonetheless, a number of well-designed studies from reputable research labs demonstrating that events in the lives of humans can effect change in their offspring without altering the DNA. For example, researchers have found that descendants of holocaust survivors have lower levels of the hormone cortisol, which aids in the body's resilience following trauma (Yehuda et al., 2016). This study and others clearly add to our thinking about the cross-generational transmission of the effects of trauma.

So why did I include my dissertation research in this book? The first and most facile reason is that this book represents a compendium of many of my publications and presentations over the span of my career. As such it also represents the beginning of my professional evolution that ensued, including inevitable twists and turns in direction.

From 1976 to 1980 I had the good fortune and opportunity to conduct my dissertation research under the supervision of Sigurd Ackerman and Myron Hofer in their Evo-Devo lab,[1] sponsored by Herbert Weiner, Director of Psychiatry at Montefiore Hospital, Albert Einstein College of Medicine.

44   Neil J. Skolnick et al.

Credit also needs to be extended to George Cicala the titular sponsor of my dissertation at the University of Delaware, where I was a doctoral candidate. He both allowed the inter-institution arrangement and made valuable contributions to the project. One could not hope for better mentors. While affording me great independence, they also provided me with patient, astute guidance, respect and support, both emotionally and financially. It was an invaluable experience for me, who at the time was considering a career in research either alone or in combination with a clinical practice.

To this day I continue to value my exposure to research in basic science. It exerted an influence on my critical thinking processes that continues to this day, be they clinical or more purely theoretical. But in 1977 I experienced a setback in my dissertation research that convinced me that I had the soul of a clinician and not a researcher. That summer in New York City there was a massive blackout. One of its numerous consequences was to shut down the air conditioning in the animal vivarium where my rodent subjects were housed. The lack of air conditioning allowed a strain of pneumonia to strike my rats that were in various longitudinal phases of the study and they all died. Upshot was I lost about nine months of work. So it goes for my illusion of having control. Of the many reasons I chose to do an animal study for my dissertation was, aside from my interest in basic science research, it allowed me to maintain the illusion that I had total control over obtaining subjects for the study and that I did not have to depend on the vagaries and inconsistencies of enlisting unreliable human subjects. This experience was one of many that cemented my interest in clinical work which, although far from reliable, held disappointments and frustrations that did not hold a candle to the disappointment brought on by my future being held up by a mechanical mishap in the lab. Of course, I was much younger and inexperienced then and had not as yet been exposed to much that can go seriously wrong in life, anywhere and at any time. That said, I do think my character ultimately proved to be more suitable for clinical work, that, as noted, has been greatly influenced by my experience with, and appreciation of, the contributions of basic research. If nothing else I can spot the dishonest attempts by insurance companies to misuse research results to justify their preference to reimburse cheaper, less reliable and less valid forms of psychotherapy. But that issue merits a longer discussion that lies outside the scope of this book.

The evolution of science is steeped in philosophical arguments that are also far beyond the purview of this book, and quite frankly, far beyond my cursory knowledge of the subject. Very broadly speaking, the foundations of psychoanalytic ideas have shifted, from a model of science rooted in the search for objective truths supported by hypothetical-deductive methods of research to models of science, rooted in relative truths, supported by hermeneutic organizations of knowledge.

Hypothetical-deductive models consider evolution in scientific truths to rely on a bedrock of scientific knowledge, which evolves via a gradual accretion of supporting or disconfirming data. It represents a linear search for an objective truth, ultimately knowable. According to Greenberg and Mitchell (1983), in their classical study of object relation theories in psychoanalysis:

> Until the last several decades, Western Philosophy of science has been dominated by an understanding of science and its theories grounded in a thoroughgoing empiricism and, in this century, elaborated by the philosophical doctrines of logical positivism. Within this understanding, termed by recent philosophers of science "The Received View," there is an assumed one-to-one correspondence between good theory and actual events and processes in the real world: facts are established irrefutably through objective observation; theories offer different explanations of these facts on the basis of which testable predictions can be made; experimentation determines the correctness or error of the theory; science proceeds through a gradual accumulation of neutral observations and confirmed hypotheses; scientific understanding changes through the absorption of earlier, more limited theories into increasingly broader and more inclusive theories.
>
> (p. 16)

In the 1950s and 1960s, scientists influenced by relativity theory and Heisenberg's Uncertainty Principle adopted a new understanding of the relationship between science and objective reality. They adopted "weltanschauung" analysis (Suppe, 1977) which holds that there are no purely objective facts and observations which lie outside of theory. Rather, one's theory or way of thinking determines what are likely to be held as facts. The truth, then, became decidedly more of a relative truth dependent on the context of a "weltanschauung," conceptual perspective. Thomas Kuhn became a chief advocate of this perspective (Greenberg and Mitchell, 1983).

He held that scientific truth was composed of a temporal series of disconnected paradigms that were useful for problem solving for a limited period of time and then were replaced by more useful paradigms, as new ideas and data became available. While in ascendance, paradigms held great power to influence reigning organizations of ideas, conceptual attitudes, research and thinking.

Scientists and philosophers are currently attempting to delineate a middle approach between a positivistic approach to an absolute truth and a "weltanschauung" emphasis on non-objective presumptive truths. It is a work in progress. In this light, Kuhn has more recently modified his theory of "weltenschauung" and the use of paradigms to account for their becoming too elastic and virtually meaningless and giving too little a nod to the role of rationality in choosing model choice. He now rejects the construct of "paradigm" and has adopted the concept of "disciplinary matrix." Matrices are not applicable to all sciences. Rather they are composed of models pertinent to specific disciplines. Psychoanalysis in particular, is a discipline in which people make commitments to metaphysical models in order to understand and organize ideas. Kuhn, according to Greenberg and Mitchell (1983), holds that psychoanalytic theories operate as models reflecting metaphysical commitments because they are based on untestable premises concerning four fundamental premises:

1. Defining the basic unit of study. What are the basic, non-derivative, building blocks of experience?
2. Defining human motivation. What do we want?
3. How do we think about development, the transformation of the infant mind to the mind of the adult?
4. How do we account for the stability of an individual's distinctive features. Or its change?

Returning to paradigms, Greenberg and Mitchell (1983) highlighted Kuhn's thinking about transitions between paradigms:

If science consists of a series of discontinuous models, how does one move from one paradigm to the next? What are the features of such a transition? His depiction of this process highlights what might be considered to be the more "political" features of the history of scientific ideas. Paradigms, because they are models of reality taken for the "truth," inspire loyalties. During the peak period of influence of a paradigm, nearly all workers within the particular field are under its sway . . . As the peak period is passed, new data, new ideas begin to emerge outside the boundaries permitted by the paradigm.

(p. 17)

For many years, Darwin's theory held that cross-generational transmission of traits was determined by the genetic makeup of the individual and extra-genetic influences were extremely rare, limited to rare mutations. Those scientists who differed, like Lamarck, were vilified and cast into oblivion.

My dissertation research took Darwin's long held theory of inheritance to task. In my study, reprinted in this chapter, it was demonstrated that an environmentally acquired ulcer susceptibility in rats could be transmitted across generations. That study was conducted before the advent of the field of epigenetics burgeoned. The recent studies of epigenetic phenomena fall, then, under the purview of a *paradigmatic shift* or, if you prefer, a change in a *disciplinary matrix*. They indeed provided data which compel a re-examination of tenaciously held reality/theory. Today, the study of epigenetics has indeed become an acceptable and respectable pursuit. It points to the powerful tendency of time wrought change to alter basic realities.

Note

1 Evolution-Developmental. Myron Hofer has argued that the increased separation between the study of biology and the study of development, which had unnecessarily veered apart during the twentieth century, was presently changing. He states, "Remarkably, discoveries in the last two decades have resulted in a new set of changes in how biologists view development in relation to evolutionary processes, bringing biological to a position that is again more compatible with psychoanalytic thinking." For more on this issue see Hofer (2014).

References

Ackerman, S.H., Hofer, M.A. and Weiner, H. (1975). Age at maternal separation and gastric erosion susceptibility in the rat. *Psychosomatic Medicine*, 37(2): 180–184.

Erdösová, R., Flandera, V., Krecek, J. and Wiener, P. (1967). The effect of premature weaning on the sensitivity of rats to experimental erosions of the gastric mucosa. *Physiol Bohemoslov.*, 16(5): 400–407.

Greenberg, J.R. and Mitchell, S.A. (1983). *Object Relations in Psychoanalytic Theory*. Cambridge, MA: Harvard University Press.

Hofer, M.A. (2014). The emerging synthesis of development and evolution: A new biology for psychoanalysis. *Neuropsychoanalysis*, 16(1): 1–20.

Klosin, A., Casas, E., Hidalgo-Carcedo, C., Vavouri, T. and Lehner, B. (2017). Transgenerational transmission of environmental information in C. elegans. *Science*, 356: 320–323.

Rosenfeld, I. and Ziff, E. (2018). Epigenetics: The evolution revolution. *The New York Review of Books*.

Skolnick, N.J., Ackerman, S.H., Hofer, M.A. and Weiner, H. (1980). Vertical transmission of acquired ulcer susceptibility in the rat. *Science*, 208: 1161–1163.

Spergel, G., Levy, L.J. and Goldner, M.G. (1971). Glucose intolerance in the progeny of rats treated with single subdiabetogenic dose of alloxan. *Metabolism*, 20(4): 401–413.

Suppe, F. (1977). *The Structure of Scientific Theories*, 2nd edition. Chicago: University of Illinois Press.

Yehuda, R., Daskalakis, N.P., Bierer, L.M., Bader, H.N., Klengel, T., Holsboer, F. and Binder, E.B. (2016). Holocaust exposure induced intergenerational effects on *FKBP5* methylation. *Biological Psychiatry*, 80: 372–380.

Chapter 2

Vertical transmission of acquired ulcer susceptibility in the rat[1]

1980

Neil J. Skolnick, Sigurd H. Ackerman, Myron A. Hofer, and Herbert Weiner

Experimental interventions during an animal's early development can result in modified behavior patterns, physiologic response characteristics and susceptibility to disease that persist for long periods. For example, it was found (Erdosova, Flandara, Krecek and Wiener, 1967; Ackerman, Hofer and Weiner, 1975, 1978) that premature separation of rat pups from their dams increases their subsequent susceptibility to restraint-induced gastric erosion, RGE.[2] We now report that this increased susceptibility to RGE is transmitted to the F1 progeny of female rats who are prematurely separated from their mothers in their own infancy. We also report that the increased RGE susceptibility of prematurely separated rats is transmitted to their progeny prenatally. To our knowledge, this is the first report of an altered susceptibility to a particular disease, acquired by an environmental manipulation during postnatal development in one generation, that is transmitted to offspring in the next.

Gastric erosions can be induced in rats by a combination of food deprivation and restraint. If rats are separated from their mothers at the customary time (postnatal day 21), approximately 10 to 20 percent develops gastric erosions during restraint on day 30. However, after premature separation on postnatal day 14, approximately 80 to 90 percent develop gastric erosions during restraint on day 30 (Ackerman, Hofer and Weiner, 1975).

To evaluate the RGE susceptibility of the offspring of female rats, we compared four groups of F1 progeny (Figure 2.1). In the parent generation, ten litters were separated from their mothers on postnatal day 14 and ten on day 21. The females from each litter were then allowed to grow undisturbed to maturity. At about day 100, one female from each litter was randomly selected and bred to a stock Wistar male. Their offspring were separated from the mothers either prematurely (day 14) or at the usual time (day 21).

On postnatal day 27 all four groups of F1 progeny were deprived of food for 26 hours and then restrained for 28 hours at an ambient temperature of 22°C. Afterwards the animals were killed and their stomachs examined for gastric erosions under a light microscope (X30). The experimenter was unaware of the origin of the stomachs.

The group of special interest was the normally separated progeny of mothers who had been prematurely separated in their own infancy. Sixty-four percent of these F1 rats developed gastric erosions, whereas in the control group (normally separated progeny of normally separated mothers), only 19 percent developed erosions ($x2 = 17.6$; $P < .001$) (Figure 2.2). If the F1 rats were themselves prematurely separated, they had a high incidence ($\sim$ 80 percent) of gastric erosions, regardless of the early experience of their mothers (Figure 2.2). We conclude that a prematurely separated rat mother transmits her acquired RGE susceptibility vertically to her normally separated offspring.

In a second experiment we cross-fostered the F1 progeny to determine whether the differences in ROE susceptibility among F1 rats is acquired prenatally or postnatally. This experiment also served as a partial replication of the first experiment. The parent females were produced by the same procedure as in the first experiment. When about 100 days of age, two estrous females, each from a different litter, were mated at the same time with a single stock male. These mothers delivered litters within 24 hours of each other. After delivery the mothers from each pair of litters were switched so that all F1 progeny were reared by foster mothers. On postnatal day 21 all progeny were separated from their foster mothers. On day 27 they were deprived of food and then restrained. (The animals were coded so that all rearing and testing was done without awareness of the experimental group to which each rat belonged.)

The incidence of RGE was 66 percent among F1 rats born to prematurely separated mothers but reared by normally separated mothers (E x N in Figure 2.2). By contrast, the incidence of RGE in the rats born to normally separated mothers but raised by prematurely separated mothers was 24 percent (N x E in Figure 2.2) ($x2 = 18.5$, $P < .001$). Thus the RGE susceptibility of normally separated F1 rats is influenced by the early experience of their biological mother, not their foster mother. We infer that the increased RGE susceptibility associated with premature separation is transmitted to the F1 progeny of female rats by prenatal factors.

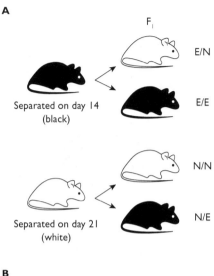
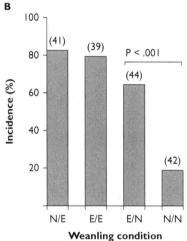

Figure 2.1 Results of the first experiment. (A) Representation of the experimental groups showing their postnatal separation treatment. Abbreviations: E, separation on day 14; N, separation on day 21 (E/N, for example, denotes the normally separated F_1 progeny of prematurely separated mothers). (B) Incidence of RGE. Figures in parentheses give the number of F_1 rats tested in each group.

In the course of conducting the crossfostering study, we also evaluated maternal behavior by inspecting home cages twice daily to obtain scores for nursing, pup grooming, pup retrieving, huddling with pups, or avoidance of pups (Leigh and Hofer, 1973). Mothers who had been prematurely separated in their own infancy spent significantly more time away from their foster F1 pups (x2 = 16.8; P < .001) and less time nursing them (x 2 = 13.0; P < .001) than normally reared mothers. However, the results of the cross-fostering study (Figure 2.2) show that these differences maternal behavior do not contribute to the differences RGE susceptibility observed among the F1 progeny.

Among the experimental groups there are no immediately apparent differences that might explain the transmission of RGE susceptibility. Prematurely separated mothers are as fertile as normal mothers. Their litters are of the same size and weight at birth and survive equally well. Their progeny do not differ in weight up to day 28 and throughout the period of restraint. The individual weight differences observed in the F1 rats could be accounted for by their own ages of separation and not by the separation experiences of their mothers.

There are analogous reports of an intervention before mating in female rats affecting both the animals and their progeny. Daily handling of unweaned rats is known to increase their activity and to decrease plasma corticosterone levels during open-field testing in their adulthood (Levine, Holtmeyer, Karas and Denenberg, 1967). Daily handling of unweaned females has also been reported to affect the open-field behavior (Denenberg and Whimby, 1963) and plasma corticosterone levels (Levine, Holtmeyer, Karas and Denenberg, 1967) in their unhandled progeny. The exposure of female rats to various drugs before impregnation has been shown to affect their progeny. For example, the treatment of young female rats with trifluoperazine produces learning deficits in avoidance conditioning in both the treated rats and their untreated F1 progeny (Gauron and Rowly, 1973). And the administration of thyroxine to neonatal female rats delays the time of vaginal opening and of first estrus in them and their untreated F1 and F2 progeny (Bakke, Lawrence, Robinson and Bennett, 1977).

We know of only one other example of a vertical transmission of an acquired disease susceptibility. A single subdiabetic dose of alloxan, administered to either a male or female rat before mating, has been associated with abnormal glucose tolerance in their untreated progeny (Spergel, Levy and Goldner, 1971; Spergel, Kahn and Goldner, 1975). The degree of glucose intolerance was found to increase in successive (untreated) generations, leading to elevated fasting blood glucose levels

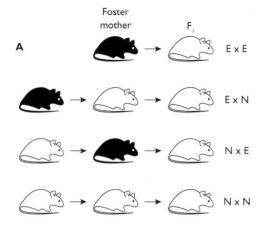

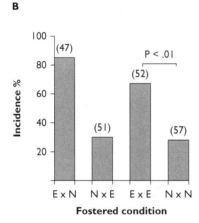

Figure 2.2 Results of the second (cross-fostering) experiment. (A) Representation of the experimental groups showing their postnatal separation treatment. The left and middle columns indicate the separation treatment of the biological and foster mother in their own postnatal periods. The right column indicates that all F_1 progeny were separated from their foster mothers on postnatal day 21. E and N (see Figure 2.1) refer to the mothers of the F_1 test animals. ($E \times N$, for example, denotes that pups born to a prematurely separated mother were fostered at birth to a normally separated mother.) (B) Incidence of RGE.

54 Neil J. Skolnick et al.

in the seventh generation. However, our experimental results may be the first example of transmission of susceptibility to a disease in which the trait was acquired in the parent generation by an environmental manipulation rather than by a drug treatment. We know of no satisfactory explanation of this phenomenon.

Notes

1 This article was originally published in *Science* (1980). 208: 1161–1163. Reprinted with permission from AAAS. Supported by research scientists development award KI MH-00077 to S.H.A., research scientist award KO5 MH-38632 to M.A.H., and by grant RO1-AM-18804 from the National Institute of Arthritis, Metabolism, and Digestive Diseases. We thank R. Shindledecker and M. Pyka for laboratory assistance. Work was conducted in partial fulfillment of requirements for the Ph.D. degree by N.J.S. We thank Dr. George Cicala, University of Delaware, for help as dissertation sponsor.
2 By RGE susceptibility we mean the probability that food deprivation and restraint will produce gastric erosions under standardized experimental conditions. Statistically, we compare the RGE susceptibility of groups of rats by comparing the incidence of erosions following restraint.

References

Ackerman, S.H., Hofer, M.A. and Weiner, H. (1975). Age at maternal separation and gastric erosion susceptibility in the rat. *Psychosom. Med*, 37(2): 180–184.

Ackerman, S.H., Hofer, M.A. and Weiner, H. (1978). Predisposition to gastric erosions in the rat: Behavioral and nutritional effects of early maternal separation. *Gastroenterology*, 75: 649–654.

Bakke, J.L., Lawrence, N.L., Robinson, S. and Bennett, J. (1977). Endocrine studies in the untreated F1 and F2 progeny of rats treated neonatally with thyroxine. *Biology of the Neonate*, 31(1–2): 71–83.

Denenberg, V.H. and Whimby, A.E. (1963). Behavior of adult rats is modified by the experiences their mothers had as infants. *Science*, 142: 1192–1193.

Erdosova, R., Flandara, V., Krecek, J. and Wiener, P. (1967). *Physiol Bohemoslov*, 16: 400.

Gauron, E.F. and Rowly, V.N. (1973). Effects on offspring behavior of parental early drug experience and cross-fostering. *Psychopharmacologia*, 30(3): 269–274.

Leigh, H. and Hofer, M. (1973). Behavioral and physiologic effects of littermate removal on the remaining single pup and mother during the pre-weaning period in rats. *Psychosomatic Medicine*, 34: 497–508.

Levine, S. (1967). Maternal and environmental influences on the adrenocortical response to stress in weanling rats. *Science*, 156: 258–260.

Levine, S., Holtmeyer, G.C., Karas, G.G. and Denenberg, V.H. (1967). Physiological and behavioral effects of infantile stimulation. *Physiology and Behavior*, 2: 55–59.

Spergel, G., Kahn, F. and Goldner, M.G. (1975). Emergence of overt diabetes in offspring of rats with induced latent diabetes. *Metabolism*, 24: 1311.

Spergel, G., Levy, L.J. and Goldner, M.G. (1971). Glucose intolerance in the progeny of rats treated with single subdiabetogenic dose of alloxan. *Metabolism*, 20(4): 401–413.

Chapter 3

Secrets in clinical work

A relational point of view[1]

Introduction

When preparing this manuscript, I spoke with Jodie about including our paper on secrets in this volume. We had co-written it 26 years ago. When I asked her if she wanted to rewrite or tweak any part of the article for publication in this book, she replied, without skipping a beat, something like, no, let it stand as it is, the very first time we both committed our thoughts on psychoanalysis to the printed page. So, in effect, our paper on secrets stands as a historical marker of the relational conceit as it existed 26 years ago, at a moment in time, before being modified, expanded or changed.

We had both recently graduated from analytic training at the NYU Postdoctoral Training Program in Psychoanalysis and Psychoanalytic Psychotherapy and were setting out, with an admixture of anxious anticipation and cautious optimism, to map out our post-training careers. Building successful private practices, teaching in a psychoanalytic institute, and writing, were just beginning to cast their imaginary, hopeful tendrils into a future time. While it was a distinct moment in the time of our careers, it simultaneously marked a distinct moment in our private lives. We were both relatively new parents. So the contextual backdrop of our writing relationship included everything inherent to our status as young parents. We were awash in the struggles of building families, acquiring real estate, and integrating children into our lives. This was no longer the stuff of the future fantasy, it was the very real stuff of the now. Future time was being woven into present time almost faster than it could be processed.

Finally, it was also a distinct moment of time in the history of psychoanalysis. Relational psychoanalysis was increasingly rearing its head in the psychoanalytic lexicon, though I'm fairly certain neither of us could confidently state exactly what it was. The relational track at NYU was just congealing and becoming an alternative to the other tracks. Jody's training at NYU was primarily located in the Freudian track and mine, the interpersonal/humanistic track.[2] We were, as were all initial members of the relational track, immigrants from other tracks. Ten years prior, Greenberg and Mitchell (1983) had published their landmark volume, *Object Relations in Psychoanalysis*. The now classic book, almost single-handedly brought the study of object relations onto center stage in the United States, and in short order, relational psychoanalysis began replacing ego psychology as a dominant force in American psychoanalysis.

To mark the introduction of the relational track at NYU, Susan Warshaw and I published *Relational Perspectives in Psychoanalysis*, a compendium of authors who considered themselves identified with the newly coined relational psychoanalysis. Relational was loosely defined, as we noted in our introduction to the book:

> As psychoanalysis prepares to enter its second century, a number of prominent scholars have noted the fundamental conceptual shifts that have occurred within the discipline, shifts that many believe present major challenges to the classic metapsychology . . . There is increasing focus on, and acceptance of, the primacy of relationships with others in the development of the personality, with major ramifications for conceptions of psychic structure, theories of motivation and pathogenesis, and clinical technique . . .
>
> There is no single relational model or theory. Rather, some who identify with this perspective are interpersonalists; others, British object relations theorists; still others, self-psychologists. Some may not completely align themselves with a purely relational model and differ in the extent to which they dissociate themselves from drive theory. All have a common concern with the centrality of relationship in the development and structure of personality.
>
> (pp. xxiii–xxiv)

Jody's and my paper on secrets was included in the book. One aspect of time that has been noted by philosophers and scientists who study time, is that it is virtually impossible to capture and freeze a single moment in time, the exact "present," as opposed to "past" or "future." By the time we note any particular moment, time has moved on, and the said "present" moment takes its place in the "past." So it is with the birth of relational psychoanalysis. Its inception will invariably overlap with other strands in psychoanalysis –classical, ego, self, interpersonal, intersubjectivity, etc. As a consequence, we look to other markers to approximate transitions and paradigmatic shifts in scientific, and philosophical trends. For example, one unobtrusive measure we can look to in order to signify the rise of a paradigmatic shift to relational thinking in psychoanalysis is the change in membership in our professional organizations. In short order, Division 39, the subsection of the American Psychological Association (APA) dedicated to relational psychoanalysis became the largest of APA's 54 divisions. Likewise, the relational track at NYU, in short, became the largest subscribed track of the NYU postdoctoral program's four teaching tracks.

We can also observe unobtrusive moments of theoretical change in shifts in the texture of our language, which can illuminate temporal transitions. When newer paradigms in psychoanalytic theorizing are being launched, the authors will wisely use the identical language of older paradigms to bridge the gap from old to new. In essence, they are playing with time. At one and the same time, readers are connected with a familiar language associated with an earlier time and sensibility while being transported to a future time where the newer paradigm might take its rightful place, in time, as being familiar. Fairbairn, notably, utilized Freudian jargon (i.e., ego, libido, object) to propose an entirely new systematic theory of psychoanalysis. Definitions of Freudian jargon were drastically redefined by Fairbairn in order to describe a theory that actually jettisoned drive theory and replaced it with object relations theory. Utilizing almost identical language, Freud's drives, considered at the time the centerpiece of human motivation, development, growth and pathology gave way to a theory that placed the establishment and maintenance of human relationships with other people as the centerpiece of human motivation, development growth and pathology. Simply put, in relationship to language, time traveled to the past in order to transport the reader to the future. Winnicott and Fairbairn utilized Freudian concepts, such as "ego" and "superego," in their theories, but totally redefined them. Freud, himself, was a master at this as he wove tales around older rationales of thinking which ultimately rendered newer ways of thinking inevitable and obvious.

Secrets in clinical work   59

In our article on secrets, you can observe us struggling to present the newer model of relational psychoanalysis. We were careful not to disparage dynamic explanations rooted in more traditional models and bowed to them as possible alternative explanations to our newer relational thinking. We eschewed an either/or duality for a both/and approach. If my memory serves me well, we did this, consciously, to ease our readers' transition to a newer model, to render the change more palatable. But if truth be told, we both needed this approach for our own change process. We still needed to expressed loyalty and fealty to the models upon which we cut our teeth during our training, Jody to a classical and me to an interpersonal model. We also needed to maintain and express loyalty, not only to older organizations of thought, but to our teachers, supervisors and patients as well. Change *involves* a village, all the people connected to the development of our professional identity to date. As we also know from our study of development, the establishment of individual growth, autonomy and identity requires a lifetime of separations, conflicts, divided loyalties, new integrations and syntheses. Professional growth can involve the same issues, work and pain that accompanies personal growth.

We also learned the hard way that sometimes we pay too much homage to the past. I recall a recent meeting when new students of psychoanalysis complained we, more experienced analysts, lingered too long in the past when trying to justify newer, more relational ideas. With justified outrage, we who were brought up under the sway of drive theory, were excoriated for always justifying the relational shift. "We get it," they protested, "we came into this discussion long after relational sensibilities became mainstream. We don't need to relive the fights of your past." Instantly, and justly humbled, we realized we no longer needed to play time travel games, we could comfortably live in the present new relational order. Period. The paradigm had shifted, the times had changed.

In regard to time, we note in the paper the very essence of many secrets is bound up with when it will, or not, be shared. While noting their relational import as transitional phenomena, a place holder between internal and external worlds, we also note the ways that a secret plays with time. Particularly with secrets that are announced but not shared, they seduce the other with an implicit "yet." The future, then, beckons with the promise that a secret will be revealed. We cautioned the reader at the time that this is not necessarily a defensive ploy against revealing something from the forbidding unconscious. Time will tell if there will be a satisfying rendezvous with increased intimacy in the form of the details of a secret. Will an expanded creative capacity for engagement be realized, or alternatively, the revelation of a sadistic taunt bound for disappointment? In the consulting room, the outcome will reveal to us something, either way, about a patient's character.

In the case of someone who has suffered an abundance of unsatisfying, unloving or abusive relationships, secrets may serve the function of freezing time. Whether Guntrip's regressed ego or Winnicott's true self in hiding, both phenomena contain a wish for a safer, life-affirming *future time* with loving others. The self, which may have experienced a sense futility in the past or the present, can maintain hope for a future time and has not completely succumbed to only envisioning a future infused with futility.

Hope, then is a repository of a life-affirming future time. But what about dread? Dread is a repository of an annihilation soaked future. It represents a sense of doom frozen in time, that, like hope, awaits a future time to materialize. And like hope, dread is also born of unbearable experiences in the present or past. Since both hope and dread are senses of time born of bad experiences, I can only conclude that both are inherent reactions to the human condition that live in constant tension within us. I will leave it to the philosophers to untangle that conundrum, but do wish to point out how much of our personal psychology and experiences of self are intimately affected by the phenomenon of time and the interweaving of past, present and future.

Notes

1 This paper originally appeared in N.J. Skolnick and S.C. Warshaw (eds.) (1992). *Relational Perspectives in Psychoanalysis*. Hillsdale: The Analytic Press.

2 At the time this paper was written, the faculty at the NYU postdoctoral program was organized into three separate tracks, Freudian, interpersonal/humanistic and unaligned. Candidates were not required to pledge allegiance to a track and could take courses in all three, though some, more aware at the time of their theoretical biases, tended to prefer one track over the other two. All faculty were hired by, and considered a member of, a single track. At the writing of this paper, a fourth track, the relational track, was just beginning to be formed. See Ghent (in N. Skolnick and S. Warshaw (eds.) (1985). *Relational Perspectives in Psychoanalysis*. New York: The Analytic Press) for a description of the evolution of the postdoctoral training program at NYU.

Chapter 3

Secrets in clinical work
A relational point of view[1]
1992

Neil J. Skolnick and Jody Messler Davies

Psychoanalysis has always been concerned with secrets. Indeed, by their very nature, secrets implore psychoanalytic speculation. They are an infinitely rich, complexly textured and inherently intriguing phenomenon. They involve the seen and the unseen, the verbalized and the unspoken, the involvement of others as well as their exclusion. It is surprising, given the nature of psychoanalytic investigation, with its emphasis on uncovering and revelation, that more has not been said about secrets. Yet from the inception of psychoanalysis as a theory and a practice, secrets have been a tacit concern of psychoanalysis, whether or not they have been addressed directly.

Implicit in Freud's earliest attempts at a "cathartic" cure was the premise that the extraction of an unconscious and noxious secret wish idea, or experience, could be mutative, if not curative. Subsequent speculation about secrets has by and large paralleled the evolution of and divergences within psychoanalytic theory. The proposed meanings and functions accorded secrets have been considered from a purely drive perspective (Gross, 1951), an ego psychological approach (Margolis, 1966, 1974) and an object relations point of view (Khan, 1978; Winnicott, 1971; Meares, 1976). Each respective theoretical treatment has tended to draw new bottom lines, placing the psychic meaning of secrets into a paradigm that gives special weight to a limited focus, be it the drives, ego functions or object-relational concerns. In this paper we first present a brief historical overview. We then argue for an updated consideration of secrets that includes a description of different types of secrets and more importantly, an attempt to understand secrets from a primarily relational perspective. To accomplish this, we rely on clinical material to illustrate our points.

62 Neil J. Skolnick and Jody Messler Davies

Gross (1951), a drive theorist, places the motivation underlying secrets squarely in the realm of an unfolding sequence of psychosexual concerns. Impressed by the temptation of the owner of a secret both to surrender its content and to retain it, he suggests that there might be, in our unconscious, a complete identity between the secret, on one hand, and bodily excretions on the other. He finds partial support for his hypothesis in the etymology of the Romance languages; the literal meaning of the Latin word *secretum* is "that which has been secreted, or secretion" (p. 38). He then makes an important distinction between the content of a secret and its function. The importance of this distinction is underlined by his contention that the secret undergoes certain changes over the course of development. At certain points in time, its content holds its meaning; at other times, its function. It is at the anal stage, Gross claims, that the content of the secret, its quality as a possession, holds most explanatory sway, whereas at later psychosexual stages it is the quality of its function that is more important. Specifically, as the genital stage approaches, with its increase in a tendency toward external effectiveness, the secret is placed in the service of exhibition (e.g., making oneself seem important by hints about a secret), and later it can be employed as a potential gift to initiate friendships, and ultimately as an aid to wooing a love object.

As psychoanalysis shifted its focus from the contents of the repressed psyche to the agent of repression, the ego, so too did discussion of secrets shift from what was kept secret, and why, to the mechanisms of the ego involved. As Sulzberger (1953) put it, "the keeping of a secret is not just simply an easy act of omission, but rather constitutes a task, involving the whole ego" (p. 43). Margolis (1966, 1974) presents the most comprehensive attempt to describe secrets from the perspective of the functioning of the ego. Indeed, he likens the keeping of a secret to the very process of repression itself. Building on what Sulzberger (1953) called the "confession compulsion," he claims that the more important a secret is, the greater the energy change it acquires and the stronger its push to re-emerge. Margolis (1974) concludes:

> Conscious secrets thus obey many of the laws of unconscious secrets (secrets) which a person keeps from himself. There is continued pressure for them to express themselves just as there is continual pressure from unconscious id impulses and the repressed for expression (the return of the repressed), requiring in both cases constant counter-pressure to keep them contained.
>
> (p. 291)

Secrets in clinical work   63

For ego psychology, not only does secret-keeping resemble the process of repression, but it is actually a precursor to repression itself. Ego psychologists hold that all the contents of the repressed unconscious involve issues, events, wishes, etc. of childhood that the child first decides to keep secret from his or her own superego and its predecessor, the child's parents. Furthermore, "the formation of neuroses proceeds from conscious secret-keeping by the child to keeping things secret from his or her own superego and ego" (p. 292). Psychoanalysis is, then, held to be a process by which patients reverse this course of events by revealing conscious secrets to the analyst and no longer having to hide unconscious secrets from their own ego and superego.

Khan (1978) promoted a radically different perspective on secrets in his conception of them as potential space. According to Khan, no longer are secrets considered to be in the province of repressive forces, ego defenses or similar processes designed to negotiate the balance between expression of the drives with the demands of the external world. Secrets, as potential space, are now accorded a life-affirming role in the development of the self. Borrowing the concept of potential space[2] from Winnicott (1971 [1967]), Khan spoke of secrets as a place where one could go to absent oneself, both from one's own internal world and from the traumatizing aspects of one's external environment. As opposed to *hiding* oneself in symptoms, a secret provides a potential space where a part of the self is absented, placed in suspended animation. The secret, Khan (1978) maintains, carries a hope that one day the person will be able to emerge from it, "be found and met" (p. 266) and thus become a whole person, sharing life with others. Like others before him, Khan emphasizes that the content of the secret is not what is important, but that the act of creating and maintaining a secret is what is meaningful. For him, however, it is meaningful because it tucks part of the self away for safekeeping. Of significance is that this piece of the self is no longer available for elaboration or alteration. It is not that the person has a secret hidden within; on the contrary, the person infuses a secret with part of the self, which then becomes frozen in time and exists apart from ongoing development. Khan describes the case of a child who, by hiding a pair of candlesticks, absented herself into a secret when her ongoing life with her mother broke down, when "her growth in mutuality with her mother had been disrupted" (p. 268). He states further that a secret will be shared only when there is an opportunity for mutuality with an object – when one perceives that someone out there is available to respond and adapt to one's needs.

The secret, then, as Khan conceived it, becomes a maneuvering by the self for protection and control when the outer world ceases to be responsive to the needs of the child. This conceptualization places secrets in a relational frame. They are born of failures in the interpersonal matrix, sustained by hope of a more hospitable environment in the future, and relinquished when a person perceives the opportunity for mutuality with an object.

Implicit in the discussion of secrets as potential space is that secrets can be appreciated for their developmental function. They can be created adaptively to protect the developing self from trauma. Perhaps their adaptive function can provide, in a more ongoing fashion and in a less pervasive manner, a means to negotiate the everyday failures of the significant object to rise to and respond to a child's needs. Meares (1976) takes steps in this direction when he proposes that some secrets can be distinguished as being "creative secrets." He suggests that the attainment of the idea of secrecy is an important feature in a child's development, specifically in its contribution to forming personal relationships. His idea is that secrets become the "coins of intimacy," shared with others as a means of establishing a close bond. Furthermore, he claims that they are related to the child's growing ability to distinguish between inner and outer worlds and establish a boundary between them.

To summarize thus far, we have attempted to outline a historical perspective of the treatment of secrecy in psychoanalytic theory. Originally conceptualized as rooted in the conflict between the drives and reality, the secret has been considered from an ego psychological approach and an object relations point of view. We find value in both approaches, particularly as they can be helpful in informing the theoretician as well as the clinician; we do not feel that any one approach has been sufficiently comprehensive to understand the multifaceted concept of a secret, with its many forms and functions, as well as the complexities of its role in the clinical process. To begin to explicate a more comprehensive viewpoint, we have chosen to approach the issue of secrecy from a clinical/ developmental point of view.

We are considering the secret from a relational perspective, which regards it not as a valuable gem to be excavated and carefully unearthed, but as a developmental/relational phenomenon involved in the growth and maintenance of the self and its inner world and in the relationship of that inner world to external reality. We expect that the secret will emerge clinically as an essential aspect of the characteristic interplay between analyst and patient. The secret is a defining element of the process by which patients induct us into their private world, make us acquainted with the internal cast of characters, and reveal through transference–countertransference paradigms their particular ways of relating to each of these internal figures, as well as to the specific developmental arrests that impinge on all these relationships in characteristic ways.

We suggest a particular typology of secrets based on the very different ways in which secrets can emerge in clinical work. Each, we believe, places emphasis on very different yet equally significant developmental issues and on the relational matrices specific to their emergence in the transference–countertransference processes. We include: (1) secrets meant to be shared with others; (2) secrets that are announced to the therapist but whose specific content is withheld; (3) shameful secrets; and (4) secrecy as a pervasive character style.

Secrets meant to be shared with others

All analysts have found themselves in the situation of being presented with a special parcel of information. This bundle, which we now refer to as a "secret meant to be shared," is typically a highly valued and affectively charged piece of information about the patient or the patient's internal world that not only is shared with the analyst, but is identified as a secret being shared exclusively (or almost exclusively!) with the analyst. "You are the only one I've ever told this to" and "I'm relieved just to tell someone" are commonly heard preceding these types of revelations. The statement is usually made in the spirit of conspiratorial playfulness, with the obvious motive of engaging the analyst.

Our contention is that it is primarily within the relational matrix that evolves from the sharing of the secret that its importance and ultimate meaning is to be found. We consider the offering of the secret to be an invitation to another to share, notice and acknowledge a piece of one's inner subjective world. Furthermore, it is an offer of a potential type of bond, which, if successful, will result in a sought-after intimacy or mutuality. It can be likened in a sense to a scout who is sent into unknown, potentially dangerous waters in advance of an exploratory expedition. Is the expedition safe to proceed? Will the group be welcomed, acknowledged and appreciated? Or will it meet with hostile forces looking to absorb the group or, worse, betray it? This type of secret appears to be a way of initiating a bond with someone in the external world, or more precisely, with an external object's internal world (subjectivity), by roping off a piece of one's own internal subjective world and sending it out, not unlike a trial balloon.

We place this type of secret in the realm of transitional phenomena as described by Winnicott (1975 [1951]). Winnicott referred to transitional phenomena as illusions set up to mediate and negotiate the distinction between internal and external realities. They are used to relinquish gradually the omnipotence a child experiences over his or her external reality and to be able gradually to distinguish between an internal reality and the limits of an external reality that is much less under psychic control. A secret, if negotiated successfully, represents a step in the relinquishing of omnipotence. By revealing an inner subjective reality (a secret) to someone out there, one is clearly making a distinction between separate inner and outer realms. But by labeling it as a secret, the person is still maintaining or attempting to maintain control over the content of the internal package as it ventures outside.

The most successful outcome of such a venture is that the other person will accept the secret and acknowledge both its importance and *its secrecy*. Thus the two people enter into a bond that gains its strength from the mutual recognition of the secret as a transitional phenomenon. Both now hold the secret precious in their internal worlds, yet both recognize that some control has been relinquished in the sharing of the secret. This relinquishing of control implies a mutual trust, at least for the moment, that one's internal world is separate and safe from both the external world and the internal world of another. Omnipotent control over the external world has been momentarily suspended and placed into the hands of another.

The two also enter into a shared world of intersubjectivity that can exclude others, thus defining their own safe interpersonal reality separate from the rest of the external world and remaining under their shared control. This process can be observed in pairs of school children of five and six who delight in forming secrets that are kept from others. The content of their secrets, often in fact freely revealed, seems much less important than the experience of having shared a secret with another. Later, these twosomes are expanded into secret groups and clubs that have the same function.

Of course, the best outcome, a mutual bond, is not always the case. The list of potential snags is endless; they range from betrayal, to non-acceptance, to a lack of recognition, to many other pitfalls in the process. Children, for instance, who have had some relative degree of success relinquishing omnipotence and distinguishing internal and external worlds, will merely pull back their trial balloons, pack up their toys and go elsewhere, looking for other uncharted territories to explore. Our point is that they *will* go elsewhere and continue to engage others in this process. We wish to stress this point because it implies that these types of secrets, secrets-meant-to-be-shared, are a manifestation of a normal and regular course of events. They can be utilized in the lifelong struggle to negotiate boundaries; and furthermore, given an environment that is reasonably safe, these types of secrets can be imbued with delight and pleasure as they are used repeatedly in establishing intimacy in relationships.

This view of secrecy has implications for the treatment setting as well. It can become all too easy to regard a patient's announcement of a secret as a defensive process, aligned with the forces of repression to maintain information out of conscious awareness. There are many ways in which an analyst might regard the offering of such a secret as a form of resistance or defense. Those more classically inclined might regard it as the acting out of a wish rooted in a libidinal or aggressive drive. Is the patient being seductive? Or overly familiar, or possibly demeaning? Others might hear an intent to idealize the analyst. Still others might attend to self-deprecating undertones. While, of course, these inferences might be accurately perceived nuances of the analytic interaction we hold that there is a risk that the analyst may be missing the patient's attempt to establish a bond or mutuality with another, that the offering of a secret represents an initial step in establishing a safe intersubjective tie.

We offer as a clinical example a character in a recent movie, *Europa Europa*, based on a true story. The movie revolves around a major secret, that of a 16-year-old Jewish boy's attempt to survive the atrocities of World War II Germany by pretending to be non-Jewish. In situation after situation, for example, his being sent to an elite school for Aryan Hitler youth, he lived in perpetual fear that his secret would be unearthed and result in almost certain death. His world revolved around his efforts to keep his true identity a secret. At one point in the story, the boy reveals his secret to a member of the enemy. He exclaims through tears, "I just had to let someone know." The audience's suspense at this moment hinges on the fate of his revelation. Will he immediately be revealed, resulting in almost certain destruction? Or will his secret be safe within the confines of a newly established mutuality? Indeed, not only is his secret accepted, but the sharing of the secret fuels the development of a powerfully intimate bond between the two. This example, while extreme, beautifully illustrates the relational needs embodied in a secret meant to be shared. It is an invitation to share one's subjective world with another, motivated by the hope for a bond with the other in which one's subjective safety and integrity is affirmed.

Announced secrets whose content is withheld

In contrast to secrets that are meant to be shared is the type of secret whose existence is announced by the patient, although the content continues to be withheld. Here the patient describes being "not quite ready," "too embarrassed," "not sure what you'll think of me," to reveal the content of the secret, though he or she clearly wants the therapist to know that the issue exists. Although this type of secret emerges periodically in almost every treatment, it can, for some patients, emerge as a predominant transferential paradigm, giving a particular coloration to the therapeutic relationship. In contrast to the mood of paralyzing humiliation evoked by shameful secrets (to be discussed later), the atmosphere has an almost playful, tantalizing, "catch-me-if-you-can" quality. The therapist, caught up in this play, clearly wants to know, discover and understand what the patient is so engagingly offering up, for there is little as truly engaging as a secret announced but withheld.

Classical analysis has traditionally regarded such an announced but withheld secret as a resistance to the reemergence of forbidden libidinal wishes; a defense against the patient's demand for drive gratification, usually within the transference; essentially, a disruption in the free associative flow of the hour. Emphasis has been on interpreting and working through these transference resistances in order to uncover the true meaning of the secret that lies embedded and encoded within the content of what is withheld. Beginning with Freud's (1913) basic description of the "fundamental rule" of psychoanalysis, the very idea that a patient could consciously withhold information from the analyst has been viewed as antithetical to the entire analytic agenda. Freud stated:

It is naturally impossible to carry out our analysis if the patient's relations with other people and his thoughts about them are excluded ... It is very remarkable how the whole task (psychoanalysis) becomes impossible if a reservation is allowed at any single place.

(pp. 135–136)

Greenson (1967) includes a special section on consciously held secrets in his chapter on analyzing resistance. His position, fundamentally consistent with the classical one, stresses the need ultimately to uncover the content of the secret by patiently analyzing why the patient feels the need to withhold it. Greenson says:

Our basic attitude is that there shall be no concession about secrets. They have to be analyzed ... The analytic attitude is that we shall attempt to analyze secrets as we would any other form of resistance. We are just as determined and just as patient. We may be aware that a patient has a conscious secret, but we know that it is the unconscious factors that have to be analyzed, before the patient can reveal the secret. The patient knows the content of the secret, but he is unconscious of the important reasons which make it necessary to maintain the secrecy.

(p. 130)

We propose here that patients who characteristically engage their analysts with a series of withheld secrets are attempting to accomplish a particularly important development shift, one that has either failed to occur or has only partially occurred. We find it most useful to define this shift in the Winnicottian mode of facilitating new capacities. The psychic shift we refer to here is thus indicative of the capacity to regard oneself self-reflectively, that is, to adequately cordon off and respect the existence of a separate, private and entirely subjective inner reality. Implied here is the capacity to move between this entirely subjective inner reality and a field of intersubjectivity without fearing undue penetration and influence by another or the omnipotent, rageful, potentially destructive impact of oneself.

What, then, of patients who routinely organize their interpersonal relationships around a series of tantalizingly withheld secrets? It is our contention that these patients have arrived at a level of ego organization and object relations that has established the potential for preliminary trials with intersubjective experience, but that certain developmental issues preclude them from further maturation in this realm. By announcing the existence of encapsulated pieces of inner reality that may or may not be available for sharing, the patient defines the field on which these issues will be played out. On this field, through the transference–countertransference constellations, the specific lacunae in ego development and self/object representations will be highlighted, and the patient's avoidance of open disclosure in an intimate setting will be analyzed.

The following case vignette highlights some of these issues. Jesse was a 29-year-old, white, southern woman, the youngest of three children. She had two brothers, five and eight years older than she, respectively. Jesse's parents owned and operated the local bar in her hometown, and this fact, coupled with the age difference between the patient and her brothers, meant that much of her early childhood had been spent alone or in the homes of neighbors and friends. In fact, loneliness was far and away the most potent affective residue of this woman's childhood as she began treatment. Also significant in her early memories was the experience of needing to fit into the homes in which she was cared for in as unobtrusive and invisible a way as possible. There were few childhood friends, and the patient reported spending most of her time in a rich, highly developed and well-articulated internal fantasy world. Though she seemed in most instances to distinguish this world from her actual life and claimed that she never experienced any confusion as a child between what was real and what was "make-believe," it was clear that the patient retreated to this fantasied place as a source of comfort, soothing and emotional sustenance. No real relationship evoked within her the same experiences of warmth, wholeness and safety that her imagined world had.

Jesse remembered her parents' relationship alternately as calm, deadening and passionless or actively engaged, volatile and emotionally abusive. She recalled her father as rather depressed, a withdrawn, almost schizoid, man, and her mother's way of making contact was to become provocative and inflammatory until both appeared out of control. Jesse recalls that her parents related to her as they did to each other. Father was withdrawn most of the time, although a certain level of coquettish flirtation could be counted on to "elicit a wan smile." Mother was most often not at home, but when she returned Jesse recalled a subtle yet insidious demand for compensatory experiences· of intense emotional and physical contact. "She would literally swoop down upon me; wrapping me up in herself; wanting to know about every minute of my day; expecting me to return her need. I felt numbed; I couldn't be with her the way she wanted."

Secrets in clinical work 71

At the time she entered treatment, Jesse was a bright, vivacious and engaging woman; she was professionally and academically successful. She had a somewhat promiscuous history with men, moving from one relationship to another as soon as the man became serious about her. She was at the time involved in a serious relationship with a young man she described as gentle, passionate and emotionally available. The patient was eager to preserve this relationship but was only too aware of what she called her "pattern of restless wandering."

Jesse entered treatment in a most striking and dramatic way. She announced at the beginning of her first session that although she felt committed to an analysis, there was one event in her life about which she would never speak and about which the analyst must promise never to ask. She would say nothing other than to reassure the analyst that her "secret" involved no illegalities about which the analyst need feel concerned. It was "simply a private matter." The analyst responded that for such a private matter, the patient certainly felt compelled to announce its existence rather precipitously. The analyst went on to wonder aloud whether the patient had certain concerns about her capacity to keep a secret and might not be setting that as one of the goals of the analysis; after all, being able to "keep someone out" is a prerequisite for the decision to "let them in." Toward the end of this initial consultation, patient and analyst agreed that revealing her secret would never be made a precondition for Jesse continuing the analysis; however, the analyst insisted on maintaining the right to refer to Jesse's secret and its possible relevance during the course of the work. This condition was acceptable, and the analysis began.

Clearly, this unusual situation raises certain clinical issues relevant to our topic. For although the contents of this secret were sure to be pointedly meaningful on a symbolic level and were, eventually, to assume some importance within the analysis, the specific content of the secret was essentially peripheral to the exploration of its place and function within the analytic relationship. By using the metaphor of "her secret," the patient was able to represent externally and highlight certain areas of intrapsychic vulnerability: the richness of her inner world as compared with the emptiness and isolation of her actual life; her difficulties with a guilty and intrusive mother who was unavailable for extended periods and alternately was invasive, controlling and disrespectful of her daughter's needs for consistent boundaries and privileges of privacy; a depressed and withdrawn father in relationship to whom the patient's "secrets" represented attempts to actively master his essential indifference to her (she had no secrets from him, for he showed no interest in her inner life). In the analysis, exploration of the patient's efforts to maintain the boundaries around her secret, her ambivalence about doing this, her fantasies about the analyst's curiosity or lack thereof, and her less conscious attempts to engage the analyst in pressing for disclosure of the secret, all emerged in different aspects of transference–countertransference engagements.

This clinical example highlights one of the therapeutic "choice points" that often make interventions based within a relational framework incompatible with those stemming from more traditional instinctually driven models. To the extent that the analyst focuses on "resistances" to revealing this secret, implying that the patient must comply with the analytic standard of uninhibited free association, exploration of the vital issues surrounding separateness, boundaries, privacy, impingement, autonomy, submission and the like will be unavoidably discouraged or even foreclosed.

Of particular interest here is that two years into the analytic work, the patient's "secret" emerged in undisguised form in a dream she reported to the analyst. Having told of a dream where she was dancing "topless" in a small disco, Jesse turned to the analyst, shrugged with a smile, and said simply, "I suppose I was ready to have you know." The patient then began her own analysis of the special meaning that this event had played in her life. Placing the secret within a relational frame did not, therefore, prevent analyzing the content of this secret but did attempt to understand its broader meaning as a transitional bridge between Jesse's internal and external object worlds, and her complex relationship to both.

Shameful secrets

These are conscious experiences, usually occurring in childhood, that patients have chosen to keep to themselves for many years. Although these may at times overlap in their phenomenology with secrets in other subtypes, they do have enough special features to warrant separate consideration. We are not referring here to those fleeting experiences of shame that often accompany the revelation of new material in psychoanalysis, but more specifically to those secrets which have been kept for so long and with such a commitment of energy that they become core aspects of the identity and self-representation of the patient, although they are known to no one. The secret itself comes to serve a characterological function for the person, and

Secrets in clinical work 73

when its defensive function is challenged by revelation within the treatment setting, varying degrees of regressive disorganization may ensue.

Shameful secrets have to do mostly with childhood experiences of a traumatic nature – incest, child abuse or illegal, antisocial acts occurring outside of a predominantly psychopathic character structure. In most of these cases, the secret is an attempt to maintain a homeostatic balance in the inner object world, that balance which allowed the child to survive in a world where parents abandoned, betrayed or failed in other ways to protect from paralyzing overstimulation. Although this type of secret involves behavior that is almost never the young child's fault, the manifest content that emerges during analytic hours involves experiences of intense shame and mortification, as well as the conviction that the analyst will certainly reject the patient if his or her behavior is revealed. Symptomatically, one often sees compulsive self-abuse behavior and intense self-hatred. In following the patient's associations we are often led to interpret, along more traditional lines, the content of the secret as a manifestation of guilt over unconscious gratification of unacceptable wishes. From a self-psychological point of view, the likelihood is that this gratification has been incorporated by the patient into a system of compensatory grandiose fantasies. For example, it is not uncommon for the adult survivor of child abuse to express, in the analytic context, the belief that as a child he or she revealed some special quality that made him a particular target of abuse, and that furthermore, by exhibiting this quality, the patient could provoke and control outbursts of parental abuse. The passive experience of parental abuse and betrayal thus comes under active control and is used as a way to refortify the child's sense of omnipotent control of his or her dangerous world. The secret could, then, be viewed as a defense against both the exhibitionistic urges that might re-emerge in the treatment situation and the overwhelming terror and fear of annihilation that would be re-experienced were the true passivity of the original trauma to be recalled by the patient.

It has been our experience, however, that an approach that focuses exclusively on the unconscious guilt of the patient or on the split-off, grandiose fantasy is often insufficient to render the secret open for association and analysis and end the patient's intense self-hatred and abuse. Although a patient may accept these types of interpretations and may begin to deal with the content of the secret during analytic hours, the shame itself remains virtually untouched. The patient's experience is one of being "worn down," and though he or she may come to understand the symbolic meaning of the secret, the shame, fear and self-hatred continue. The interpretive process, thus conducted, may become a retraumatization itself.

That the shame, humiliation and self-hatred often prove to be the most immutable aspect of this clinical picture is in itself an interesting paradox. For it is clear that this kind of secret, once revealed, is almost never anything for which the young child was himself responsible. Most often the secret concerns something that was "done to" the child by a person of some significance in his or her life. The importance of keeping the secret, then, stems not only from the guilt and shame processes already described, but, on a fundamental level, from a primitive, primary identification with the painful object in its aggressive or abandoning aspects. It is, in fact, the very blamelessness of the patient in the context of a struggle with powerful ties to bad objects that provides the most powerful motivation for maintaining the secret. It is the child's need to protect himself or herself from the crushing experience of betrayal and aloneness that is operative. The assumption of guilt and shame reflects the idea that it is safer to think oneself a bad person, deserving of punishment, in an otherwise good world, than a blameless victim, abandoned and surrounded by evil (Fairbairn, 1952). One is reminded here of Fairbairn's classic description of a patient whose dream reflected a choice between eating poisoned pudding or dying of starvation. The child, helpless and dependent, cannot choose aloneness; therefore, the tie to the object is established, the evil internalized and converted to shame, and the patient's continued security maintained. As Fairbairn himself put it,

> The essential feature, and indeed the essential aim of this defense is the conversion of an original situation in which the child is surrounded by bad objects into a new situation in which his objects are good and he himself bad.
>
> (p. 68)

There is, then, a danger in approaching such a patient either from a classical Freudian perspective, which would stress the patient's unconscious guilt over the gratification of unacceptable wishes, or from a self-psychological model, which would emphasize the therapist's empathic bond to the helpless and victimized child. In our opinion, the crucial clinical question asks: which approach to this patient will allow for all the more classical and self-psychological issues to be analyzed, and at the same time set the stage for the emergence onto the clinical scene of the sadistic/abandoning introject? It is only, we believe, when this introject is given full reign to act upon the therapist and to understand through the therapist how he or she acts upon others in the world that the vicious projective/introjective cycle of abuse–counterabuse and self-abuse can be broken.

The secret, ultimately, is a secret coexisting on many levels: libidinal, narcissistic and object related. The working-through process is long and complex; it entails gratification of unconscious wishes, compensatory omnipotent and grandiose fantasies with external idealizations of sadistic figures, and finally the attempt to make real and therefore analyzable the early sadistic introject. The last of these tasks is the most formidable because the process involves something of a therapeutic paradox. On one level, the patient works through several different defensive positions: I was abused and am bad; I was abused, but I am not bad; I was a victim and should not continue to punish myself. However, a parallel process also begins to emerge: I am a part of someone who would abuse/abandon a blameless child, and that someone is a part of me. If I deny that contact, I am a part of no one, and anyone who is a part of no one must truly be bad after all.

Secrecy as a character style

We now turn to a discussion of a type of secret we believe accompanies the experience and functioning of a more pathological level of adjustment. This type of secrecy occurs frequently in those patients presenting with severe character disorders, whom we refer to today as borderline or narcissistic and whom the British object relations theorists commonly referred to as schizoid. Rather than a delineated, discrete secret, or series of secrets, we are referring to a pervasive style of secrecy that casts its shadow over large areas of a person's experience, behavior and functioning. The person acts as though guided by an imperative to relegate a wide spectrum of his or her experience, actions or thoughts to the realm of secrecy. Nothing is spared. Mundane, routine events can be included, as can symptomatic behaviors such as bulimic episodes or compulsive rituals. Even, and sometimes especially, major triumphs and successes are shielded by secrecy. Clinically, this type of secrecy can manifest in many ways. Lengthy, withholding silence can signal such a style, or perhaps glaring omissions, as when a patient announces some future event that, the therapist realizes at some later point in time, has never been mentioned again. At times a belated announcement of a major incident or event, leaving the therapist wondering, "Why am I just hearing about this now?" can signal such a process. Sometimes it is announced directly, as in the case of a severely reclusive and narcissistically impaired man who stated several years in to treatment, "I have a fantasy of getting better, living a rich, full life, and keeping it all a secret from you."

This man did, in fact, keep much of his life shrouded in a veil of secrecy. From a very early age, he would keep not only his needs, wants and actions, but also his successes and failures, from his family and others. It became apparent that he relished his world of secrecy. It was not a world to which he retreated, but rather it was a world that contained and protected his self and his self in relation to the world of others. It was a world in which he could interact with others safely and not include them at all. Paradoxically, the only available, safe and acceptable means of interacting with others did not include them. In the continual struggle to define the boundaries between inner and outer realities, objects in the outside world were brought into the inner experience and related to, acted upon or reacted to, through the vehicle of secrecy.

The realm of secrecy does not represent a divorce or retreat from reality, but rather a harnessing of what is perceived to be an unbearable and uncontrollable reality. Thus, we are not describing a retreat to a fantasy world. Secrecy, as we understand it, involves real people and actions. Contact with reality is maintained. It is, therefore, unlike the world of psychotic experience, in which reality is generated from and dictated to by an internal fantasy world and its contents. Indeed, the reality that is brought into this secret world probably is composed, to a large extent, of an array of part-object representations, rather than fully integrated wholes, and to that extent reality testing may be somewhat impaired. Furthermore, since much relating to others (these part-object representations) occurs in a safe and secret world, the constraints and limitations of real others are rarely confronted, thus perpetuating unrealistic knowledge of others and a further need for secrecy. So a sense of reality is maintained, but reality testing may never be given adequate opportunity.

The motive to hide oneself also does not appear to emanate from shame or embarrassment, nor does it appear to represent a libidinally rooted tendency to withhold. While shame, embarrassment or withholding can be operative, they are not the primary motivating force and are better understood as derivatives of a type of failed object relationship that seems to underlie this tendency toward massive secrecy.

It is our contention that where secrecy becomes a pervasive style, there has been a severe disruption in an early relationship with a primary other. Either severely depressed or markedly focused on their own narcissistic needs (or both), the parents are physically present but severely detached and unavailable. Often, issues of control may dominate. Furthermore, we have noted powerful, usually unconscious, murderous desires occurring in the parents toward the child. The external world provided by such parents is extraordinarily frightening and unsafe. This creates a situation in which the normal use of secrets as transitional phenomena is radically aborted. As noted, we maintain that secrets can be utilized for the developmentally necessary task of relinquishing omnipotent control, initiating intersubjectivity and gradually achieving a more realistic sense of one's own limitations and the limitations of the external world. In the situation we are describing here, the child experiences his or her world as massively unsafe, and attempts at transitional phenomena are met with either no response or a murderous (disavowing, unconfirming) response. Omnipotence, then, is not gradually relinquished but, rather, tenaciously retained. Illusions of omnipotence, both about one's self and one's objects, are not given the opportunity for disillusionment. One's objects are maintained as dangerous and potentially destructive, to be reckoned with only within the confines of a safe, removed and secret world where one can omnipotently control all the contingencies.

Crucial to understanding this form of secrecy, and indeed secrecy in general, is that a secret, or secret world, does not exist without an object. A secret is a piece of experience kept from somebody, and the object is inherently and inextricably involved in the phenomenology of keeping the secret. For a person who creates a world of secrecy, objects are abundant. Actual interactions with others need no longer occur; the person need no longer be frustrated, or worse, destroyed, by a world of others who are either absent or harbor murderous impulses. These others are brought into the internal subjective world by virtue of their exclusion from it, without an opportunity to act, react, destroy or control. The resulting pervasive style of secrecy represents a contact with the outside world that, for purposes of safety, control and even survival, remains tucked inside of an illusion. Consider the case of a 25-year-old woman who entered treatment (with a supervisee of one of the authors) after having been evicted from a prior therapy. Her previous analyst, reciting a litany of complaints, had become uncontrollably enraged at this patient and found that she could no longer tolerate the patient's antics; particularly her unremitting, relentless efforts to stalk the therapist. The patient, a high-achieving medical resident, would repeatedly walk or drive by her analyst's house and office, calculating when she might catch a glimpse of her, however briefly. She always remained inconspicuous, hiding unobtrusively in the shadows, never allowing her presence to be known. Faithfully, however, at the next session she would reveal, in exquisite detail, the nature of these stalking expeditions. The patient's repertoire of enraging behavior was not limited to her stalking. During most sessions, she was childlike and provocative, taunting her analyst with personal questions and persisting even as limits were set or an analytic frame was reinforced. The analyst became increasingly unable to tolerate what she referred to as the patient's "acting out." She decided her countertransference reaction (primarily rage) precluded the opportunity for further treatment, and she transferred the patient. Two aspects of this woman's initial presentation were immediately apparent. One was the enormous disparity between her regressive, childlike demeanor in the therapy situation and her high level of functioning elsewhere. She had successfully completed an Ivy League education and medical training; she had friends and was engaged to be married. While it is not uncommon for patients to present with similar inconsistencies (though not always as extreme or immediately apparent), an additional feature was puzzling. There was a playful quality to her antics, an almost tongue-in-cheek shading to her "bad" behaviors. Indeed, her stalking, manipulating, provoking or generally enraging behavior had a compulsive quality and was distressing to her; but she exercised a noticeable degree of control in that she never got caught, never actually crossed boundaries (i.e., she would call the therapist at home only when fairly certain no one would, be there), and she faithfully confessed to all her transgressions. While she engaged in many of the same behaviors that characterized her previous therapy, there seemed to always be an enticing invitation to her therapist to "come play with me." The analyst's initial stance was to enlist her cooperation in exploring the meaning of what she did and to set limits on what was intolerable (i.e., stalking the analyst's house). The patient proceeded to figure out the analyst's work schedule and purposely lingered at certain places hoping to see the analyst without being seen. This was accomplished at the expense of tremendous time and energy, as when she would traverse town, in the middle of a work day, and circle the office block for up to an hour, hoping to get a glimpse of the analyst. She became obsessively ruminative about all aspects and every corner of the analyst's life, attempting to smoke out every activity, every acquaintance. One particular ritual she performed provided valuable insight into the nature of what was going on. After figuring out which car belonged to her analyst, she would routinely pass the car en route to sessions, hoping to catch a glimpse of something, anything, in the car, that might provide a clue about the analyst's life or recent activities. The analyst, in turn, repeatedly found herself surveying the car for artifacts of her recent out-of-office-life (a map, a car seat, a candy wrapper). She was struck by the enormity of the power, the outright omnipotence, she was attempting (at times successfully!) to wield. While typically experiencing anger or rage in response to such a patient's omnipotent machinations, the analyst remained amused, feeling she was being drawn into something that could be stopped at any time, perhaps some form of play.

What did gradually emerge was that this woman had an enormous secret world in which she reveled and from which little in her life was spared. She delighted in erecting and maintaining secrets from the major cast of characters in her life. For example, when she and her husband bought a car, she named the car after her analyst and delighted in this secret name and secret knowledge. Indeed, by far the most encompassing secret in her life was her therapy. Since adolescence she had been involved in a series of therapies in which she lived an entire existence parallel to, apart from and outside her life. These worlds were her special secret, and she carried them around with her perpetually. She was master of these worlds; she created them, ruled over them, determined their edges, and filled in their substance. They gained much of their significance not just from the power she wielded, but from being kept secret from others. The others – her parents, husband and colleagues – populated her secret world by virtue of her keeping the secrets from them and lording the secrets over them in her thoughts.

Her secretive existence began early in childhood. Her mother was an extremely controlling, narcissistic and erratic woman, prone to wild, unpredictable and explosive tantrums. Her younger brother was labeled the "bad" one of the family, and she repeatedly observed her mother physically strike him. She developed a compliant "good" self, which she defensively erected and presented to her mother and the world. Her father appeared to be well meaning but was largely absent and unable to control her explosive mother. Neither parent seemed able to set effective, consistent limits and enable her to feel protected from her own impulses and omnipotent desires. While presenting her "good" self to· the world, early on she secretly harbored her "bad" self, a world composed of her own impulses and identifications with her impulsive mother, as well as her more spontaneous wishes and desires, which could not be expressed in her mother's controlling world. This self was cordoned off and expressed increasingly in the safety of her secret world. First it was expressed privately (i.e., secret eating binges), then in her play, and eventually in her therapies. For her, therapy represented an invitation to another to participate in her secret world ("come play with me"). She, of course, was the master of ceremonies, and the therapist was to be at the mercy of her omnipotent control. It became clear that whether the analyst allowed her antics (e.g., her stalking) or protested, becoming enraged like her previous therapist, or benignly set limits did not actually matter. In all eventualities, the analyst was responding to her omnipotent demands. The way out of this morass was for the analyst to respond to her secretiveness as an illusion of control existing in a transitional space. More and more the analyst approached her secret world as a parent might a transitional object. She had set up this world to maintain the omnipotence that had never been disillusioned in either her own internal world or that of her mother. In the therapy her secretive control became more of a transitional game. The analyst could recognize it, even allow it, but also remind her of its limits. Thus therapy became an arena wherein she could use transitional phenomena (her secret world) not just to maintain her omnipotence, but gradually to relinquish it. Therapy provided an opportunity for a safer exploration and discovery of an intersubjective world and allowed for a diminution of a need for a secretive style of existence. She began to chance real encounters with both her analyst and the major people in her life and recognized the limits, boundaries and subjectivity of each. She could increasingly tolerate the controls on her wishes mandated by the realities of another's internal world. She felt freer to risk revealing her inner world to others without fearing destruction. With an increasing tolerance for the limits of her control, and of others', she could begin to venture out from her secretive world.

We have presented this case in order to illustrate a pervasive style of secrecy, as well as to emphasize the importance of taking a relational perspective in order to inform the treatment. The patient had been evicted from a previous therapy. Did her enraging stalking behaviors represent an expression of sadistic, destructive impulses? Were they aimed at a therapist who could no longer tolerate her own rage and the threat to her own omnipotence evoked by the seemingly uncontrollable acting out? While we do not discount these formulations, we believe that a relational perspective can expand our understanding. It appears that the patient succeeded in transforming her first therapist into her explosive, murderous mother with the ultimate expression of this transference–countertransference enactment being her ejection from therapy.

It is our conviction that the first therapist was unable to recognize and respond to the patient's attempt to negotiate an intolerable situation with her own mother by creating a world of secrecy in which all who entered were held under her omnipotent sway. The patient, by inviting her therapist to participate in this secret realm, was attempting to maintain omnipotent control and at the same time chance relinquishing the same control. Her secret world, then, operated on the level of transitional phenomena (Winnicott, 1975 [1951]) in which she could maintain illusory control over external others, in this case the analyst, while struggling to acknowledge the limits of that control. Once the second analyst was able to recognize the transitional nature of her secret behavior, she was able to respond to her antics with the tolerant distance of apparent observing and occasionally participating in a child's play enactments. While the content of her secret world may indeed have included sadistic, exhibitionistic and self-destructive wishes, the treatment was endangered as long as the analyst failed to recognize the relational configurations to which those impulses were brought.

Concluding remarks

We have argued for a conceptualization of the secret that places relational configurations at the heart of our understanding of this ubiquitous phenomenon. We have described several core relational commonalities of secrecy that, at times, emerge from the background into the foreground of analytic work. So encapsulated, such phenomena can imply the normal unfolding of developmental processes, aberrations of psychopathology or significant transference–countertransference patterns. We have demonstrated how they can be constructed and maintained as part of a lifelong effort to support the requisites of self-development and continuity. They can be employed as an aid to the discovery and experience of intersubjective bonds, as transitional phenomena providing an opportunity to relinquish primitive omnipotence, and as a vehicle for the establishment of safe, secure boundaries between inner and outer, between self and others. In pathology, they can be adaptively erected to negotiate severe environmental trauma. We do not discount that drive impulses or strictly defensive concerns may be implicated in the complex meanings and textures of a secret.

We do not, however, agree with the heretofore held conceptualization of secrets as serving the sole purpose of keeping forbidden instinctual wishes out of consciousness. Rather, we view impulses embedded in secrecy to be of secondary importance to and a product of the developmental/relational concerns we have attempted to explicate.

Notes

1 A previous version of this paper was published in Skolnick, N.J. and Warshaw, S.A. (eds.) (1992). *Relational Perspectives in Psychoanalysis*. Hillsdale: The Analytic Press. Relational perspectives in psychoanalysis by WARSHAW, SUSAN C; SKOLNICK, NEIL J. Reproduced with permissions of ANALYTIC PRESS in the format Book via Copyright Clearance Center.
2 In his paper "The location of cultural experience," Winnicott (1971 [1967]) states: "From the beginning the baby has maximally intense experience in the potential space between the subjective object and the object objectively perceived, being nothing but me and there being objects and phenomena outside omnipotent control" (p. 100).

References

Fairbairn, W.R.D. (1952). *Psychoanalytic Studies of the Personality*. London: Routledge & Kegan Paul.

Freud, S. (1913). On beginning the treatment. In J. Strachey (ed. and trans.), *The Standard Edition of the Complete Psychological Works of Sigmund Freud* (Vol. 12, pp. 121–144). London: Hogarth Press, 1958.

Greenson, R. (1967). *The Techniques and Practice of Psychoanalysis*, Vol. 1. New York: International Universities Press.

Gross, A. (1951). The secret. *Bulletin of the Menninger Clinic*, 15: 37–44.

Khan, M.M.R. (1978). Secret as potential space. In S.A. Grolnick, L. Barkin and W. Muensterberger (eds.), *Between Reality and Fantasy*. New York: Aronson.

Margolis, G.J. (1966). Secrecy and identity. *International J Psycho-Anal.*, 47: 517–522.

Margolis, G.J. (1974). The psychology of keeping secrets. *International Revue Psycho-Analysis*, 1: 291–296.

Meares, R. (1976). The secret. *Psychiatry*, 39: 258–265.

Sulzberger, C.F. (1953). Why it is hard to keep secrets. *Psychoanal.*, 2: 37–43.

Winnicott, D.W. (1975 [1951]). Transitional objects and transitional phenomena. In *Through Paediatrics to Psychanalysis*. London: Hogarth Press.

Winnicott, D.W. (1971 [1967]). The location of cultural experience. In *Playing and Reality*. New York: Basic Books.

Winnicott, D.W. (1971). *Playing and Reality*. New York: Basic Books.

Chapter 4

The good, the bad and the ambivalent[1]

Fairbairn's difficulty locating the good object in the endopsychic structure

Introduction

This paper was written to present at a conference on Fairbairn I put together in 1998 in New York City. It was subsequently included in *Fairbairn: Then and Now*, a collection of the papers from the conference. It was a time when Fairbairn's ideas were being reprised and considered, along with the ideas of Ferenzci, to constitute one of the seminal cornerstones of relational psychoanalysis.

In regard to my evolution as a relational analyst, this chapter starts with a rather inelegant exposé of my struggle at the time (Skolnick, 1998), to integrate drive and object relations theory. My conclusion was in essence to punt. I resorted to highlighting the ambiguities inherent in our work in order to rationalize a rather weak eclecticism. Today, embracing the more solid theoretical changes wrought by the passage of time, and the contributions of countless relational authors, too numerous to give credit to all, I can state with greater certainty an argument which transcends an "anything goes" sensibility. Briefly, today I consider the basic building blocks of human character, development, pathology and psychotherapy to be our relentless pursuit to establish and maintain loving connections with others. While we harbor powerful biological urges and forces, I conceive of them not as primary determinants of our characters, but rather, as being shaped by and gaining meaning within the matrices of our relationships with others. More on this in Chapter 9 where I provide an assessment of relational theory today.

Shortly after the Fairbairn conference in 1998, I taught a class on object relations theory and assigned the paper presented in this chapter. One of my more perceptive students remarked that he experienced the paper as both homage to Fairbairn, and of even more significance, a love letter to Fairbairn. I nodded and smiled, but I must admit I was not exactly certain what he meant. Many years later, as I was reviewing the paper to include in this volume, it immediately became obvious to me what he was observing that I was not. In an *après coup* moment I noticed, somewhat to my embarrassment, that the paper was not written in my usual style, which is typically more straightforward and accessible, with a minimum of jargon. I intentionally write to elucidate my ideas as clearly as I can. Not a hint of post-modern obfuscation or excessive jargon appear anywhere in my usual text. While reading this article, at this point in time, years after it was written, I was thunderstruck when I realized that my ideas were drowning in meticulously constructed theory peppered with more jargon per sentence that seemed in excess of the sum total of all jargon I had placed in all my previous papers combined. In other words, I was thinking and writing in the impossibly dense style of my theoretical hero, W.R.D. Fairbairn. And if imitation is the greatest form of flattery . . . I finally discovered what my student meant by a love letter. I was arguing a point of Fairbairn's, that the unconscious is devoid of good objects, in a dense style of writing that appeared to emanate directly from his pen. I have always held, and still do, that the ironic feature of Fairbairn's opus is that while he was one of the purist, most experience-near object relations theorists, who wrote from a totally different level of discourse from drive theorists, his humanistic, person based speculations were wrapped in an almost incomprehensible, mechanical, impossibly dense spewing of jargon.

Moreover, I was attempting to rescue his theory from one of its greatest criticisms, its refusal to find a place for good objects in the unconscious. As I will attempt to explicate, his mistake entailed a matter of time and timing. Briefly, Fairbairn opined that repression was evoked by necessity only as a defense. He viewed the process of repression to be a maneuver to protect a person from the intolerable associations with actual bad, non-loving objects. For him, since good objects are, by definition, not intolerable, there is no need to repress them and they remain available, internalized in what he called our "central ego" for referencing and usage in our conscious or preconscious experience.

While our earliest objects are internalized via normal identificatory processes during Fairbairn's so-called period of infantile dependence, there is, for Fairbairn, no need to repress them if they remain good. Only the intolerable, e.g., bad, objects are internalized *and repressed*. And here is where the issue of timing becomes of the utmost importance.

Temporal issues play a starring role in the experience of splitting during our earliest days of development, which are organized psychically in the paranoid/schizoid position. Experiences organized in the paranoid/schizoid position do not contain ambivalence. They are governed by a life or death, black or white, good or bad attitude toward part self and part object experience. It is only when the organizations of the life instinct are supported by internalizing life-affirming contact with good objects, that the threats organized by the death instinct no longer threaten annihilation. This temporally later state of affairs ushers in the depressive position, with its accompanying experience of ambivalence, heretofore not particularly a hallmark of experience. The lifetime struggle to maintain integrated whole self and object representations now occupy present time and then travel into the future. By omitting the crucial element of temporality in the transition from splitting to ambivalence is where I believe Fairbairn ran into an error.

His theory works only if we are regarding the earliest days of life, when splitting is in ascendance as a defense mechanism. At this earliest juncture, the infant has virtually no experience with its environment and those who populate it, virtually no experience with the need or ability to modulate its responses to its immediate world of objects. The child has basically only two responses with which to greet the others in its world – to accept those people who feel life-affirming and to reject those who feel threatening to the continuity of life. The former evoke loving responses and the later powerful feelings of annihilation, the primary anxiety of the earliest stages in life. Put in terms coined by Melanie Klein, the child whose psychic organization is operating in the paranoid/schizoid realm is operating in roughly the equivalent of Fairbairn's absolute dependence. The primary anxiety for both Fairbairn and Klein's early infant is fear of annihilation. It is a time in life when good and bad objects present the child with a binary life or death choice; good objects signal psychic life and bad objects signal psychic death. Splitting is the reflexive defense that keeps the organizations of safety and life psychically separate from the organizations of danger and death.

Then, as time passes and the child has gathered sufficient good-enough experiences with primarily loving, life-affirming others, the child enters Klein's depressive level of psychic organization, approximately the equivalent to Fairbairn's late oral and transitional stages. The primary developmental task changes. Up to now, the child has been concerned with life and death issues, its experiences vacillating from taking peaceful comfort and assurance in the continuity of its own existence as well as the continued existence of others. The child's defensive preoccupation, as noted, is focused on splitting, on keeping its organizations rooted

The good, the bad and the ambivalent 87

in interactions with life-affirming objects as far away as possible psychically from the interactions with frightening, threatening and decidedly non-life-affirming others.

But in time, with enough experience with loving others, the developmental task shifts. The child, in normal development with good-enough objects (Winnicott, 1954), is emboldened by its interactions with loving, life-affirming others and is no longer wrestling with life and death issues or survival issues, but with conflict. It must now integrate the good, life-affirming part objects with the bad, life-threatening part objects. This results in an extremely painful experience in which the child needs to accept both the goodness *and the badness* in its primary attachment figures and in him or her self.

Likewise, the primary anxiety experienced by the child at this point in time shifts from annihilation to ambivalence. Fear of annihilation is unbearably dreadful; ambivalence is painful. It is painful to contain these contradictory feelings toward a single whole person. And this dilemma is precisely where Fairbairn ran into difficulty understanding how good part objects can wind up repressed into the unconscious. To appreciate the child's dilemma, it becomes an imperative that we understand what is meant by ambivalence. Ogden (1990) provides a solution, and his solution is rooted squarely in the child's growing sense of time.

Ogden (1990) claims that, "Ambivalence is not simply a matter of consciously and unconsciously loving and hating the same object at a given moment" (p. 88). Nor, for Ogden, is ambivalence loving a person consciously and hating them unconsciously or vice versa. For Ogden, ambivalence involves a temporal factor. For him:

> The critical achievement in the attainment of ambivalence is the fact that the person one hates is the *same person* whom one has loved and unconsciously still loves and hopes to openly love again. There is no rewriting of history; there is no feeling that one has uncovered the truth of which one was previously only dimly aware.
>
> (p. 89)

There is increasing acceptance that the person whom one has loved is actually in fact also bad; has always been bad and will always be bad. During the attainment of ambivalence one needs to accept that the bad and good object are the same person. This process involves a temporal sequence of loving an object, then hating the object when it becomes bad, and holding on to the hope that it will become good again in time.

Splitting destroys time. When operating in the paranoid/schizoid psychic organization, time does not exist in the familiar continuous ways it contextualizes our experience in the depressive position. During the paranoid/schizoid organization of experience, history is not preserved. Ogden, in fact refers to this as the child having a lack of historicity. What this means is that moments in time are split off and discarded. Experientially, this means that the surge of a murderous impulse toward a cherished person ceases to exist in the next moment. Via the processes of splitting and/or repression, they are magically disappeared. The landscape of the world shifts moment to moment. That I cursed at you, insulted you, disrespected you or humiliated you five minutes ago can now be magically erased and rewritten. I do not have to deal with any conflict it caused because one minute does not flow into the next. Rather, it no longer exists, it has evaporated and no longer plagues me with the conflicting desires of loving you and wanting to annihilate you at the same time. No need for guilt or remorse. No need to repent. No need for reconciliation or reparation. I can take it all back, it never happened, don't worry, be happy.

In the depressive position, sadness pervades. Ogden again, "The 'depression' of the depressive position is more accurately thought of as a feeling of sadness in the acknowledgement that history cannot be rewritten" (1990, p. 89). One cannot omnipotently take back the hurt or damage one has inflicted on one's cherished object, nor the accompanied feelings of guilt or remorse. Sadness can no longer, as in the paranoid/schizoid organization, be disappeared and has to be dealt with. One can attempt to make the situation more palatable with reparations, but one cannot magically disappear the hurt and sadness. He states, most poignantly, "The feelings of sadness involved in mourning, guilt and the renunciation of omnipotence are among the 'prices' one pays for becoming human in the way that one does in the depressive position" (Ogden, 1990, p. 89).

In the depressive position one must reach some peace with the fact that history cannot be rewritten. Largely because the temporal modes of past, present and future become forever and intimately interrelated, each mode influencing the other, and none of them easily dismissed; Ogden considered Klein's depressive position to herald the birth of historicity.

The good, the bad and the ambivalent 89

Once the child transitions slowly into the depressive stage, the burden of conflict rises as moments of time are not disappeared, they cannot be taken back and rewritten. Rather they are held in perpetuity where one must wrestle with the pain and guilt that accompanies ambivalence. Feeling guilt or remorse or regret for the transgressions of one moment as they linger into the next is decidedly painful. Splitting no longer magically erases and rewrites the past. The developmental task that confronts us all, at times for life, is to be able to accept the badness in our loving others as well as the badness in ourselves and maintain an integrated, sturdy sense of our flawed humanity, and that of others. All while maintaining a primarily loving attitude.

But this takes time and repeated experiences of "the good, the bad and the ambivalent" interactions as they accompany our lives and relationships forever. It is my contention that one way to ease the pain of ambivalence inherent in conflict, which in turn is inherent in being alive, is to implant not only the bad experiences with others into unconscious realms, but also *good* interactions with others can be banished as well. Life becomes infinitely easier and the pain of conflict is neutralized when either branch of a good vs. bad conflict is eliminated.

This is the point of this chapter. In essence, I am making a plea for a measure of temporality to be highlighted in relational theory. Relational theory replaces the psychosexual drives as the primary motivators of our aliveness with the primary importance of establishing and maintaining loving connections with others. The timing of connections in development can, as I demonstrate in this chapter, determine the nature of the connections; determine whether they mitigate or enhance annihilation anxiety or ambivalent anxiety. Whatever one considers to be the "cornerstones" of our character, be it the paranoid/schizoid dynamics, depressive position dynamics or even the Oedipal conflict complications, they are all contextualized by temporality. The past, present and future all contribute to our ability to create and maintain solid, reliable and vital connection with others.

Moreover, as I described in Chapter 1, the development and quality of our sense of time is influenced by the quality of our relationships. A child whose parents are out of step with her needs, like the child of a divorced father who is inconsistent in keeping to a visitation schedule, coming many hours late or even not at all, can develop a distorted perceptual sense of temporal intervals. Hours can feel like days and days can become an eternity. Time and connection are intimately and endlessly intertwined.

Our characters both embed time and are embedded by time. Relationships, the fuel of our psychic survival, contextualize and are contextualized by temporal factors.

Moreover, I am proposing that Fairbairn did not distinguish between the splitting processes of our earliest psychic organizations in the paranoid/schizoid position, and the integration processes of the depressive position. The primary anxiety accompanying the paranoid/schizoid position is annihilation, while the primary anxiety of the depressive position is ambivalence. This temporal distinction allows us to posit the possibility that during the depressive position, in order to mitigate the pain of ambivalence, good part objects can be repressed.

Closely related to the issue of the internalization and repression of good objects is the issue of hope. Hope provides a temporal link to the future and, of course, it can reign eternal. I maintained that some forms of hope and its cousin, optimism, are expressions of the loving ministrations of the internalized good-enough mother, whether conscious or unconscious. Even when it might be difficult to locate goodness in a deficient, unloving parent, I maintain that few people are totally devoid of some scintilla of goodness that can be internalized and fuel a measure of hope. With many of our patients hope operates inconspicuously in the background, propelling a person into and through the rigors of therapy. With patients who have suffered through trauma and major family disruption, realistic (as opposed to idealistic or taunting) hope can appear, at time mysteriously, its genesis arising seemingly out of nowhere. I will often remark to myself when working with someone from a horrific set of life circumstances that I cannot imagine how this person can put one foot in front of the other and keep marching inexorably into the world. Yet they seem to thrive on hope and optimism about the treatment. Even in the throes of a virulent negative transference, they continue to come to sessions, time after time, angry or enraged, yet riding on a ray of invisible hope that relief will be forthcoming. It can be both helpful and comforting when working with a difficult patient to remind myself of the possibility that they still harbor hope that may be accessed in our work.

Note

1 An earlier version of this paper appeared in N.J. Skolnick and D.E. Scharff (eds.) (1998). *Fairbairn: Then and Now*. Hillsdale: The Analytic Press.

References

Ogden, T.H. (1990). *The Matrix of the Mind*. Northvale: Jason Aronson.

Skolnick, N.J. (1998). The good, the bad, and the ambivalent. In N.J. Skolnick and D.X. Scharff (eds.), *Fairbairn: Then and Now* (pp. 137–161). London and New York: Routledge.

Winnicott, D.W. (1954). The depressive position in normal emotional development. In D.W. Winnicott (eds.) (1958), *Through Paediatrics to Psychoanalysis* (pp. 262–278). New York: Basic Books.

Chapter 4

The good, the bad and the ambivalent

Fairbairn's difficulty locating the good object in the endopsychic structure[1,2]

1998

Neil J. Skolnick

Taken by Melanie Klein's (1935, 1946) elaborate descriptions of the dramas that unfold in, and determine the internal psychic reality of, the infant, Fairbairn also focused his attention on explicating the processes by which a child incorporates and then situates self and object relationships in the internal world. He (Fairbairn, 1940, 1944) frequently addressed his theoretical revisions to both Freud and Klein, and gradually his respectful disagreements with their ideas could be found to do nothing less than offer major alterations of both their theories. His radical departures are still being discovered and rediscovered today. Those who study Fairbairn's remarkably elegant theoretical opus are often amazed by the extent to which he presaged many of the paradigmatic shifts that characterize much of the relational theorizing today. Where Freud (1923) spoke of an ego that was empowered by the forces of the id, Fairbairn (1946) posited dynamic structures that are in nature similar to the contemporary concept of self as put forth by self-psychology theorists (Kohut, 1971; Robbins, 1992) as well as current trends in intersubjective theory (Stolorow and Atwood, 1992) that caution against static reifications of psychic structures. In fact, Fairbairn did away with the id as Freud had conceived it and replaced it with an irreducible need for people to establish and maintain relationships with others. Whereas Klein (1935, 1946) opined on the darker forces of the death instinct and accorded their aggressive essence primary importance in determining psychic structure, motivations and developmental course, Fairbairn, by contrast, focused his theoretical attention on the primary importance of the child's early environmental objects. Whereas Klein spoke of the influence of our instinctual phantasmagorical inheritance on shaping the fate of the external world as it

The good, the bad and the ambivalent 93

lodged within the psyche, Fairbairn, by contrast, turned his attention to the real aspects of the real environment and their fate in the internal endopsychic structure, particularly as it ran up against the need of the child for human loving connections. Whereas Klein described the earliest knowledge of the world as rooted in projection, Fairbairn started the developmental ball rolling with introjection. These are just a few of the fundamental shifts he proposed and wrote about. And like his psychoanalytic predecessors, he rooted his ideas in the time-honored method of clinical observation.

I have for years, in my own clinical work, been struck by the somewhat embarrassing quandary that I find both Klein's and Fairbairn's diametrically opposed ideas equally useful in informing my thoughts about, and actions toward, patients. I can ignore the gross, and at times grotesque, inconsistencies and incompatibilities between these two theoretical systems. I can, without appropriate chagrin, lapse into holding mutually exclusive theoretical explanations about my patients and ignore obvious contradictions as if they were merely inconvenient. I resolve such inconsistencies in a number of ways. My presumption is that the readers of this volume are familiar with some of them. I can unabashedly ignore them. That's the easiest route. I can also, although with some unease, claim "different theoretical strokes for different folks," squashing some patients into some models and other patients into others. This could be labeled a sloppy eclecticism. Or – and this is personally the least satisfying alternative – I just shrug my shoulders and relegate theoretical inconsistencies to the inherent ambiguity embedded in our work. So where my analytical mind, as informed by Klein, might hear the rumblings of predetermined, phylogenetically programmed narratives as primary determinants of current psychic functioning, my Fairbairnian ear wonders about the early experiences of the person and the abilities of early others to love and convince of their love. In the same breath that I talk about the effects of sadistic parental attacks, I might refer to the patient's same masochistic fantasies as determining the internalized identification with a sadistic parent (or sadistic analyst). This approach to resolving theoretical inconsistencies, by the way, has received new sanctioning by appeal from post-modern deconstructionist thinkers who often call for embracing, and even celebrating, the paradoxical. Thus we can synthesize dialectical poles or deconstruct them, both at times useful and both at times clouding inconsistencies in our thinking. Unfortunately, and as we all know too well, sadly, we cannot always have it both ways.

With this in mind, I present here for your consideration a way in which we might begin to think about a possible integration of one aspect of Fairbairn's and Klein's differing conceptualizations of the internal world. Specifically, I address the somewhat glaring discrepancy the two have in their place for good objects in the unconscious. Very briefly stated, Klein puts them there and Fairbairn does not.

The divergent conceptualizations of Fairbairn's and Klein's good objects have been explicated by a number of theorists, notably Winnicott (1965, 1975), Grotstein and Rinsley (1994) and Mitchell (1981) among others. Winnicott (1965) describes the state of the theoretical conundrum by claiming that "I think more has been written about bad internalized objects similarly disowned than about the denial of good internal forces and objects." Moreover, to highlight these differences, Mitchell has described a number of incompatibilities between Klein's and Fairbairn's concepts of the origin, nature and functions of internal objects. In this paper, I focus a critical spotlight on Fairbairn's idea that the internal unconscious world of objects is devoid of good objects. I propose that a clarification and alteration in Fairbairn's theory of development can allow for the place of good objects in the unconscious, while maintaining the basic integrity of his fundamental concepts.

For Fairbairn (1944), the endopsychic unconscious is structured by the child's internalization of interactions with aspects of his or her parents that fail to meet his or her psychological needs, that is, with bad or unsatisfying objects. The child, when faced with the intolerable feelings that arise in the face of not being loved or having his love recognized, resorts to a disintegration of ego or consequently, he or she establishes a closed internal world that contains organizations of split-off pieces of self, dynamically structured by and in interaction with split-off pieces of the other. Whether the split-off pieces of the other are exciting or taunting, rejecting or failing, they all have their roots in parental provisions that were lacking; that is in bad objects. Others, most notably Sutherland (1963), Kernberg (1980) and Grotstein and Rinsley (1994), have modified Fairbairn's conceptualization of the internal self and object tie to make way for a larger role for the affects as providing self- and object links. They nonetheless adhere to his basic plan of the endopsychic structure as separate self- and other systems fashioned out of bad interactions with early others. Sutherland maintained

Fairbairn's focus on the failing parent as influencing these structures, Kernberg focuses on constitutional factors while Grotstein insists that constitutional factors and environmental factors can be "simultaneously encompassed" (p. 133) despite their seeming incompatibility (as an aside, Grotstein has mounted the most ambitious attempt to integrate Fairbairn and Klein's perspectives and his "dual track" approach presents us with a good example of our being asked to embrace the paradoxical).

Noting that for Fairbairn the internal world of objects is a gratuitous concept in the economy of healthy as opposed to pathological functioning, Mitchell (1981) has criticized Fairbairn's inability to account for the internalization of good objects. He states, "Perhaps the greatest weakness of Fairbairn's system is his failure to account for the residues of good object relations and the structuralization of the self on the basis of healthy identifications" (p. 392).

This paper, in large part, picks up where this criticism leaves off, and I will argue for a correction in Fairbairn's theory. Fairbairn's notion of a primarily evil endopsychic underworld lacking much influence by good objects is unsatisfactory. From several levels of discourse, both theoretical and clinical, I believe there is an argument to be made for including a process by which good objects are internalized, repressed and identified with, and structured into the endopsychic self, where they remain out of conscious awareness but where they exert an active influence on interactions with the external world much the same way bad internalized objects do.

In order to provide a context for critiquing of Fairbairn's ideas about the internalization of good objects, allow me to begin with a very brief review of his description of the development of the endopsychic structure.

For Fairbairn (1944), the establishment of an endopsychic structure, while universal and inevitable, represents a fall from grace. Buffeted by the inability, both expectable and those ranging to the traumatic, of early caretakers to respond to what the child needs, especially in the realms of dependency and love, the child's ego shatters from its pristine integral unity and, by way of the processes of splitting, introjection and repression, ensconces the failing characteristics of one's early objects in the repressed internal object relationships of the endopsychic structure. Indeed, for Fairbairn, our unconscious exists as a kind of intrapsychic hell, populated only by split-off pieces of bad objects (either exciting or rejecting), along with the fragments of ego structure that abscond with and relegate to the unconscious, in particular, the libidinal and antilibidinal egos.

Identifications with good objects are, conversely, accorded express tickets to healthy, well adapted functioning, the realm Fairbairn (1944) dubbed the Central Ego, the workhorse of our quotidian mental health. As structured into the central ego, good objects remain conscious and readily available for open, flexible interaction with worldly matters and people. Thus according to Fairbairn (1944), good objects are nowhere to be found in the internal unconscious world. Good objects, that is, those pieces of our parents that meet Winnicott's (1965) criteria for "good enough" mothering (p. 145) remain integrally connected to our central ego. These central ego/good object self-units influence and potentiate, if not determine, our healthy functioning. The integrity, strength and robustness of our ego in our numerous pursuits is, for Fairbairn (1944), derived from our early interactions and identifications with adequate parents.

How does this happen? Fairbairn (1946) maintained that the child is born with a whole integral ego oriented toward whole others and ready to connect, wired to relate, if we may. Indeed, current mother–infant observational research (Stern, 1985; Beebe and Lachmann, 1992) has provided support for the idea of an infant possessing an ego that has great ability to affect and be affected by others from birth.

Should the parents fail to love the child for whom he or she is and fail to accept the child's spontaneous offers of love, the experience for the child becomes unbearable at the least and traumatic at the extreme. In reaction to the failures to provide psychological provisions, the infant defensively splits the object into good and bad part objects and internalizes the bad, which it further splits into its taunting and rejecting aspects. These split-off "bad" aspects of the parents are banished to the unconscious along with pieces of the child's ego, those pieces of the self that develop in the context of and interactions with the unsatisfying aspects of the parents. These split-off bundles of part-self and part-other in dynamic interaction with each other exist in the unconscious, as Rubens (1984) argues, as "split off subsystems of the self" (p. 434), which continue to exhibit powerful effects on conscious thought, affect and behavior. The person caught up in repetitious, self-defeating and painful patterns is somehow enacting powerful unconscious self-and-other relationships that were structured through repeated interactions with a failing parent.

Ogden (1983) expands this idea and notes that a person is identified with both the subject and object in these internal dramas, and can therefore enact either role. He states:

Fairbairn's insight that it is object relationships and not solely objects that are internalized opened the way to thinking of both self- and object components of the internal relationship as active agencies, "dynamic structures."

(p. 89)

In this light I would suggest that the internalization of an object relationship . . . would result in the formation of two new sub-organizations of the ego, one identified with the self in the external object relationship and the other thoroughly identified with the object.

(p. 99)

And what is the intrapsychic fate of the parent who is responsive to the child? What becomes of the parental attributes that rise to the occasion and provide love and recognition? How does the "good enough" (Winnicott, 1965) parent become internalized and ensconced in the child's self- and object subsystems? Fairbairn had a lot of difficulty consistently accounting for the internalization of the good object, and his theory is riddled with inconsistencies and confusion regarding this subject. He at different times accounted for the internalization of the good object in the following different ways:

Fairbairn (1943) stated that the good object is internalized by way of the moral defense. This is in essence a temporal model of internalization. In response to internalizing the bad object, the child subsequently internalizes the good object to compensate for the possible threat to self-organization that comes with being identified only with unsatisfactory object experiences. As he is oft quoted, "It is better to be a sinner in a world ruled by God than to live in a world rule by the devil" (p. 67).

By 1944 he maintained there is no primary internalization of a good or satisfying object. For him, internalization was a matter of defensive coercion. The bad part-object, the part of the parent that does not satisfy the infant's needs, is internalized in order to shift the locus of control to the infant. There is no need then to defend against the satisfying experiences of relating to a good object who meets the infant's needs.

Fairbairn (1944), in a 1951 addendum, posited that the earliest internalization is that of a preambivalent object, one that "presented itself as unsatisfying in some measure as well as in some measure satisfying" (p. 135). It is only later, when the parent fails and the infant confronts an ambivalent internal object, the infant splits off the overexciting and overfrustrating aspects of this object and represses them (as the exciting and rejecting objects) along with the pieces of the central ego with which they are in interaction, namely the libidinal ego and the antilibidinal ego, respectively.

While Fairbairn left it for future theorists to resolve the inconsistencies in the timing and nature of the internalization of good objects – and indeed, the issues appear to get murkier the closer one looks – my reading of where he landed was that, while good objects may be internalized (although the timing is never quite clear), they are never repressed. They are never forced by the central ego to dwell in the unconscious endopsychic structure, maintaining self- and object ties that defy conscious awareness. Instead, what remains of the good object, after being shorn of its unsatisfying badness, remains attached to and interaction with the central ego. It takes the form of an ego ideal informing the core of the superego.

Rubens (1984) has advanced Fairbairn's thought by making qualitative, rather than a topographical, distinction between the internalization of good and bad objects. In essence, he posits that objects are internalized in two ways, structuring and non-structuring. Bad objects are subject to structuring internalization. As they are repressed, they form fairly rigid self- and object subsystems that are structured into the unconscious endopsychic structure. Here they reside, in fairly closed off systems that remain vital as they manifest in maladaptive patterns and psychopathology. By contrast, good objects are never subjected to structure-generating repression. There is no self-splitting and no formation of endopsychic structure with a good object. Instead, non-structuring internalizations of good experiences with an object result in either memory or the conscious organization of experience. As Rubens states:

> It is clear from this position that non-structuring internalization does not result in the establishment of any "entity" within the self, but rather results in an alteration of the integration of the self, or in the production of a thought, memory or fantasy within the self.
>
> (p. 437)

While his conceptualization of non-structuring internalization of good objects represents a thought-provoking enhancement of Fairbairn's concept of central ego, it still fails to account for repressed good objects.

Clinical evidence for unconscious good objects

Shifting to the clinical arena, a fairly common outcome of psychoanalytic treatment is that as a person demonstrates improvement, one overt reflection of the improvement is the return to consciousness of a heretofore unconscious, yet decidedly good, object relationship. Take, for example, a father who is inexorably recounted during the course of treatment as a brutal man but now is reorganized in the patient's experience as a caring, though somewhat inept, man struggling under the constraints of his own conflicts, and a memory appears of his caring concern for a child's unhappy disappointment on a first date. Or consider the bitter, depressed and removed mother who is recalled as relaxed, singing and happy on a picnic outing. Consider the following dream fragment:

A patient of mine, Derek, reported this dream within a week of his father's death. He was standing in an exquisitely appointed lobby. As he was admiring the rich architectural compositions his father entered the dream and embraced him lovingly. Derek experienced an unexpected welling of powerful and reciprocal loving feelings toward his father.

This brief dream fragment came as a total and utter surprise to Derek, who was not aware of ever having experienced loving emotions toward his oft-described tyrannical father. In his 37 years, he was not aware of a single moment when he regarded his father with anything but intense fear and contempt. Indeed, he seemed particularly unmoved by his father's recent death and was conscious only of a pervasive relief to be "rid of the bastard" at last. Prior to this dream his father existed for him almost exclusively as a demeaning and destructive tyrant, with no shades of ambivalence around the edges, a unidimensional tormentor. Of particular note was Derek's attitude toward the dream: He expressed true puzzlement and dismissed it as an aberration unworthy of any attempts at associations or analysis.

Derek had entered analysis with the dual complaint that he lacked an ability to experience love toward others and that he was not productive at his chosen profession, songwriting. That he possessed significant talent and creativity was substantiated some eight years prior to our meeting, when he wrote a song that achieved critical acclaim. Subsequently, he was unable to write and, feeling exceedingly blocked and frustrated in his work, he resorted to drugs and brief sexual encounters with women to fill a life largely occupied by nothing. He conducted a relationship with a woman that spanned the time of his professional success, but he became disenchanted and emotionally dead as his professional success deteriorated. He regarded this woman initially as an angel who evoked his creativity in muse-like fashion. He was, however, now unable to muster positive feelings toward any woman and entered treatment despairing of loving again.

Following the dream, Derek began to have an increasing number of fond recollections of his father. Earlier scenes of his father in a dictatorial rage competed with momentary memories of a kind, caring man who had great difficulty expressing his warmer feelings. Alongside a father who only criticized and discouraged was one who was encouraging and proud. His father's business successes, once seen as exploitation, now gave him the admirable shadings of a self-made man. At first Derek was puzzled. Preferring to hold on to an image of his father as a petty tyrant, he resisted these memories. He could not entertain an image of his father that included both fond and hateful memories, although he slowly began to acknowledge that they both existed and that his struggle to accept the kinder father was perplexing to him.

In the transference almost the reverse situation was occurring. His previous and tenaciously held positive attitude toward me began to show cracks as I became increasingly worthy of his contempt. Actually, to say that this represented the reverse situation is not entirely correct. The emergence of positive feelings toward his father and less than positive feelings toward me could be considered two manifestations of the same process, that of a foray into what Kleinians might consider the depressive position with its hallmark event, the advent of ambivalence. He was indeed gradually able to embrace a more ambivalent attitude toward his father, and he was likewise able to recognize his own identifications with both the loving and tyrannical aspects of him. These changes paralleled a similar shift in his ability to embrace loving and not so loving feelings toward me and others. He began dating a woman for whom he had strong loving feelings, and, while bemoaning her shortcomings, he decided to marry her.

Derek's evolution in treatment was not unlike that of many of our patients, who, as they progress in psychoanalysis and become more able to tolerate ambivalence, begin to access not only bad memories of early others but also surprisingly loving ones as well. Attempts to understand these memories within the framework of Fairbairn's split self and object systems lead to unsatisfactory dead ends.

The psychic situation for Derek might, from a Fairbairnian perspective, consist of a structured unconscious in which he would have split off and repressed the tyrannical aspects of his father (the rejecting object) in interaction with a split-off part of his ego, identified with the rejecting object (the antilibidinal ego). This system would continue to manifest in his creative and loving blocks, his attacks on his creativity and his inability to love. Similarly, the enticing, taunting aspects of his father (the piece of him that promised recognition but failed to provide it) would remain ensconced in the endopsychic structure in interaction with an unrealistically hopeful organization of self. This organization might be reflected by the part of Derek that searched endlessly for a muse, one who would enable him to fulfill his grandiose strivings for stardom. The kinder, more accepting and encouraging aspects of his father that appeared in the dream and during the course of treatment might be viewed as a good object ensconced in and suffusing Derek's central ego, where it might exist in memory, but not subject to repression. If we consider the force with which Derek resisted these memories of a kind father, however, we might then posit that they indeed had been repressed and were no longer easily understood as unstructured connections to a central ego.

Alternatively, through another Fairbairnian prism we might be tempted to view these favorable memories as manifestations of only bad self and object organizations in the endopsychic unconscious. These kinder memories would represent, then, exciting objects in interaction with the split-off libidinal ego, that is, his hopes for his father's recognition that were repeatedly dashed. This explanation, however, is equally unsatisfying because, for Fairbairn, exciting objects typically exist in taunting, aggrandized or exaggerated forms; and Derek's descriptions of his father as a kinder soul were modulated and realistic.

Therefore, neither of these attempts to understand the retrieval of Derek's good memories in accordance with Fairbairn's pronouncement that there are no good objects in the unconscious appears satisfactory to me. There is too much resistance to their becoming conscious for us to locate them unequivocally in the memories of the central ego. And they lack the aggrandized or idealized nature of an exciting object in the unconscious. Derek's surprise at the fond memories and his struggle to keep them conscious bespeak some psychic force, or resistance, that actively maintains them out of awareness. For Fairbairn (1943) such a force would not be an acceptable explanation because for him the psychic force maintaining repression was the unbearable nature of the bad object which interfered with the child's desire for connection. Instead, Derek's dream and his uncovered memories appear to embody the sustained and satisfactory aspects of a good object relationship that were lost to repression.

To turn now to another clinical observation, Fairbairn's object relational approach, not unlike other relational approaches that relegate the drives to secondary importance, runs into difficulty when trying to account for the intensity of our motives, their qualitative forays into the extreme. Once we denude our behavior of the primary and powerful underpinnings of sexual or aggressive tensions seeking quiescence, where are the constructs by which we can understand the motivational thrust and intensity of our everyday passions? By everyday, I am referring to the more or less healthy intensity that can imbue any pursuit, romantic or otherwise. Such scenarios include the at times inexplicable yet powerful investment of our selves in a person or endeavor – be it the passionate pursuit of a desired romance, the passions that fuel our professional goals, the passionate enjoyment of a cherished hobby, or the fleeting enjoyment of a night on the town. The seething underworld of steamy, tumultuous, instinctual forces have great appeal, often greater appeal than some of our less charged relational constructs.

It is important to note that, when considering passionate experience and phenomena, I am not referring to the self-defeating masochistic, and ultimately painful, connections to the world that are overt manifestations of a more or less closed internal world of bad object relationships. The split-off and at times inexorable pursuit of bad objects motivated by the structures of the endopsychic unconscious might appear passionate (like Derek's passionate pursuit of a muse or his quest for fame) but it is probably more correctly called compulsive. Indeed, Fairbairn (1943) did make the point that the greater the amount of ego relegated to the closed world of the unconscious, the more compulsive the pursuit of bad objects will be.

Although Fairbairn (1944) never addressed the issue of passion directly, he most likely would have located the sources of healthy passion in the success of the central ego in seeking sought-after object ties. As the mother greets the child's needs with pleasure and a measure of her own passion, so would the child identify with and incorporate into its self a potential for passionate investments. This process would fall under what Rubens (1984) described as the "unstructured internalizations" of the healthy central ego as it internalizes the satisfying provisions of the good object. It seems to me, however, the Fairbairn's concept of the strivings of a central ego, shorn of its badness, as providing the wellspring of our passions seems to fall flat. It lacks the stormy and inexorable strength of our passions, at times inexplicable, but realistic enough to fuel the pursuit of dreams and follies embedded in our lives, literature and culture.

One additional clinical experience suggests the presence of good, though repressed, self- and object-organizations. As noted, the workings of the central ego shorn of its badness seem insufficient to account for the tenacity of our patients, particularly our most disturbed, who come to analysis regularly, repeatedly and harboring hope, despite the affect storms, disintegration and chaos that can pervade the therapeutic relationship. Why do they keep coming, even when their experience of us is primarily of us as taunting devils or outright persecutors? Of course, this issue overlaps that of hope, but I think it also contains a degree of what we might consider to be realistically optimistic, hopeful self-organizations fashioned in large measure by contact with satisfying aspects of a parent but remaining out of conscious awareness. Consider the learning of a new skill, say, playing an instrument. The difficulties, disappointments and narcissistic injuries inherent in the learning process, and the perseverance we can muster in spite of them, have parallels in the persistence with which our patients consistently return to our offices, over and over, despite vitriolic attacks, empathic disappointments and experiences of disintegration. Are these just the workings of the central ego's connection to fulfilling objects? I don't think so. Persistence is informed by a certain inexplicable quality in which an understanding of the driving force and intensity is not readily apparent. It seems to me that this experience cannot be rooted in a more or less conscious or preconscious functioning of a central ego. I maintain that it too is a manifestation of a part of oneself that developed in interaction with hopeful and encouraging pieces of one's parents – the good objects – but operates from a place out of awareness.

These three clinical phenomena – the appearance of heretofore unconscious good object relationships released during the course of treatment, the often inexplicable imbuing of our behaviors with a passionate charge, and the persistence with which our patients continue in treatment – suggest the existence, in the unconscious, of a world of repressed good objects that remain out of awareness, but very much vital, as they affect our conscious motivation, affects and behavior much as do the torturous, unconscious bad objects.

The unconscious good object

Fairbairn's difficulty in locating these good object relationships in the unconscious can be traced to two separate but overlapping confusions in his theory. The first involves the timing of the structuring of the endopsychic unconscious; and, the second, his failure to distinguish adequately between split object experience and ambivalent object experience. To elaborate these points, let me briefly digress to review several more of his key concepts in order to provide a context for these criticisms.

In 1941 Fairbairn elevated the importance of the quality of the of the object relationship to center stage. In one fell swoop he redefined the oral, anal and phallic stages of development by focusing on the changing nature of a child's dependent relationship on the object and not the libidinal excitation of changing bodily zones. Thus, a child navigates a developmental course from absolute dependence on a caretaker to a mature mutual dependence on others, not by way of the successful resolutions of the oral, anal and phallic crises. Fairbairn's earliest stage in development, corresponding to Freud's (1918) and Abraham's (1924) oral stage and centering on the child's unconditional dependence on the object, he relabeled the period of infantile dependence. He divided this stage into early and late periods, each with its accompanying conflict, which is exacerbated by a depriving environment. The early period encompasses relations with an essentially pre-ambivalent whole object. The child relates to the object through primary identification and internalization, processes that, for Fairbairn, are essentially indistinguishable at this stage. There is no ambivalence toward the object; the choice for the child is to accept or reject the object. The accommodations, ranging from the pathological to the more or less normal, that are necessitated when the object fails to meet the child's needs are coterminous with the establishment of the endopsychic structure.

The late oral period, by contrast, involves an ambivalent relationship with the object. The conflict for the child at this later point is how to love an object without destroying it by hate. These early and late periods correspond roughly to Klein's (1946) paranoid/schizoid and depressive positions (1935) respectively.

One of the hallmarks of Fairbairn's (1944) theory is his emphasis on the earliest period of development, the period of infantile dependence, as the time when endopsychic structure is laid into the cornerstone of character. Further development of ego and object structure is basically overlaid onto,

The good, the bad and the ambivalent 105

or fused with, these earliest structures. A careful reading however, reveals that he was unclear and inconsistent about the actual timing of events. At times he treated the early and later stages as one stage contributing to the establishment of the endopsychic structure; at other times he (Fairbairn, 1941) made a clear distinction between the early and the later stage. He considered the earlier, schizoid period to be the crucial time for establishing the endopsychic world and relegated the later period, with its depressive issues to one of lesser importance.

He was similarly inconsistent about the appearance of ambivalence during early development. According to Fairbairn (1941), there is no ambivalence in the early schizoid period. Later, however, Fairbairn in 1944 claims that the structuring of the endopsychic structure is, indeed, the structuring of the child's original ambivalent attitude toward the mother: "For what the obstinate attachment of the libidinal ego to the exciting object and the equally obstinate aggression of the internal sabateur (antilibidinal ego) toward the same object really represent is the obstinacy of the original *ambivalent* attitude" (p. 117; italics added).

One wonders how ambivalence can be structured if it has not yet appeared on the scene.

Seemingly a minor, hairsplitting point, this inconsistency becomes of utmost importance when one considers the phenomenology of ambivalence. As I have already noted, Fairbairn failed to make an important distinction between the experience of ambivalence and the experience of splitting. Ogden (1986) makes the well-taken point that ambivalence is not

> a matter of consciously and unconsciously loving and hating the same object at a given moment . . . The critical achievement in the attainment of ambivalence is the fact that the person one hates is the *same person* whom one has loved and unconsciously still loves and hopes to openly love again.
>
> (pp. 88–89)

Thus, ambivalence requires the temporal maintenance of affects or attitudes toward the same person, despite moment-to-moment fluctuations and swings. And, more importantly, ambivalence fuels a hope that one will return to a loving state again.

Splitting, on the other hand, lacks a historical continuity; it involves affects and attitudes that are constantly and magically being created, reversed

106 Neil J. Skolnick

and re-created. The person one loves one moment is not the same person one hates the next, and the "I" who does the hating is not the same "I" who does the loving. In one state, there is no knowledge of or communication with the other state; realistic hope has no meaning in splitting. I maintain that the original attitude toward the primary object structured into Fairbairn's unconscious endopsychic structure is not one of ambivalence, but one rooted in splitting. When the original object fails to meet the emotional need of the child, the intolerable feelings that arise lead to a splitting of the object and self and these split self and object systems remain very separate. Like hope, ambivalence has no experiential meaning in splitting.

Fairbairn's early and later stages of primary dependence need to be more clearly distinguished, as they are in Klein's (1935, 1946) paranoid/ schizoid and depressive positions. A clear delineation between the early and late oral periods sets the stage for an understanding of how the repression of the good object might occur in Fairbairn's model without excessive strain on the theory's internal consistency.

The stages can be more clearly delineated by considering their core conflicts and defensive operations. The task for the child during the early oral period is to accept or reject the object, and the default mechanism used by the ego to negotiate failure of the object is splitting. By contrast, the primary task of the later oral period is to maintain a whole object when it fails and is attacked by the child's aggression, which is coterminous with the problem of establishing ambivalence. And it is in dealing with the problem of ambivalence, with its at times painful conflicts, that the action of repressing good objects, along with their attachments to loving pieces of self is in ascendance.

The development of the endopsychic structure as Fairbairn described it, particularly with its establishment of the three ego/object subsystems (Central Ego/Ideal Object; Libidinal Ego/Exciting Object; and Antilibidinal Ego/Rejecting Object) continues to hold reliable merit in this new system. It is an early part-object structure, predicated on splitting, pre-dating and devoid of ambivalence. It is formed when the needy infant meets an unsatisfying bad object that fails to meet the infant's needs. The infant, fearing annihilation, splits the object and himself and represses the dreadful situation of exciting and rejecting part objects into the unconscious endopsychic structure. (For an excellent description of the differences between splitting and repression, see Davies and Frawley (1994).) My patient Derek's unyielding idealization of women serving as potential muses can be understood as illustrating splitting processes as described by Fairbairn.

In the later oral stage, largely ignored by Fairbairn, the problem of a failing object changes. It no longer threatens annihilation, it now threatens the pain of conflict. With the establishment of the endopsychic structure, and its compensatory internal split-off self and object subsystems, the child is left with a relatively whole good object, shorn of its badness, firmly connected to and interacting with its conscious central ego. But good objects are not always good. Being inevitably "good-enough" (Winnicott, 1965; Kohut, 1971), they can fail a child in countless ways. But the child, stronger now shorn of its bad objects, experiences the failures not as annihilating, but rather as painful yet bearable. When faced with the failures of these basically good, but flawed objects, already structured into the conscious central ego, the child must now struggle with the problem of ambivalence and struggle not with annihilation but, rather, with the fear that their reactive anger could do damage to the object they love. The challenge is to maintain the object as good, despite powerful angry feelings being directed at it.

This is an extremely painful conflict, not unlike the one described by Klein (1935) during the onset of the depressive position. There are several important differences, though. In keeping with his (1943) disavowal of the death instinct, the problem of ambivalence for Fairbairn resides in the child's angry responses to a failing object. Aggression for Fairbairn (1944) is always reactive. The imperative for the child is to maintain a relationship with a real object that does not meet its needs, that actually frustrates and evokes anger. A failing object for the Kleinian child is, early in development, always a projection onto the caretaker of the child's own endogenous aggression, not an actual failure by the mother.

Another important difference is that, for Fairbairn, the task is for the child to *maintain* whole object functioning, despite it being buffeted by ambivalence; whereas for Klein the task is for the child to integrate and *achieve* whole-object functioning. Fairbairn throughout maintained that the human infant is born a whole self, oriented toward whole objects. Inevitable failures by the mother cause the child to defensively split and internalize bad objects in order to control them. So that for Klein, integration of a whole self and object is an achievement aided by interaction with good, loving others, while for Fairbairn, we are born whole and split when confronted by environmental failure.

As I noted, having feelings of both love and hate toward the same person present the child with an enormous problem. It is just this struggle to maintain a good connection with a whole but failing object that ushers in ambivalence, with its concomitant feelings of painful conflict. It is this conflict, then, that can propel the child during Fairbairn's later oral stage to split off and repress *good* part and whole objects. This conflict-driven maneuver serves a function not unlike Klein's manic defenses; the splitting and repression of good object ties eases the child's conflict through a denial of the value possessed by the good object. The maintenance of the connection with the whole object who fails, a whole object who evokes ambivalence, is a Herculean and probably lifelong task. Not unlike Klein's manic defenses, the repression of goodness can aid in the achievement of integration and ambivalence.

One ramification of this alteration to Fairbairn's theory is that it places conflict back on center stage as a primary mover and shaker of the internal world. Often, in discussions of early splitting, the motivating force of conflict is ignored or relegated to later developmental significance. As Mitchell (1988) has noted, relational theories that employ the metaphor of the infant tend to ignore the significance of conflict in psychic development and functioning. Fairbairn's internal world, devoid of good objects as he would have it, can take on the proportions of cataclysmic battle between life and death, a psychic Armageddon. Allowing for the presence of conflict can temper this tendency and substitutes for Armageddon the complex debates of a Mideast peace negotiation – neither side is on the side of the angels or devils and God is on neither or perhaps both, sides. This internal scenario more accurately represents the state of affairs when we are attempting to understand our patients' experience of ambivalence.

The inclusion of good objects in the unconscious internal world might also enhance the ability of those working from a Fairbairnian perspective to remain closer to a patient's experience of ambivalence. All too often the emergence of good interactions (either in the transference or actual interactions in the external arena) are conceptualized by the analyst as the manifestation of an exciting object tie that needs to be made conscious *as a bad object relationship*, one that need to be ultimately disavowed. In this fashion, the appearance of my patient, Derek's, loving father in his dream (or perhaps the transference implications of the image) might have been dismissed as but another example

The good, the bad and the ambivalent   109

of a split-off expression of his idealized relationship with a taunting, and ultimately rejecting, father. Viewing the image as a loving aspect of his father that has been repressed, the patient (and analyst) can begin to embrace this life affirming aspect of the father and ultimately integrate it into an expanded perception of his father as a whole, though ambivalent and complicated person. Likewise the patient could attain an increased ability to view and accept himself and others in a more integrated, expanded, albeit ambivalent manner.

My guess is that many of us who work from a relational perspective are already helping patients to embrace passionate and life-affirming aspects of themselves and others that have been lost to repression. The problem for me is that unless one subscribed to a Kleinian conception of the depressive position, and its emphasis on the developmental imperative that we must tame our aggressive drive derivatives in order to achieve object integration, there is no place within Fairbairn's theory that allows us to acknowledge the presence of unconscious good-object relationships, relationships with roots in actual interactions with real, loving others. Good objects for Fairbairn, while internalized, are never repressed to the unconscious.

Which brings me back to my stated quandary at the outset of this chapter, that I may find myself working from diametrically opposed theoretical positions. This can feel duly discomforting, that not only have I surrendered to some form of reckless abandon, but have crossed a line into theoretical illegality. I comfort myself by maintaining that my contradictory ideas are but preliminary to a potentially heuristic and fruitful theoretical integration. The inclusion of repressed good objects in the Fairbairnian schema may help bridge the gaps between Klein's and Fairbairn's blueprints for the unconscious inner world. It should also be noted that the alteration I am suggesting, that good objects are repressed *after* the depressive position crisis has set in developmentally, underlines a temporal distinction I believe Fairbairn had overlooked.

Notes

1 A previous version of his paper was originally published in N.J. Skolnick and D.E. Scharff (eds.) (1998). *Fairbairn: Then and Now*. Hillsdale: The Analytic Press. Reproduced with permissions.
2 I would like to thank Stephen Mitchell for his helpful comments in preparing this chapter.

References

Abraham, K. (1924). The influence of oral eroticism on character formation. In *Selected Papers of Karl Abraham*. London: Hogarth Press.

Beebe, B. and Lachmann, F. (1992). The contribution of mother–infant influence to the origins of self- and other object representations. In N.J. Skolnick and S.C. Warshaw (eds.), *Relational Perspectives in Psychoanalysis* (pp. 83–119). Hillsdale: The Analytic Press.

Davies, J.M. and Frawley, M.G. (1994). *Treating the Adult Survivor of Childhood Sexual Abuse*. New York: Basic Books.

Fairbairn, W.R.D. (1940). Schizoid factors in the personality. In *Psychoanalytic Studies of the Personality* (pp. 3–28). London: Routledge and Kegan Paul, 1952.

Fairbairn, W.R.D. (1941). A revised psychopathology of the psychosis and psychoneuroses. In *Psychoanalytic Studies of the Personality* (pp. 28–58). London: Routledge and Kegan Paul, 1952.

Fairbairn, W.R.D. (1943). The repression and return of bad objects (with special reference to the "war neuroses"). In *Psychoanalytic Studies of the Personality* (pp. 59–81). London: Routledge and Kegan Paul, 1952.

Fairbairn, W.R.D. (1944). Endopsychic structure considered in terms of object relationships. In *Psychoanalytic Studies of the Personality* (pp. 82–136). London: Routledge and Kegan Paul, 1952.

Fairbairn, W.R.D. (1946). Object relations and dynamic structure. In *Psychoanalytic Studies of the Personality* (pp. 137–151). London: Routledge and Kegan Paul, 1952.

Freud, S. (1918). From the history of an infantile neurosis. In J. Strachey (ed. and trans.), *The Standard Edition of the Complete Psychological Works of Sigmund Freud* (Vol. 17, pp. 17–122). London: Hogarth Press.

Freud, S. (1923). The ego and the id. In J. Strachey (ed. and trans.), *The Standard Edition of the Complete Psychological Works of Sigmund Freud* (Vol. 19, pp. 12–66). London: Hogarth Press.

Grotstein, J.S. and Rinsley, D.B. (eds.) (1994). *Fairbairn and the Origins of Object Relations*. New York: Guilford.

Kernberg, O. (1980). *Internal World and External Reality*. Northvale: Aronson.

Klein, M. (1935). A contribution to the psychogenesis of manic-depressive states. In *Love, Guilt and Reparation: And Other Works 1921–1945* (pp. 262–290). New York: McGraw Hill, 1964.

Klein, M. (1946). Notes on some schizoid mechanisms. In *Envy and Gratitude and Other Works, 1946–1963* (pp. 1–25). New York: Delacorte Press, 1975.

Kohut, H. (1971). *The Analysis of the Self*. New York: International Universities Press.

Mitchell, S.A. (1981). The origin and the nature of the "object" in the theories of Klein and Fairbairn. *Contemporary Psychoanalysis*, 17: 374–398.

Mitchell, S.A. (1988). *Relational Concepts in Psychoanalysis*. Cambridge, MA: Harvard University Press.

Ogden, T.H. (1983). The concept of internal object relations. *International Journal of Psycho-analysis*, 64: 227–241.

Ogden, T.H. (1986). *The Matrix of the Mind*. Northvale: Aronson.

Robbins, M. (1992). A Fairbairnian object relations perspective on self psychology. *American Journal of Psychoanalysis*, 53: 247–261.

Rubens, R.L. (1984). The meaning of structure in Fairbairn. *International Review of Psychoanalysis*, 11: 429–440.

Stern, D. (1985). *The Interpersonal World of the Infant*. New York: Basic Books.

Stolorow, R. and Atwood, R. (1992). *Contexts of Being*. Hillsdale: The Analytic Press.

Sutherland, J.D. (1963). Object relations theory and the conceptual model of psychoanalysis. *British Journal of Medical Psychology*, 36: 109–124.

Winnicott, D.W. (1965). *The Maturational Processes and the Facilitating Environment*. New York: International Universities Press.

Winnicott, D.W. (1975). *Through Paediatrics to Psychoanalysis*. New York: Basic Books.

Chapter 5

What's a good object to do?

A Fairbairnian perspective

Introduction

Early in my career, before relational psychoanalysis made its prominent appearance on center stage, I was in a session with a 20-something-year-old man when the skies opened up in a torrential, and perhaps for me, prophetic, thunderstorm. The session was about to end and I noted that my patient had not brought an umbrella. As I describe in this chapter, I deliberated for several moments about whether to break classical psychoanalytic protocol and offer him an umbrella, and landed upon – of course I would; it was the decent thing to do. So I gave my patient an umbrella and dealt with the aftermath later. We explored a range of issues connected to the incident, such as: Why wasn't he carrying one? (He never does.) What was his reaction to my offering him an umbrella? (He felt infantilized and ashamed but appreciative.) Anything else? (He was concerned he might misplace it, damage it, or forget to bring it back.) I describe the incident in this chapter and how it became one of the cornerstones of my shift to a more relational approach to my work. I did not try to rationalize my behavior as belonging to the "working alliance" (Greenson, 1967) or the "real relationship" between analyst and patient (Greenson, 1967, 1971; Greenson and Wexler, 1969) as opposed to the transference relationship. Greenson (1967, as noted in Greenberg and Mitchell, 1983) attempted to make a distinction between the transference relationship, born of "instinctual frustration and the search for gratification," and the "working alliance," the cooperation between the patient's and analyst's reasonable, analyzing egos. He also noted that a piece of the "working alliance" was soaked up by the "real relationship," the patient's accurate perceptions of the actual qualities and weaknesses of the analyst.

At the time, I was not convinced that I could be, with such facility, divided into separate "real," "working" and "transference" personae. I doubted my patient saw it that way either. It was me, myself and I who acted in the many ways that comprise my character. Sometimes my different self-states were

What's a good object to do?   113

consistent and sometimes they were not. We all are infinitely complicated and endlessly unique. I pondered that maybe we needed to reconsider what transference is all about? Is it a projection of a drive, internal object, or object relationship upon the blank-screen analyst, or does it have to do more with a patient's reaction to the actual analyst who can no longer hide behind the camouflage of a mythical blank screen? Maybe it's a confluence of the two, a two-way projection or interaction (soon to be labeled as intersubjectivity).

In any event, I was clearly not the only one thinking along such radical lines. Relational theory was in the air. And the air held harbingers for greatly expanding possible explanations for transference and countertransference, considering a number of one- and two-person relational configurations. There was clearly no one moment when a critical mass was reached, but voila! Relational perspectives on transference and countertransference were spun out in exciting, new, cohesive, comprehensive, and internally consistent theory. I think it more likely the case that, gradually, time performed its repetitive magic and what people first observed clinically, thought about, and then tentatively voiced, began to loosen analysts' tenacious hold on conventional theoretical beliefs. Largely by virtue of slow change tucked into the passage of time therapists were enabled to surrender old paradigms and adopt new models of organizing clinical data. Often the tiny but inexorable changes in themselves went unnoticed until, in retrospect, psychoanalysts could observe large changes in their clinical and theoretical sensibilities.

One way I tend to think about how these slow, time-dependent evolutions in our technique occur is similar to the way I think about how our patients change; I think of them as changes incurred through a combination of Fairbairn's "dynamic structure" (1952; also see Skolnick, 2006) and what Lyons-Ruth (1999) of the Boston Change Process Group refers to as either implicit or unconscious enactive relational procedures. Both are means by which we internalize relationships in non-reflexive, unsymbolized fashion, which may or may not at some future time be translated into words. The significance of what changes in the way we do what we do (enacting), become evident in the future, with their seeds traced to what we did in the past, often beyond our awareness. For a rich discussion of implicit knowing and change I refer the reader to *Change in Psychotherapy: A Unifying Paradigm*, published by Norton, in 2010, by the Boston Change Process Study Group.

The changes I am describing when shifting to a relational paradigm from a drive theory paradigm represent a reversal of figure and ground. In the older drive theory model of the psychoanalytic relationship, the emphasis in the development of transference/countertransference was rooted in a drive deprivation model of treatment, and the "real" relationship existed as a kind of error variance that had to be factored out of the mutagenic equation. In the newer model, the real relationship (no longer in quotes), consisting of both transference and countertransference, takes center stage as the mutagenic engine of the change process, holding the key to understanding and, ultimately, to change. I am referring to the subliminal, non-reflexive adjustments and changes we make in our own technique, often out of awareness, until at a later time we become aware of major alterations in what we do, in our implicit procedural model of conducting an analysis (Lyons-Ruth, 1999).

The paper in this chapter represents my clearest break from the traditional psychoanalysis of my training, though some conflict and struggle visibly remain. I am no longer attempting to squeeze relational concepts into traditional metapsychological holes. From Freud on, many attempts have been made historically to alter classical metapsychology in efforts to make it conform more to the clinical observations garnered from the consulting room (Greenberg and Mitchell, 1983). For example, Freud, who at times bravely, and with integrity, challenged his own theory, revising his thinking about the clinical observation that symptoms often tenaciously re-appeared following transference interpretations and subsequent working through (Freud, 1920). Bottom line, though, he finally settled on the operation of the repetition compulsion to explain this phenomenon. Moreover, the repetition compulsion, for him, was a manifestation of the death instinct, a theoretical mainstay of classical drive theory. Perhaps because of political pressure to maintain the integrity of his "project," and defend it against would be interlopers or traitors, or perhaps because of his own narcissistic needs to remain "Papa Freud" to his followers in the psychoanalytic movement, or perhaps both, or other personal needs, while he was open to the need for theoretical alterations, he paradoxically remained tenaciously protective of what was later to become known as classical one-person drive psychology, and contemptuous at best, and totally dismissive at worst, of those who endeavored alternative theoretical bottom lines.

I personally answer more of my patient's questions now. The reasons I do this are manifold, and rooted primarily in my clinical experience. Historically, this issue changed for me when I was in the clinical habit of exploring a patient's curiosity about where I would be taking my vacation.

After the umpteenth time I heard from them their "fantasy" that I vacationed in either the Hamptons or Martha's Vineyard (often, but not always correct!), I decided to answer the question, and then explore the aftermath. This typically revealed more to me about a patient's experience of self and other than having them guess or fantasize. One time I dared to answer the question and informed a patient I was going to the American Southwest for my vacation. The patient, looking crestfallen, told me it was a disappointment that I wasn't planning a more intellectually oriented vacation to cultured Europe. In fact, Europe, and his identification with his German grandmother, was at the center of his intellectual aspirations. For him all other places and identifications paled in comparison. The answer spurred an exploration of the allegiances and dynamics he internalized from his extended family. That was enough to convince me that to give an answer revealed much more about a person's internal experience. Better to answer and see where the associative chips fall. I still will withhold answers at times, particularly if I am intuiting a boundary problem, but as a rule I answer most questions, and then ask for reactions and associations to my answers.

I note in this chapter that one indication of the change toward a relational model of psychoanalysis has been the changes in the psychoanalytic language used by relational psychoanalysts. By the time I wrote this paper the use of language that was rooted in drive theory had decreased dramatically. For example, terms such as transference neuroses, regression in service of the ego, neutralized libido or aggression, and countertransference (as indicating an analyst's error), to name just a few, were rarely seen in contemporary relational literature. This diminution of terms rooted in drive theory had been accompanied by a corresponding uptick in relational language, such as mutual enactments, intersubjectivity and countertransference (not used to indicate analyst error but rather to indicate the new royal road to understanding a patient's experience). These changes, for me, had reached a critical mass over time.

However, rather than noting the changes, each as they occurred, I notice them in retrospect, by comparing present usage with that of the past. This is not unlike another trick of time, often reported by patients, who can report an appreciation of their personal change not moment by moment, but only as they compare the present moment with times past, noting important, sometimes global, changes. How do we understand this time-lapsed recognition of change?

A lesson from the multidiscipline study of time can contribute to understanding this issue. As I have noted previously, physicists who study time note repeatedly that we cannot stop or capture a moment in time exactly when it is occurring. The moment we think we have caught it, time has moved on. This axiom can be applied in a broad fashion to the evolution in the use of our psychological theories. It is often only in retrospect that we note major theoretical changes. Marking any specific point of change in psychological trends serves more to satisfy our need for order in our comprehension of a continuous history than to represent either actual continuity or change. Typically, theoretical changes, as with changes in our patients, are not easily charted. Instead changes are captive to the hurdy-gurdy movements of time forward and backward, or balletic loop-de-loops, and like the coin in a nickelodeon, it comes out "here."

I frequently make reference in this chapter to the possibility of this or that change occurring via the interaction with a relational therapist "over time." A major criticism of psychoanalysis has been the length of time it takes for it to effect change. I think this question entirely misses the essence of psychoanalysis. Psychoanalysis is about time and meaning and their relationship to each other. Any psychotherapy that does not address temporality or meaning, is, for me, devoid of the humanity of the process and might as well be dispensed through a vending machine. By examining the mysteries of the presence of the present in the past and the past in the present (i.e. *après coup* and *nachträglichkeit*), and the presence of both in the future, is bypassing a cornerstone of our human existence, our inherent connection with time. It is doomed to superficiality and a disconnection from continuity. It may be helpful in alleviating a painful state, but unless it has tendrils that reach and embrace complexities, paradoxes, conflicts and even the unknown, it is more likely to serve as a quick fix as opposed to an enduring shift in the potential richness and uniqueness of a person's existence.

The British psychoanalyst, Dana Birksted-Breen (2016), actually states outright that, "Issues concerning time are at the basis of psychoanalytic theory, of the analytic setting and of the clinical phenomena we encounter. They also underlie important technical approaches, implicitly or explicitly" (p. 139). She posits that the British school and the French school of psychoanalysis each operate according to two different forms of temporality, developmental (linear) and *après coup* (non-linear) respectively. She claims they "go inherently together, one being a requisite for the other" (p. 139).

What's a good object to do? 117

Before I get totally engulfed in an elitist tantrum, I of course am respectful of personal preferences not to undertake a psychoanalytic (aka, long) journey. For many, the alleviation of psychic pain is, of course, a valid and worthwhile end in and of itself. I do think, however, those practitioners who offer such abbreviated work should not hold out hope to their patients that their shorter, more limited forms of therapy will be as transformational as an extended course of psychoanalysis, one steeped in the examination of the vicissitudes of time, past, present and future.

References

Birksted-Breen, D. (2016). *The Work of Psychoanalysis: Sexuality, Time and the Psychoanalytic Mind*. London: Routledge.

Fairbairn, W.R.D. (1952). Object relationships and dynamic structure. In *Psychoanalytic Studies of the Personality* (pp. 137–152). New York and London: Routledge.

Freud, S. (1920). Beyond the pleasure principle. In J. Strachey (ed. and trans.), *The Standard Edition of the Complete Psychological Works of Sigmund Freud* (Vol. 18, pp. 3–64). London: Hogarth Press.

Greenberg, J. and Mitchell, S. (1983). *Object Relations in Psychoanalysis*. New Haven: Columbia University Press.

Greenson, R. (1967). *The Technique and Practice of Psychoanalysis*, Vol. 1. New York: International Universities Press.

Greenson, R. (1971). The "real" relationship between the patient and the psychoanalyst. In *Explorations in Psychoanalysis* (pp. 425–440). New York: International Universities Press.

Greenson, R. and Wexler, M. (1969). The non-transference relationship in the psychoanalytic situation. *Int. J. Psycho-Analysis*, 50: 27–39.

Lyons-Ruth, K. (1999). The two-person unconscious: Intersubjective dialogue, enactive relational representation, and the emergence of new forms of relational organization. *Psychoanalytic Inquiry*, 19(4): 576–617.

Skolnick, N. (2006). What's a good object to do? *Psychoanalytic Dialogues*, 16(1): 1–27.

Chapter 5

What's a good object to do?

A Fairbairnian perspective[1]
2018

Neil J. Skolnick

Introduction

Psychoanalytic technique has periodically been modified to reflect historical and theoretical shifts (Lipton, 1983). Over the course of the last 25 years the psychoanalytic landscape has changed to reflect the mounting importance context is accorded in the structuring of our developmental and motivational selves. The relational evolution has ushered in mind-numbing changes to psychoanalytic theory and technique. Mainstays of our contemporary technique that were relegated to the heretical just a few years ago are regarded as standard fare today. Witness the debates on the efficacy of the self-revealing analyst (Burke, 1992; Davies, 1994; Greenberg, 1995; Hirsch, 1994; Tansey, 1994) or the use of enactments to further the goals of treatment (Davies, 1994). Increasingly, contemporary models of psychic functioning and organization (Bromberg, 1998) are informing expanding emergent twists and turns of technique.

Our theoretical language similarly has been altered to reflect these changes. Consider the last time you referred to a patient's loving affects as neutralized libido, or a regression in the service of the ego, or evidence of a developing transference neurosis? This was the language with which many of us cut our psychoanalytic teeth. Much of it has already been relegated to the psychoanalytic dustbin, or resurfaced as two-person jargon. "Acting out" and "acting in" have been reborn as "enactments," "transference" has been slowly morphing into "co-creations," and "psychological mindedness" now makes its comeback as "mindfullness."

When examined, the practice of psychoanalysis during its infancy contained informal customs that appeared to have violated the dictates of classical technique as it came to be. Freud at one time or another acted as a moneylender, dinner host and matchmaker to his patients. These seeming lapses become more forgivable when we consider them within the context of what was a new, evolving science. Freud and his associates were experimenting with new forms of technique that had a way to go before being codified into a set of standard practices, and by implication prohibited transgressions. Their "mistakes" awaited future contextual models to be defined as mistakes.

It is my impression that a similar situation exists today. We have ventured into new realms of technique with alternating gusto and caution. The jury is out, I would caution, as to whether these newer techniques, both clinically and theoretically derived, have proven *clinical* value. For example, analyst self-revelation has been held up by some as an important clinical option. Others even consider it an imperative of relational technique. Unfortunately, its use can at times be misused in the service of a political statement to mark allegiance to a theoretical camp, rather than a statement of its actual clinical validity. Does it work? And with whom? When might it be decidedly unhelpful? Should we be telling patients our dreams? Do we run the risk of mistaking growing precedence as bestowing validity or efficacy on newer technique?

Post-modern theories of mutuality, co-construction, interpersonal principles or relativistic truths have infused our modern sensibilities and by implication our analytic styles. Perhaps our contemporary technical innovations will also be scorned in years to come as contradictory to evolved relational practices in the same fashion that we hold up Freud's match-making with patients as a transgression of his later thinking. It is too soon to tell, just as it was too soon to reach a verdict on Freud's new "talking cure" at or near its inception. Our strong convictions can understandably outpace time proven wisdom.

The evolutionary groove we currently traverse under the broad umbrella of relational perspectives (Skolnick and Warshaw, 1992) for the most part is anchored by theorists who are reluctant to codify technical recommendations (e.g., Fairbairn, 1958; Hoffman, 1983; Mitchell, 1988; Stolorow and Atwood, 1992). The increasing acceptance of relativistic truth in our theories has organically led to relativistic angles on technique (Skolnick, 2015). For today's analyst, there are many more proverbial roads than ever leading to Rome. It is my observation that while relational theories play an important role in guiding newer techniques, many of our contemporary theorists rely more on their clinical experiences to expand technical possibilities.

I have no trouble with this. Although far from objectively reliable or valid, clinical data is the best data we have. We are at a point of hypothesis generating in our literature on technique. This paper, as well, can be considered a heuristic, hypothesis-generating endeavor. I hold no claims to new technical theory. My clinical data is garnered from years of practice and changing theoretical contexts. It is my belief that actual clinical experience with patients (our hermeneutic data, if you will) accompanied by careful, intense and honest circumspection and debate will lead to more reliable statements about higher levels of abstraction to accompany an evolving theory of relational technique. But we are not there yet.

When I reflect on my own evolution as a relational psychoanalyst, I am reminded of when I was treating my training control case, over 20 years ago, when toward the end of a session it started to rain heavily. Noticing that my patient had not come with an umbrella, and would surely be soaked on this cold day in March, I tortured briefly over the wisdom of lending him one of the orphaned umbrellas that had gathered in my closet. Would this be a major transgression, a libidinal gratification forever sullying the development of the transference neurosis and fatally derailing the treatment? Was I involved in a major countertransference acting out requiring my own continued analysis? Or was it simply a thoughtful, non-sexual but loving gesture required by the serendipitous forces of Mother Nature, forces that as far as I was concerned might fall outside the purview of transference? Damning Charles Brenner, and every supervisor I ever had, I gave the guy an umbrella, figuring we would deal with the interpretive aftermath in future sessions. In fact we did deal with the conflict laden dependency issues evoked by my act of giving, and his reluctance to accept, and the analysis continued. I was beginning to learn that my interventions, per se, at choice points in treatment were often not as important as analyzing the patient's reactions to my interventions as well as the internal or co-constructed precipitants of my interventions. The umbrella episode, for me, marks the beginning of my shifting clinical sensibilities, and these shifts have been channeled into altered theoretical organizations.

For example, years after the analysis ended, the patient told me he considered my abandoning an analytic stance by offering him the umbrella one of the pivotal points in his treatment. He had observed my discomfort (aka my self-torture), my humanness and my decency as another person, who, like him, did not always have perfect answers. Today I would say he discovered the good object in me. This was not an encounter with the idealized or exciting object, but rather the authentic, fallible, integrated object with which he could identify thereby expanding the purview of his ego or self. Risking a new, decidedly non-analytic intervention that actually furthered the treatment likewise expanded me, both clinically and theoretically.

For the purposes of this paper, I do not attempt to provide a comprehensive definition of the essence of a good object. As suggested by its title, this chapter focuses on what a good object *does* and not the essence of its nature. Others have noted that the legacy of psychoanalytic theory and technique may rest more with careful descriptions of what analysts *do* than with the explanatory validity of the theory. Moreover, psychoanalysis as a theory no longer aspires solely to the constraints of a hypothetical-deductive model of scientific inquiry. While empirical research has been considered an important contributor to the accretion of psychoanalytic knowledge, with the shift in emphasis of relational theory to studying subjective experience, and co-creating relativistic and hermeneutic truths, the cornerstones of empiricism – observation, reliability and validity – do not always apply to the understanding of psychoanalytic phenomena. This paper presents a description, gleaned from years of clinical practice, of what an analyst, as good object, does, not what a good object is.

Moreover, as techniques aligned with relational psychoanalysis increasingly disentangled themselves from many of the technical dictates of drive theory, the importance of the role of the analyst has shifted from passive, neutral observer and interpreter to active participant. A relational analysis can (though not for all who consider themselves relational) insist that the analyst participate *as* a good object. To the skeptic, visions of analysts portioning out a never-ending supply of need satisfactions clouds their ability to attend to the more textured and complex nature of what a good object does. To the converted, objections and cautions to this relatively new technical turn can be unheeded with a cavalier acceptance of its validity. What I intend to explore in this paper are some broad technical strokes describing how an analyst might function as a good object.

Before turning to a consideration of what actions determine a good object in treatment, I do, however, wish to provide a brief description of what I consider a good object to be. To illustrate this less than comprehensive account, I refer to the good object as an amalgam of object imagoes as provided by the theories of Klein, Fairbairn, Winnicott and Kohut. Whether rooted in nature or nurture or an admixture of both, the good object is mostly on the side of life. It is a mature (Fairbairn, 1952; Kohut, 1984), loving (Appelbaum, 1999; Klein, 1975a, 1975b; Fairbairn, 1952; Winnicott, 1965), whole, integrated self or other (Klein, 1975b; Kohut, 1984) who has acknowledged and accepted the goodness *and* badness in oneself and others. It occupies either internal or external space (Klein, 1975a, 1975b; Kohut, 1984). This is an integrated object who does not deny the existence of our more grandiose, idealistic strivings and illusions which pull us with endless hope through life (Winnicott, 1965; Kohut, 1984). Nor does it deny our ever-present sinister affects or destructive motivations (Klein, 1975a, 1975b). It has managed to accept their inevitability, to struggle with the tensions they evoke, to adapt to them, integrate them, and continue to be able to love and accept love (Klein, 1975b; Fairbairn, 1952; Winnicott, 1965; Kohut, 1984).

Again, a good object is not a perfect object, one that Klein (1975a, 1975b) referred to as idealized and Fairbairn (1952) referred to as exciting. An idealized or exciting object, when too pervasive or rigid, is ultimately a bad object. It represents neither a loving, a whole nor an integrated object. Instead, it is a one-dimensional fiction, sometimes engaged with for survival, that denies the existence of complexity, ambivalence, or doubt. The achievement and acceptance of doubt, which is a lifetime struggle of good objects, is an anathema to bad objects. Bad objects require immutable truths, truths that demand absolute adherence in order to survive. All doubt must be destroyed. If any uncertainty is entertained, the absolute truth and meaning of a bad object is in mortal jeopardy. For meaning to be maintained by bad objects, anything smacking of ambivalence, uncertainty or doubt must be defended against, if not wiped out. In psychoanalysis we refer to this process as the deployment of primitive defense mechanisms, such as splitting, projection, introjection or denial. For Klein (1975b), the obliteration of doubt was the hallmark of a paranoid-schizoid organization. For Fairbairn (1952), overwhelming doubt lay at the very heart of our universally split egos. For Osama bin Laden, death to the infidels obliterates those who might suggest the existence of doubt.

Fairbairn and Klein differed markedly on the origins of the good object. Briefly, a good object for Klein is a part object originally rooted in the innate life instinct. Present at birth it is originally projected onto the mother (to protect it from one's own destructive impulses) and later introjected along with the mother's gratifying attributes. The good object ultimately

What's a good object to do? 123

evolves into a whole, integrated object if the mother loves and provides for the child's needs.

Fairbairn, on the other hand, never fully described a good object. He referred to it alternatively as the accepted object and ideal object. As opposed to Klein, who posited that we are born with internal good and bad part objects which achieve integration during development, for Fairbairn we are born as a unified whole and it is only as a consequence of the failures of the environment that we split into good and bad object organizations. The good object is an aspect of the real (not fantasized) loving mother that remains once the bad objects have been split off. The child then ensconces the good object into its central ego (self) in order to fend against the split off and internalized bad objects which are aspects of the mother which have failed to love the child. Fairbairn's labeling of the good object as "ideal" is, to me, a confusing misnomer, and not to be mistaken with Klein's idealized object, which, as I noted, is a bad object. I tend to equate Fairbairn's "ideal" with Winnicott's "good-enough" object.

It is important to distinguish a good object from both Klein's idealized and Fairbairn's exciting object. Idealized and exciting objects are bad objects. They are not loving, whole or integrated. Klein's idealized object is an aggrandized object defensively created in fantasy in order to combat and withstand the attacks to the self by bad objects. Fairbairn's exciting object is a split-off piece of the good object that holds out the taunting promise of satisfaction but ultimately fails the child. These bad objects (idealized and exciting) are one-dimensional fictions, sometimes engaged with for survival, that deny the existence of complexity, ambivalence or doubt. The achievement and acceptance of doubt and ambivalence, a lifetime struggle, is anathema to bad objects. Bad objects require immutable truths, truths that require absolute adherence in order to survive. All doubt must be destroyed. If any uncertainty is entertained, the absolute truth and meaning of a bad object is in mortal jeopardy. For meaning to be maintained by bad objects, anything smacking of ambivalence, uncertainty or doubt must be defended against, if not wiped out. In psychoanalysis we refer to the processes of eliminating doubt as those which use primitive defense mechanisms such as splitting, projection, introjection or denial. For Klein, the obliteration of doubt is the hallmark of a paranoid/schizoid organization. For Fairbairn, the denial of doubt lay at the very heart of our universally split egos.

124   Neil J. Skolnick

In his seminal paper written on technique published nearly a half-century after Freud and a half-century before now, Fairbairn (1958) demonstrated far-reaching clinical insight:

> In terms of the object-relations theory of the personality, the disabilities from which the patient suffers represent the effects of unsatisfactory and unsatisfying object relationships experienced in early life and perpetuated in an exaggerated form in inner reality; and, if this view is correct, the actual relationship existing between the patient and the analyst as persons must be regarded as in itself constituting a therapeutic factor of prime importance. The existence of such a personal relationship in outer reality not only serves the function of providing a means of correcting the distorted relationships which prevail in inner reality and influence the reactions of the patient to outer objects, but provides the patient with an opportunity, denied to him in childhood, to undergo a process of emotional development in the setting of an actual relationship with a reliable and beneficent parental figure.
>
> (p. 377)

By virtue of this statement, remarkable for its time, he catapulted the primary influence of analysis out of the arena of dispassionate drive interpretations and placed it squarely in the space created by the coming together of two vital, continuously interacting people, the therapeutic dyad. Fairbairn's revolutionary idea was that the therapeutic relationship offers the provision of a good object (or more correctly, a good object relationship).

But what is a good object to do?

What does a good object look like in the analytic setting? Where are the lines between provisions of analytic goodness and provisions of exciting, taunting or seductive false promises? How might a good object alter the therapeutic frame, including where, when and how the boundaries are drawn or redrawn? Does the goodness of an analyst relate to the authenticity of the analyst? Or the spontaneity of the analyst? Or the behavior of the analyst? Relational analysts struggle with these and similar questions today (Hoffman, 1998), when many of the rules of the analytic process have been thrown open for reconsideration.

In what follows I attempt to describe a sampling of characteristic actions of a good object contextualized by the therapeutic relationship. The list is not exhaustive, by any means, and it is not intended to be used formulaically.

Fairbairn (1958) for one was reluctant to spell out specific technical recommendations, fearing a slide to the rigid and mechanical, which, he bemoaned, might serve more to allay the clinician's anxieties or take care of the therapist's needs, than to help the patient.

In this paper, I consider three categories of activity that can be provided by the analyst/good object. The first, which I have coined "dynamic identification," is derived from what I consider Fairbairn's most seminal postulate, that of dynamic structure. I discuss here the mechanisms, not of identification with the analyst, but of the internalization of a new object *relationship* provided by a relational analyst.

The second category is also rooted in Fairbairn's theory. His theory of motivation posits its bedrock in the basic nature (Mitchell, 1996) of man to establish and maintain loving connections. For Fairbairn, loving relationships, from birth, require a two-way reciprocal street. It was not news that a parent needs to love a child. What was news, and has often been ignored, is that a child, from birth, spontaneously offers its love to others. Fairbairn stressed the crucial need that the child's love be accepted and cherished. The acceptance of love provides the thematic glue for the second category of good object activity I describe.

In the third category, I expand upon Fairbairn's emphasis on the provision of a loving object relationship to a developing child. He stressed that a loving relationship was one based upon the parent empathically perceiving and providing for the child's needs, as distinct from the needs of the parent. It is this provision of loving empathy that that I offer as another example of what an analyst, as good object, does. More specifically, the analytic provision of empathy is discussed as it relates to Klein's conceptualization of positions in development. The psychological organizations of the paranoid/schizoid position are qualitatively different than the organizations of the depressive positions. Likewise, the two positions generate markedly different self and other experiential modes. I will delineate the nature of the empathic response required by a good object when interacting with a patient functioning in the paranoid/schizoid experiential mode and its distinction from empathy necessitated when a patient is operating in a depressive organizational mode.

Dynamic identification

As noted, dynamic identification is a construct I have derived from Fairbairn's (1952) overarching principle of dynamic structure. Briefly stated, Fairbairn pronounced that psychic structure and psychic energy were equivalent. "Both structure divorced from energy and energy divorced from structure are meaningless concepts" (Fairbairn, 1952, p. 149). In an Einsteinian moment he eliminated Freud's distinction between dynamic id energy and an inert ego fueled by the drives. Paralleling the precepts of Einstein's relativity theory, egos represent dynamic, ongoing systems, imbued with their own energy rather than discrete, singular entities. An ego (or self), for Fairbairn[2] is what the ego does, and does in concert with an object and an accompanying affect tie. Ego, object and energy, for Fairbairn, are inseparable and inextricable and are spoken of disjointedly only for linguistic clarity.

What are internalized, then, for Fairbairn, are neither good nor bad *objects*, but good or bad *object relationships* including the ego/self, the object and the affective tie between the two. An ego cannot exist without reference to the objects, either internal or external, that structure it and perpetuate its essence. To interpret, then, becomes a useful cognitive exercise, but change itself becomes a problem of object relationships.

The provision of a good object, then, requires a dynamic interplay between analyst and patient. No longer is the analyst a detached imparter of wise, timely mutagenic interpretations. He or she is an active engager of the patient's self in an ongoing mutual constructive process. He or she is a relational analyst resuscitated from Fairbairn's circa 1940s opus.

It follows, then, that an important aim of the good object in the therapeutic process is to provide the patient with an opportunity to dance with the analyst's self in multiple new configurations. The internalization of new dynamic interactions will serve to restructure the patient's ego/self in as much as Fairbairn understood the self as always interacting with and being structured by an other's self. This is the process I refer to as *dynamic identification*.

Dynamic identification needs to be distinguished from identifications with static traits, preferences, sensibilities or ideographic qualities of the analyst's character, though these sometimes enter the mix. By dynamic identification I am referring to the unearthing and making one's own, the psychic processes, both conscious and unconscious, the analyst's self engages in when relating to the patient in the analytic space. In as much as the analyst's self is also understood only in the context of its interaction with an other, the process of dynamic identification is inherently an intersubjective two-way process.

The good object provides something unique. In addition to the standard activities of labeling distortions, unearthing unconscious material and providing interpretations, the good object engages with the patient in new ways of being, repeatedly, over time. The interaction with the analyst gradually becomes coterminous with the patient's expanded self. The analyst's provision of new ways-of-being, both cognitively and affectively, become structured into a patient's expanded and expanding self. Each participant retains his/her own autonomous uniqueness while, at the same time, each is being informed, stretched and restructured by the interaction with the other. Expanded, more flexible, adaptive and endurable selves are spun out and tried out. Over time, patients accumulate new ways of being with an other woven and textured into their existing dynamic structures.

As noted, the process of dynamic identification is intersubjective. In as much as the analyst struggles to understand and adapt to the ways in which a patient is interacting with him or her, the analyst's self is also subject to modification and expansion, it being no less dynamically structured than the patient's. Indeed, a profound understanding of the patient's experience is accompanied by reciprocal dynamic identifications in the analyst. In order for empathy to transcend the prosaic or formulaic, it requires the analyst being prepared to suspend preconceptions and be shaken to his or her own dynamically structured core. Indeed, mutagenic empathic response can arise from concordant identification with a patient. But from the perspective of the argument I am making, true empathy calls upon analysts to step out of their own familiar ways of being in order to resonate to and be influenced by interaction with a patient and the patient's experience.

The fomenting space for the dynamic interaction of the analyst and patient's subjective selves to meet and generate new ways of being I would place in the realm of experience described by Ogden (1994) as the intersubjective third. This is a space that belongs neither exclusively to the analyst nor exclusively to the patient, but is created by the admixture of two interacting subjectivities.

Dynamic identifications between the analyst and patient are infinite in nature, and will typically though not exclusively concern themselves with the particular trouble spots that impede a patient's pursuit of satisfaction and pleasure. Of crucial importance is that analysis provides an arena in which these trouble spots can emerge. They emerge in ways we alternately, depending on theoretical preference, have labeled transference, transference/countertransference interaction, acting out, acting in, enacting, or a search for archaic and mature self-object provisions, to name a few.

For example, if we are working with a person who struggles with containment of overwhelming, intolerable negative affect, the patient will interact with the many ways in which the analyst demonstrates an ability to contain. The patient will then, through dynamic identification, internalize a new object relationship in which affects toward another are being negotiated and contained. But that process remains just part of the story. The analyst, through dynamic interaction with the patient, has come to profoundly empathize with the patient's experience of difficulty containing affect. This enables the analyst to provide a new experience for the patient that is uniquely created out of their interaction and that transmit to the patient an experience of profound, in the moment, understanding.

Interpretations may contribute to the process but they are not sufficient, being more or less a cognitive exercise and rarely mutative. As per Fairbairn's prescription, the patient needs to observe and actively participate in an actual fully experienced interaction with the containing analyst who variously struggles, stumbles, survives, accepts reparations, remains calm, or loses and recovers calm, to name a few of the component activities of containing.

A dynamic identification might also, as another example, include the process participated in when the analyst makes a mistake and recovers from a mistake, without becoming defensive or inauthentic. We can extend these experiences to include most activities of the analyst such as the working-through analyst, the forgiving, integrated analyst, the modulating analyst, the analyst who struggles with conflict, the analyst who gets angry and recovers, the fallible analyst, and so forth.

For this to happen requires from the analyst concentrated devotion and unwavering commitment to venture as part of a dyad to wherever the patient leads and regardless of the disturbance the analyst experiences. We must be prepared to roll up our sleeves and enter the patient's inner world, as well as our own. We need to, as Pick (1985) prescribes, become greatly disturbed as we are made to experience, via dynamic identification with the patient, the object relationships inhabiting a patient's inner world. *En route*, via concordant and complimentary countertransference (Racker, 1968) we might be called upon to re-experience and once again

What's a good object to do? 129

work through the painful disturbances of our own inner object relationships. As we do, both consciously and unconsciously, so does the patient, who comes to identify with the struggles, failures and successes of our own self/other dilemmas and how we negotiate them. The more we have resolved our own issues, or are at least able to tolerate them, the further the patient can safely travel. The further we have ventured ourselves, the further the patient will feel safe to go.

But as I have stressed, the two-way street of dynamic identification can also transport the analyst to new ways of being as she is buffeted by the patient's dynamic self. Here too the analyst can be made to experience new realms of being, born of interaction with the patient, that are frightening and disorienting in their newness. The analyst needs to be disturbed by this experience, be willing to tolerate unformed or poorly comprehended new experience until a more certain foothold on the experience is obtained. The patient will also then, through dynamic identification with the analyst's struggle, come to be able to tolerate the process of integrating new ways of being, a process that can travel through frighteningly disorienting waters before being comprehended and integrated.

Let me try to illustrate. A patient of mine, Marianna, a 40-something-year-old attorney, was rather successful in her work world. By contrast her romantic life was in shambles. She was haunted by the long shadows of a mother who in many respects was loving and providing but who was enormously anxious and would, at times, become impulsively and physically abusive. She remembers episodes when her mother would smash her (the patient's) head against a wall, at times drawing blood. These incidents were never spoken about or resolved.

Marianna was in a long-term relationship with a man in which she would luxuriate in comforting thoughts about the hopeful possibilities of a life together. These hopes stood in marked contrast to the couple's actual experience with each other. Inevitably, when together, their interactions would rapidly deteriorate into verbally abusive fights that were repaired, not by resolution, but rather, only by being tucked into the passage of time.

On one occasion she entered my office following her vacation only to discover that I had replaced the old, worn patient chair with a new one. Complaining that I had not forewarned her about the change, she instantaneously entered into an enraged state, one I had not heretofore observed. She pelted me with virulent abusive language. She attacked my ability as an analyst and threatened to bring me up on ethical charges for not giving her an advanced heads-up about the change. At some point I became visibly addled, sputtering lame interpretations, while feeling a fine blend of helplessness and exasperated rage. This only fueled her sadism as she upped her attacks while simultaneously announcing that, actually, she was getting great pleasure out of bashing me. In fact, she exclaimed, she had not had this much fun in years. I was thrust into that paralyzed place, familiar to most analysts at one time or another, of feeling that my understanding of her experience was hopelessly limited and any intervention would meet with utter futility.

So, what's a good object to do?

First and foremost we must, as I'm sure most would agree, survive the attack. Whether seen as a ruthless attack by a Winnicottian, a dip into the paranoid/schizoid position by a Kleinian, or the result of empathic failure by a self-psychologist, survival of the analyst is a must and a prime requisite of a good object.

Let's examine this more closely. What do we mean by survival? Allowing for nuanced differences by analysts of different theoretical creeds, we are referring to the analyst not succumbing to the patient's omnipotence, not disappearing either consciously or unconsciously in the face of the patient's conscious or unconscious fantasy of having destroyed us. We do not abandon, retaliate or fall apart.

That we survive insures that the patient's subjective omnipotence is challenged so that gradually he or she can tolerate the ongoing tension of surviving and tolerating an existence in which one must share the stage with others, while being allowed some measure of prime time as well. But, it is not only by virtue of the experience *that* we survive that helps our patients. As, if not more importantly, *how* we survive ultimately contributes to the expansion of the patient's ego or self, and by implication therapeutic change.

Surviving is not enough. To paraphrase Winnicott (1965), we can fob off a patient with a good survival. Survivals can be as staged and lifeless as a formulaic interpretation. In the face of a murderous attack, we can manage to maintain a calm veneer while internally we fume, struggle, disorganize, become massively ashamed, sadistically attack, or settle into a lifeless remove, to name a few possibilities. While technically we have visibly survived, the patient does not get to experience or identify with *how* we survived. Patients of course, can usually detect a storm raging below our best attempts to display calm.

We need to straddle an impossible line between maintaining professional control and experiencing emotional upset. While maintaining a relative professional calm, we try not to affect a false remove, an aloof "nothing you say can affect me" attitude. Whether we are working with a more disturbed patient or a patient who is experiencing temporary paranoid/schizoid disorganization, we need to get stuck in our own psychic mud and experience our own painful disruption, which, through our own dynamic identification, provide us with clues about the patient's experience of us. To do otherwise (i.e., avoid, deny, etc.) we risk missing an empathic understanding of the underside of our patient's skin. We also can appear inauthentic; typically signaling to a patient it is not safe to venture further.

Then, we work through, once again, as we had in analysis or self-analysis this place of disruption in ourselves, whether it resides in a more neurotic, conflict-ridden arena or a more primitive, paranoid/schizoid place. We reinstate our integrity, our wholeness and the survival of our subjectivity, without enacting revenge on the patient whose reparations we lovingly accept and whose life we permit to continue. In the episode with Marianna I needed to allow and be disturbed by my own experiences with precipitous losses, failures of omnipotence, uncontrollable rage and sadistic pleasures, my own experiences of paranoid/schizoid organizational states, my own shameful disturbances. And equally as important I needed to recall my own recovery from these places.

Moreover, these disruptions and recoveries occur in active participation with the patient (either consciously or unconsciously). Through these repeated interactions, the processes of our dynamic self become available for the patient to structure into their own internal worlds. Through the mutual experiencing of our disruption and recovery, we get to intimately understand the patient's object relational world while patients dynamically identify with the *how* of recovery. They gradually, over time, can internalize and incorporate our recovery processes into their own dynamic self structure. Their own dynamic self is in turn strengthened, becoming more integrated and resilient. Their interactions with others likewise become more the realm of integrative, whole object experiences and the time needed to achievement or return to integration shortens.

Let's return to Marianna whom we left enraged, in attack mode and feasting on sadistic pleasure from the experience. Without yet understanding the vehemence of the attack, my first task was to survive. I could have sat back in my chair, staying attentive, remaining calm, attempting to explore, offering interpretations, containing the rage with empathic attunement, or just remaining silent. All of the above could be considered forms of survival, which indeed they are. Unless, however, I had allowed the attack to get under my skin, to disturb me in places I'd rather not be disturbed, to touch rage or sadism within my own experience, my survival would have, in my opinion, been doomed to be experienced by the patient as formulaic, inauthentic or, worse, another display of enviable perfection on my part, to be either idealized and/or destroyed. I would be saying to the patient that, "I am not ready to go to that place with you. I am overly anxious, it will not be safe."

In order for the patient to internalize how we contain, organize or negotiate such powerful overwhelming experiences they need to likewise experience that we have gone to a place of madness and worked it through ourselves. They need to detect, either consciously or unconsciously, that we have jumped into the muck like them, and despite our fears we have reorganized and reconstituted a secure self/other vitality. This is the point of connection needed between self and other that patients observe, experience and internalize. It is not only that we survive, but how we survive, how we venture to insanity and back, that defines the process of dynamic identification.

When Marianna precipitously attacked, I was unprepared. Unwittingly I experienced and displayed a measure of stunned disturbance. She observed my discomfort, which in the moment I neither went to great lengths to express nor hide. My unsettling and shameful sadistic impulses bubbled up, fueling an inner and pleasurably charged string of invectives. My internal voice gleefully, though guiltily, complained, "I can't just buy a fucking new chair without you giving me grief," and the like. Continuing to curse to myself, I pressed my imaginary eject button and pleasurably watched her fly out the window, sail uncontrollably over Central Park and land in a strong, icy current in the East River. I was now, in an experience paralleling hers, getting pleasure from my fantasized sadistic attack.

Through my expressions of sadism, I became identified with her precipitously assaultive mother. I inwardly cursed and delighted in my sadistic fantasies. Also, during the interaction I was not spared from experiencing the opposite pole of her internal self/object relationship. I was made to feel the horror of being the subject of her mother's attacks, the surprise and shock of receiving abject hatred from a previously safe and loving mother.

What's a good object to do? 133

Then, experiencing an admixture of painful guilt and shame, I caught myself, did not act on my fantasies and I recovered. I reasoned that I had identified first as a victim and then as a victimizer. I had been, via projective identification, made to experience both poles of her internal object relationship. As a victim, I became precipitously shocked, ungrounded and frightened. I had, to date, never experienced such an unpredictable storm from this patient with whom I had worked with for years and with whom I developed a fondness. I was clueless as to what had actually happened and frightened about what might ensue next.

With insight rooted in experiential identification and reason, I recovered and reintegrated. Had I disavowed and/or acted on my sadistic pleasure, had I denied my fear, shame and guilt, I do not believe progress would have been made. Similarly, progress would have been truncated had I not allowed myself to react visibly to her sudden outburst.

Once recovered I utilized my experience to formulate an intervention. I said to the patient that it appeared she was more inflamed from my being visibly shaken than my having not told her about the new chair. She concurred and went on to tell me that her most terrifying experiences as a child had been when her mother appeared confused and anxious. These times typically preceded physical abuse. We began to understand that my anxiety had aroused a similar fear of abuse and her sadistic attacks were an effort to ward off my impending attack.

Through her identification with my upset and recovery, a dynamic identification began to emerge. Our minds met on a paranoid/schizoid plane and we both experienced these strange dangerous feelings of self and other. We had gained some awareness of each other's struggle with powerful drive experiences, particularly sadism, as well as fear of being suddenly shamed and humiliated. Of greater import, she began to experience how I recovered through insight, reason and cognitive control.

Over the course of the next series of sessions, we gradually achieved a more related calm, we continued to be able to explore and resolve the episode. We had both been through hell, working our way over hot coals, and we both came through grounded on the other side, my regaining, and she achieving, an experience of integration of our selves and each other. Had I disavowed my sadistic pleasure, fear or guilt, as well as my working through the shame and humiliation, I do not believe progress would have been made. Being a good object is not easy.

I should add here that I was also concerned that our recovery might have been only cosmetic, both of us staging a recovery by clinging to convenient historical myths and narratives to escape the tumult of our disruption. As with much of our work, we are rarely given direct confirmation of our success. Indeed, many treatments appear to shift endlessly through enactments, disruptions, repairs, reparations, deaths, and any of the infinite possibilities of nuanced and shifting object connections. I have become increasingly more comfortable surrounded by uncertainty. While Bion (1967) instructs us to greet each session without memory or desire, I prefer to recall when George Kaufer, a wise, experienced supervisor of mine, advised me to "trust the process." Indeed, with Marianna, the ultimate proof came with the gradual, forward and back and forward improvements in sustaining integration in relationships with me and others, all leading ultimately to a satisfying marriage and children. Perhaps trusting the process is another route toward being a good object.

I need to add that a similar process is advisable when a patient reveals idealizing, loving or intense sexual feelings toward us. Whether we immediately dissuade a patient of their idealized myths about us, or not, is not to me the crucial issue. We need to climb into the heavens with the patient's positive feelings, just as we dove into the mud of their negative feelings. We need to find those places in us, and rework our own struggles with grandiosity, or perfection, or need for adoration. Consciously or unconsciously we communicate this process to the patient, allowing them, without fearing great shame, humiliation or destruction, to identify with a similar process of disillusionment.

Relational needs require acceptance of our patients' love

Recently, psychoanalysts have turned their attention to deciphering the nature of love in a deconstructed world and, by extension, in the analytic relationship. Stephen Mitchell (2001), in his last work was attempting to shine new light on love and passion's trajectory through the lifespan, and others (Appelbaum, 1999; Davies, 1994; Hoffman, 2009) have been exploring love's sexual and nonsexual presence in the analytic relationship. Freud and Klein considered love to be a derivative of our most basic instinctual inheritance and ultimately a sublimated expression of the sexual drive, at times in fusion with aggressive drive elements. Love was thought to be the ultimate mature expression of our bestial inheritance and childhood wishes. Fairbairn reversed this primal scenario, proclaiming sex to be a well-suited, though by no means exclusive, expression of mature mutual love. Speaking on a different, less drive infused level of discourse, he located a person's involvement with love at birth. He located love's essence at the heart of our fundamental human nature, our need for establishing and maintaining loving connections. Mental health, for Fairbairn, was virtually insured with parental love; pathology arose from its disruption or absence.

But Fairbairn went further than that, though little of it has carried over to today's sensibilities and conversations. As noted, he placed a need for love at the very center of the child's psychic inheritance at birth. Love is not only a requisite of the child, needed for safe passage across developmental challenges. A child likewise enters the world with a need to *express* loving desires, desires that guide the child toward, and assure the child of, needed connections with others. In this Fairbairn was greatly influenced by Ian Suttie (Harrow, 1998), a Scottish psychiatrist who wrote about the deleterious psychological effects of society's taboo on intimacy.

With this in mind Fairbairn emphatically stressed the importance of parents not only being able to love their child without excessive narcissistic investment, but also, and equally as crucial, they need to accept the child's offerings of love. For infants and adults alike, the acceptance of loving gestures affirms and reaffirms our secure connections and membership in a world of other like beings. Whether it be a child's offer of a smile, a scrap of paper, or an actual gift, its acceptance by a parent, in neither exaggerated nor devalued manner, is a crucial signal to the child of a secure, valued connection; a connection partially contributed to by the child's loving and creative gesture.

A shortage of experience with a parent's heartfelt embrace of their offerings of love can render a child with a weakened sense of efficacy, self-worth regulation and ability to believe in the loving intent of others. It can also lead to a devaluation of ambitions and dreams, creations and productions, whose loving offerings are also felt to be of no consequence.

The importance of analysts not retreating from their patients' loving offerings has not been emphasized nearly enough in our technical recommendations. I wholeheartedly add this wrinkle to the list of therapeutic activities required by the good object. We certainly encourage our patients to express their anger and rage at us, yet we can have enormous difficulty accepting their loving gestures. These we tend to interpret, entirely missing the point.

A patient's loving gestures can take on an infinite variety of expression. It is important that we try to distinguish them from non-adaptive enactment or other collusive enticement. For example, sometimes a patient can offer an expression of sincere gratitude. Before dismissing it with interpretations of idealization, manipulation or sexual bidding, which it certainly might be on occasion, I have found a simple "thank you" to be of enormous value. An interpretation at such a time can be experienced as a devaluation, attack or rejection. Some other, but by no means exclusive, examples I have come across have included receiving appropriate gifts, realistic compliments, constructive criticism or real concern about real illness.

As an illustration, I think of another patient of mine. He is a 30-something-year-old man, the son of a successful celebrity father. His father would engage in frequent contact with adoring audiences to whom he likewise blessed with visible adoration. When in the presence of his son, my patient, he remained distant, aloof and reticent. My patient reported frequent attempts to connect with his father that were shunned, ignored or criticized. He especially recalled repeated attempts to enter his father's study, a place where his father isolated himself most of the time when at home. He craved a connection of any kind with his father, whether it was to shoot the breeze, get advice or talk about his own endeavors. He had both athletic and artistic ability that went mostly unnoticed. When he entered the study, his father would typically regard him with a blank stare and remain eerily silent until my patient would quietly exit, nursing the sinking feeling of an unwelcome and deplorable intruder in his father's life. I remarked that while his father had rarely expressed generous feelings of love and pride toward him, what was equally, if not more unbearable, was that his father could not accept his offerings of love and friendship. My patient concurred, breaking into deep sobs. He desperately wanted his father to receive his adoration, to accept his kudos and offerings of friendship. Being the youngest by many years in a house with much older siblings and a self-centered narcissistic mother he looked toward his father lovingly, as an ally. Unable to tolerate his father not accepting his offers of "sonship," he retreated to an invisible, withdrawn and dejected place he continues to occupy as an adult.

Empathic attunement to psychic organization

Relational analysts routinely hold up empathy or empathic attunement as a requisite provision of a good object. It is far beyond the scope of this paper to explore the development, phenomenology or nuanced processes of therapeutic empathy. I would like, however, to note an observation on a specific use of empathy, gleaned from my work, that holds consequence for both theory and therapy.

While empathy is a concept more associated with self psychology than Fairbairn, it is my contention that when Fairbairn bases healthy development in the parent's ability to love the child *for who the child is* and not for what the narcissistic parent requires the child to be, he is appealing essentially to the parent's ability to be empathic to the needs of the particular child. By adding *for who the child is*, he is implying that the provision of love will be unique for each child and their level of development. By extension, he is implying that a key provision of the love one expresses to a child is rooted in the capacity of a parent to be empathic to the uniqueness of each child, his or her temperament, developmental stage, experience, and needs. The love of a parent who does not have the ability to be empathic will be compromised.

Likewise, a therapist needs to hone his or her loving empathy for the patient. It is my contention that a specific and crucial form of empathy involves the analyst being aware of and empathizing with the level of psychic organization of the patient, including the accompanying powerful affects. By psychic organization I am referring to the positional psychic organizations identified by Klein (1975a) and more recently expounded upon by Ogden (1986), namely the paranoid/schizoid and the depressive. These forms of psychic organization each beckon for a different form of empathy as they emerge in treatment. I wish to describe here a variant of empathy needed by a patient operating in the paranoid/schizoid position. When a patient functions in this position, the empathic attunement is strengthened by the analyst recognizing an understanding of the patient's *experience* of their psychic level of organization, and a diminution of attention to interpretation of psychic meaning or conflict. It also involves the analyst being responsive to the strength of the powerful accompanying affects, particularly murderous rage and fear of annihilation, which are hallmarks of the paranoid/schizoid psychic organization. I often will refer to this type of empathic attunement as having empathy for the *state of the state*.

The experience of the paranoid/schizoid psychic organization, as expanded upon by Ogden (1986), devolves into a state of "it"-ness. Emotions, thoughts and even behaviors do not feel to be arising from a locus within the patient. Instead, they are experienced as happening to the patient. As such, the truth of moment to moment psychic meaning is, for the patient, derived from an absolute external truth. The patient has no sense that they are in any way the arbiters of meaning, the masters of their own perceptions. The contemptuous patient does not *imagine* you are a hopeless incompetent, they *know* that you are a hopeless incompetent, with no room for degrees of freedom. The adoring, idealizing patient experiences the truth of their feelings similarly. Consequently, his or her rancor or adoration toward you is not debatable; it is the only reasonable response from a reasonable person whose reasoning follows from the absolute truth. Furthermore, since this organization contains split-off islands of experience, in which time has collapsed into an eternal dimensionless plane, not only do the experiences of the paranoid/schizoid organization contain no past or future, there is also no communication with other states. These patients, in the moment, have no awareness they possess alternate feelings, or could imagine the possibilities of other feeling perspectives at any point in time, past or future.

The a-historicity of a paranoid/schizoid organizational truth requires that the analyst address his or her empathic attunement to just this experience. For example, a patient of mine who functioned in a relatively healthy (e.g., depressive position) state of mutuality with me most of the time came to her session the day following her mother's death from chronic alcoholism. I greeted her with an appropriate expression of sympathy. She instantly flew into a vitriolic spewing of rage at me, declaring that my sympathy had nothing to do with her, it was rooted solely in my selfish preoccupation with my desire to be liked. I was merely a "touchy-feely leftover from the Sixties."

So once again, what's a good object to do?

I wondered, then, was she right? Have my 1960s sensibilities, honestly honed in the 1960s, appeared in as immature a fashion as they existed then? Was my expression of sympathy formulaic or just an expression of self-interest? Or did her rage represent a displacement of her rage toward her mother, who, now dead, became a more guilt evoking target? Do I empathize with her rage? Or do I interpret? Or what?

As per what I have been arguing, I first discerned that my patient, at that moment, was ensconced in a paranoid/schizoid organization of self and other. In that place, she lacked capability to understand an interpretation, be it transferential, interpersonal, intersubjective or whatever.

The depressive organization that could process the self-generative meaning of her experience was split off and unavailable to her. An interpretation at that moment would have appeared useless at best, and attacking at worst. Likewise, an empathic response to her affects would similarly fly out the window unless they had been offered with a full resonance to the extreme severity of their essence. "You're in a rage at me," would be experienced as a lame attempt at stating the obvious.

I maintain that what was needed in the situation was an empathic communication of the state of her state, the immediate experience of her paranoid/schizoid way of organizing and enduring her mother's death, including a connection with the accompanying affects. Paranoid/schizoid states are usually accompanied by primitive, powerful and unbearable affect states, most notably, annihilation anxiety and rage. It is important that we do not shy away from naming and being empathic with the experience of these disorganizing, annihilating and murderous affects. Focusing on the temporal discontinuity of her experience of me as a whole integrated person, I offered to my patient a statement something like, "It must be terrifying to trust me one minute, and have that trust evaporate entirely the next. Now it must seem that our relationship is permanently damaged and that hopes for it ever being re-established, futile." I made no interpretive ties to her mother, no identification of internal conflicts. I'd like to say she immediately responded, settled down and returned to a higher level of psychic organization. Truth be told, she flew out of the room in an exasperated rage. I believe what I failed to do was to connect with her immediate experience of annihilation anxiety that was evoked by any words I might have offered.

She returned the following day, ready for business as usual, with no mention of the previous day's events. Tossing aside my attempts to bring up the previous session, dismissing it as silly, she continued to proceed, calmly as always. This cycle of disruption followed by nonchalant calm began to occur with increasing rapidity, with fewer and fewer calm sessions. Gradually (a good object needs to have patience), and with empathic attunement to the paranoid/schizoid states of chaos, futility and hopelessness, she began to internalize my kind and loving offerings of holding (Slochower, 1996). Finally, after many months of this, during one outburst, she exploded into tears, wanting to know how I could stay so calm. In fact, she hated my calm. My calm, we discovered, felt like a sadistic attack, highlighting by distinction, the disruption of her explosions. Ultimately, she felt mortified and annihilated in the face of my calm.

We continued to understand that her hateful experiences of me were fueled by intense powerful envy. During her tumultuous paranoid/schizoid states, her envy and hate blinded her to other aspects of my character, past or present. She rebuked my calm, empathic holding with scathing envious attacks. This rendered her tragically unable to absorb, by dynamic identification or any other means, a more adaptive containing process.

Gradually, over a long time, and with the use of empathic attunement to her states of timeless futility and hopelessness, she could tolerate and internalize my calm offerings of holding. The process of dynamically identifying with a good (in this case surviving) object was jump-started as she returned to her previously rather high level of depressive position integration. Despite her disapproval of my rather lame "sixties" type responsiveness, she could also regain her equanimity toward me. This led to fewer stormy eruptions and increasing expressions of gratitude, which I heartily accepted.

It also led to a greater understanding of her original outburst following her mother's death as an attempt to hold onto her internalizations of her mother (who was prone to vitriolic outbursts) that she required in order to prevent further disintegration of her self experience. While the meaning of her outbursts was of course important, it could not be of use to her until the strengthening of her ability to regain access to a more integrated appreciation of self and other, a strengthening she gained in interaction with a new, loving good object.

Conclusion

I have attempted to describe and illustrate the use of the analyst as a good object in the mutagenic arena of the good object relationship. I have discussed its use from a pluralistic consideration of concepts taken from distinct and varying relational theories. Drawing mostly from Fairbairn, Winnicott and Klein, as well as my own clinical experience, I described categories of good "object-ness." These included the process of dynamic identification, the acceptance of a patient's offering of love, and the use of empathy for patients in a paranoid/schizoid organization.

Notes

1 Previous versions of this paper appeared in *Psychoanalytic Dialogues*, 2006, 16: 1–28, and in Clarke, G.S. and Scharff, D.R. (2014). *Fairbairn and the Object Relations Tradition*. London: Karnac Books, published with permission by Taylor and Franics.
2 In my opinion Fairbairn's use of the term ego was similar to Freud's earlier (prestructural model), more encompassing meaning of ego as the center of self- expression.

References

Appelbaum, G. (1999). Considering the complexity of analytic love: A relational perspective. Paper presented at the Focus Series of the National Institute for the Psychotherapies Psychoanalytic Association, New York, 1999.

Bion, W. (1967). Notes on memory and desire. In E.B. Spillius (ed.), *Melanie Klein Today*, Vol. 2 (pp. 17–21). New York: Routledge, 1988.

Bromberg, P.H. (1998). *Standing in the Spaces*. Hillsdale: Analytic Press.

Burke, W.F. (1992). Countertransference disclosure and the asymmetry/mutuality dilemma. *Psychoanalytic Dialogues*, 2: 241–271.

Davies, J.M. (1994). Love in the afternoon: A relational reconsideration of desire and dread in the countertransference. *Psychoanalytic Dialogues*, 4: 153–170.

Fairbairn, W.R.D. (1952). *Psychoanalytic Studies of the Personality*. London: Routledge and Kegan Paul.

Fairbairn, W.R.D. (1958). On the nature and aims of psycho-analytical treatment. *International Journal of Psycho-analysis*, 29: 374–385.

Greenberg, J. (1995). Self-disclosure: Is it psychoanalytic? *Contemporary Psychoanalysis*, 31: 193–247.

Harrow, J.A. (1998). The Scottish connection-Suttie-Fairbairn-Sutherland: A quiet revolution. In N.J. Skolnick and D.E. Scharff (eds.), *Fairbairn, Then and Now* (pp. 3–17). Hillsdale: The Analytic Press.

Hirsch, I. (1994). Countertransference love and theoretical model. *Psychoanalytic Dialogues*, 4: 171–192.

Hoffman, I.Z. (1983). The patient as interpreter of the analyst's experience. *Contemporary Psychoanalysis*, 19: 389–442.

Hoffman, I.Z. (1998). *Ritual and Sponteneity in the Relational Process*. Hillsdale: The Analytic Press.

Hoffman, I.Z. (2009). Therapeutic passion in the countertransference. *Psychoanalytic Dialogues*, 19(5): 617–637.

Klein, M. (1975a). A contribution to the psychogenesis of manic states. In *Love, Guilt and Reparation, 1921–1945* (pp. 262–290). New York: Free Press, 1964.

Klein, M. (1975b). Love, guilt and reparation. In *Love, Guilt, and Other Works, 1921–1945* (pp. 306–). New York: Free Press.

Kohut, H. (1984). *How Does Analysis Cure?* Chicago: University of Chicago Press.

Lipton, S.D. (1983). A critique of so-called standard psychoanalytic technique. *Contemporary Psychoanalysis*, 19: 35–45.

Mitchell, S. (1988). *Relational Concepts in Psychoanalysis*. Cambridge, MA: Harvard University Press.

Mitchell, S. (1996). Fairbairn's object seeking: Between paradigms. In N.J. Skolnick and S.C. Warshaw (eds.), *Fairbairn: Then and Now* (pp. 115–136). Hillsdale: The Analytic Press, 1998.

Mitchell, S. (2001). From angels to muses: Idealization, fantasy and the "illusions of romance". Paper presented posthumously at the National Institute for the Psychotherapies' Annual Colloquium, New York, 2001.

Ogden, T.H. (1986). *The Matrix of the Mind*. Northvale: Aronson.

Ogden, T.H. (1994). *Subjects of Analysis*. Northvale: Aronson.

Pick, I.B. (1985). Working through in the countertransference. In E.B. Spillius (ed.), *Melanie Klein Today*, Vol. 2 (pp. 34–47). New York: Routledge, 1988.

Racker, H. (1968). *Transference and Countertransference*. New York: International University Press.

Skolnick, N.J. (2015). Rethinking the use of the couch: A relational perspective. *Contemporary Psychoanalysis*, 51: 624–648.

Skolnick, N.J. and Warshaw, S.C. (1992). Introduction. In N.J. Skolnick and S.C. Warshaw (eds.), *Relational Perspectives in Psychoanalysis* (pp. xxiii–xxix). Hillsdale: The Analytic Press.

Slochower, J.A. (1996). *Holding and Psychoanalysis: A Relational Perspective*. Hillsdale: The Analytic Press.

Stolorow, R.D. and Atwood, G.E. (1992). *The Intersubjective Foundations of Psychoanalytic Life*. Hillsdale: The Analytic Press.

Tansey, M.J. (1994). Sexual attraction and phobic dread in the countertransference. *Psychoanalytic Dialogues*, 4: 139–152.

Winnicott, D.W. (1965). *The Maturational Processes and the Facilitating Environment*. New York: International University Press.

Chapter 6

Termination in psychoanalysis

It's about time

Introduction

The meaning of the concept of termination can be traced back to Joan Riviere's 1937 translation of Freud's paper, "Analysis terminable and interminable." There still remains a curious mystery as to how her translation led to the use of the term *termination* to connote the end of an analysis since, as pointed out by Schlesinger (2005), there are no roots to the word termination in the German language. Nonetheless, moving forward from Freud, the evolution of the focus on termination, as an entity and a process, has shifted in meaning from the loss of a drive satisfaction, to the loss of an object, to the loss of a multiplicity of self-states to the loss of intersubjectivities. All models of the process, regardless of their aforementioned foci, however, have remained connected to a death and mourning ritual. Historically, death and mourning models of termination were enhanced by the technical prescription to disallow any contact between analyst and patient once the analytic clock ran out and the patient left treatment. The temporal realities of *Chronos* dictated that in order for termination to signify the end of a treatment, all neurotic wishes and hopes, whether rooted in the abandonment of drive satisfactions, object relation wishes, etc. needed to be resolved, period.

In this chapter, alternative models of termination are considered, models that are not rooted solely in death and mourning and, moreover, are derived from other models of time that are more closely allied with relational theory. Winnicott's concepts of somatic and object time are introduced, as are Bollas' interpretation of them, to theoretically justify leaving the door open for future contact between analyst and patient following termination. Also woven in are models of time stemming from infant research (Priel, 1997) that suggest other models of termination are possible. Specifically, I refer to the non-linear construction of time in our internal subjective worlds that respects what I refer to as the "dance of time," a random movement of our constructed realities of time among the tenses, for example, from present to past to future to wherever. The "dance" frees patient and analyst from a fixed amount of time, energy or linear directionality. Moreover by freeing termination from the strict, tick-tock linear constructions of *Chronos* allows both analyst and patient to wander freely to past, present and future internal clocks, exploring new meanings attached to the termination process, yet ultimately not ignoring the tragic, inevitable implications of a "last" session and death.

The dance also obtains its power and meaning from what Loewald (1962) refers to as the reciprocal relations between past, present and future as active modes of psychic life. Again, he is referring not to actual tick-tock time (*Chronos*) but our subjective perceptions of time (*Kairos*) that arise from interactions and interrelations between the three temporal modes – past, present and future, each mode both defined and negated by the other and, at times, infusing each other.

Loewald's (1972) opus occupied a space between classical metapsychology and contemporary relational thinking. Listen to him as he struggles with the issue of psychic determinism and time:

> There is another aspect of the experience of time which deserves mention here. Is the course of our lives seen as propelled by forces of the past, by a *vis a tergo* (absolute determinism), or is it seen as pulled by the attraction or prospect of future possibilities or purposes (conscious or unconscious)? In the early stages of psychoanalysis, with its emphasis on id psychology, there was a decided tendency to understand psychic life as wholly determined by our unconscious past: unconscious forces from the past explained the development and vicissitudes of life; and future was nothing but a time when a past state would be attained again. With the ascendency of the structural theory and ego psychology, with the growing importance of object relationships in psychoanalytic theory, this time perspective shifted. The shift is perhaps most clearly exemplified by Freud's stipulation of a life or love instinct, which works in opposition to as well as in cooperation with a death instinct. The idea of a life instinct bespeaks an orientation toward a view in which life is not altogether motivated by forces of the past but is partially motivated by an attraction coming from something ahead of us. Our experience, I believe, tends to oscillate between these two time perspectives.
>
> (pp. 140–141)

Termination in psychoanalysis 145

This quote, to my ears, captures what psychoanalysts struggled with as they wavered between an adherence, or rather a loyalty, to a drive theory paradigm and a growing intrigue with a newer object relational paradigm. Drive theory is given the explanatory priority, while a more relational paradigm is sort of tucked in as an afterthought. With the transition to a relational paradigm, or model, we no longer need to be encumbered by the weightiness of drive theory. We can relegate it to incidental importance, not primary. But Loewald was also reluctant to disavow drive theory. He could have easily explained a pull toward the future without invoking Freud's introduction of a life instinct. He could have, perhaps, invoked the anticipation of a satisfying encounter with a loving object relationship to understand the pull toward the future, with all the complexities, conflicts, hopeful fantasies and experiences with good objects that this forward thrust might entail. So while nodding toward increased involvement with object relations, he falls back into step with drive theory to explain the pull of time into the future.

Loewald, in the same paper, tackles an understanding of two opposite poles of time that he relegates to pathological states, though today we might see them more as existing as state-driven possibilities in normal functioning. These poles are that of the experience of eternity and the experience of fragmentation. The experience of eternity he describes as a complete absorption in the present moment such that the past and the future no longer exist. He likens this state to a mystical experience or even what some people describe as getting lost in a particularly intense emotional experience or the ecstasy of a sexual moment. He contrasts the experience of eternity with the experience of fragmentation, where the world exists in bits and pieces, and any sense of meaning has evaporated. The links between moments disappear and any sense of past, present and future has disintegrated. As Loewald (1972) aptly describes:

> While in the experience of eternity – which objectively may last only for a small fraction of time – temporal relations have vanished into a unity which abolished time, in the experience of fragmentation time has been abolished in the annihilation of connectedness . . . in the experience of eternity all meaning is condensed in the undifferentiated global unity of the abiding instance . . . and may flow out from there again to replenish the world of time with meaning; while in the experience of fragmentation, meaning, i.e., connectedness, has disappeared, each instant is only its empty self, a nothing.

(p. 142)

Interestingly, Loewald, the ego psychologist, refers to eternity and fragmentation as defenses against anxiety, whereas in our contemporary relational world we would probably describe such states as dialectically related self-states, each defining and negating the other and not necessarily pathological, but in tension with each other throughout our lifespans. They would fall under the purview of *Kairos*, subjective senses of time perception that are a distortion of more objective, observable measures of time. While not of much use in the physical sciences *Kairos* is invaluable to psychoanalysis.

Kairos moments come into particular emphasis during the termination of an analytic treatment. During an analysis, the non-reversible linear relationships between past, present and future are suspended. They are permitted to wander and interrelate in random and novel ways in order to create new narratives and meaning, which help to expand and redefine a person's definition of their unique self. While enormously useful to a patient attempting to construct creative and resonant narratives of their existence, at termination patients need to transfer their senses of time back to a primarily *Chronos*-ruled, objective appreciation of reality. This can entail painful loss and require a real interval of time to accomplish, this being one reason why a termination *process* is a requisite to all endings of a psychoanalytic treatment.

One particularly fascinating episode I refer to in this paper is when a number of my patients, all coincidentally at around the same period of time, returned to therapy after significant stretches of time, from 15 to 25 years, away from treatment. This real life, naturalistic "design," i.e., not contrived or planned ahead of time in a carefully constructed longitudinal study, allowed me to observe, as I would in a hypothesis-generating study, a number of variables. Questions proliferated. What in the treatment dyad's experience remained the same, and what changed? What memories of each other succumbed to the forces of *nachträglichkeit, après coup* or any other process that reconfigures, reconstructs or distorts our memories? Some findings were predictable, and some were surprises, as when a returning patient who had left treatment in a rage not only had no memory of his rage toward me, but had held tenaciously onto an internal image of me as one of the more significant positive influences on his life and career. Who knew? And how did this happen?

A word about surprise seems appropriate here. One of the more salient lessons I received from my wiser teachers and supervisors was never to

Termination in psychoanalysis 147

make any assumptions about my patients, never take anything for granted. Always inquire, be curious and do not be quick to force closure in my understanding of anyone I work with. This sage advice echoes Bion's (1967) recommendation to approach each session sans memory or desire. It also has distant rumblings of Bollas' sage advice (1987) to tolerate not knowing. To rush to understand can foreclose closer approximations of a patient's truth, and can serve more to quell our own anxieties about the analytic process with its endless ambiguities and uncertainties. Premature assumptions fall into what Fairbairn warned against in his one paper on technique (1958) when he wrote:

> In general, I cannot help feeling that any tendency to adhere with pronounced rigidity to the details of the classic psychoanalytic technique, as standardized by Freud more than a half century ago, is liable to defensive exploitation, however unconscious this may be, in the interests of the analyst and at the expense of the patient; and certainly any tendency to treat the classic technique as sacrosanct raises the suspicion that an element of such a defensive exploitation is at work.
>
> (p. 81)

The experience with my treatment returnees, and the accompanying surprises that arrived with them, once again affirmed my career-long commitment to never assume, to minimize categorization, and to respect the uniqueness of each patient and the uniqueness of my relationship with each of them.

My experience with them also reconfirmed my emphasis on the importance of respecting, rather than reducing and eliminating, error variance. The scientific method, with its emphasis on reducing error variance in order to support widely applicable, reliable and valid results, has been invaluable in increasing our stock of knowledge. But it fails miserably when applied to the deeply personal, creative, individualized therapeutic relationship that occurs between a person and their analyst engaged in the analytic process. Our understanding of our patients does indeed need broad strokes, like knowledge of diagnostic categories or attachment levels to help establish the broad rules of the engagement. It helps to guide us, especially at the beginning of therapy, to locate the psychological neighborhoods in which we and our patients live. We will listen differently to a depressed patient than we will to an agitated hysteric or a trauma victim or a person with bipolar disorder, for example. But I have found that people rarely fit neatly into any diagnostic category or combination of categories. We also need to appreciate a large measure of what sets each patient apart from the other, what makes each person unique, what unfortunately gets discarded when we eliminate the error variance. Once I become genuinely connected to and engaged with something akin to a person's unique idiom, an ineffable quality that sets them apart from others, I am then able to relinquish categories and diagnoses, characterological generalizations and facile explanations. This takes time! No one is that quick a study. But this profoundly intimate and unique intersubjective space is, I believe, the arena where a mutagenic interaction is more likely to occur.

References

Bion, W.R. (1967). Notes on memory and desire. *Psycho-analytic Forum*, 2: 271–280. Reprinted in E. Bott Spillius (ed.), *Melanie Klein Today*, Vol. 2, *Mainly Practice* (pp. 17–21). London: Routledge, 1988.

Bollas, C. (1987). *The Shadow of the Object*. New York: Columbia University Press.

Fairbairn, W.R.D. (1958). On the nature and aims of psycho-analytic treatment. *International Journal of Psychoanalysis*, 29: 374–385.

Loewald, H.W. (1962). Superego and time. In *Papers on Psychoanalysis* (pp. 43–53). New Haven: Yale University Press, 1980.

Loewald, H.W. (1972). The experience of time. In *Papers on Psychoanalysis* (pp. 138–148). New Haven: Yale University Press, 1980.

Priel, B. (1997). Time and self. *Psychoanalytic Dialogues*, 7: 431–451.

Schlesinger, H.J. (2005). *Endings and Beginnings: On Terminating Psychotherapy and Psychoanalysis*. Hillsdale: Analytic Press.

Chapter 6

Termination in psychoanalysis

It's about time[1]
2010

Neil J. Skolnick

Termination, the end or ending of a psychoanalytic treatment, presents the analyst and the patient with challenges both unique to the occasion and emblematic of the entire treatment endeavor. Issues analyzed and reanalyzed throughout the therapy rear their heads as if to give one more dying gasp before crossing over the line into post-analysis space and time. Enactments of multiple self and other configurations (Davies, 2005), both internal and external, once again take center stage, also preparing for their flying solo following the final session. At the same time, the very real here and now inevitability of separation casts its wary glance on the two players as they struggle to reconcile the closeness they achieved with the ultimate end of that very same closeness. Similar to a loss, but not quite the same, how do both analyst and patient maintain an internal connection while losing the other? The concept of termination appeared in the psychoanalytic lexicon following Joan Riviere's translation of Freud's (1937) paper, "Die Undliche und Die Unendliche Analyse," as "Analysis terminable and interminable." Actually, the etymological understanding of the word *termination* to indicate the end of a psychoanalytic treatment is somewhat puzzling. As pointed out by others (Schlesinger, 2005), Riviere's translation was a curious one because there are no roots to the word *termination* in the German language. Others (Leupold-Lowenthal, 1988) suggested alternate translations such as "Analysis *finite and infinite*" which capture the greater richness of the original German.

Interestingly, Freud's intent in writing the paper did not have much to do with the process of ending an analysis. He was primarily concerned with spelling out the criteria for a successful ending of treatment. These criteria provided a bookend to his earlier considerations of the specific criteria for analyzability. Appealing to the structural hallmarks of id and ego, he pronounced that those patients who suffered from a traumatic event were the most likely to achieve a successful analysis. He maintained that the most successful therapeutic outcomes occur in patients in whom there had been a genuine trauma. Conversely, he pronounced those patients with either excessive libido or alterations the ego unable to achieve a viable conclusion to their analytic work. So we see that Freud was not particularly concerned with the process of ending a treatment in the very article that, through a slip of translation, gave us the name to the process of ending a treatment. The term he used to refer to the end of treatment, *Undliche*, was not translated aptly into English to capture the richness of the process that occurs at the end of a psychoanalytic therapy. Nevertheless, the word *termination* stuck and has been used widely to refer both to the end of a psychoanalysis and the process of ending a psychoanalysis.

This paper will examine aspects of termination from a relational model. I maintain that a relational model applied to the end of an analysis captures more of the fluidity and texture than traditional models. It sits squarely in a two-person psychology so that it wrestles with the end of a mutual relationship that has focused on the analyst's process, the patient's process and the interaction of the two. The loss of the analytic relationship, by relational definition, includes the struggles, both internally and externally, of both the analyst and the patient as they prepare to, and ultimately do, separate. More traditional models focus primarily on the patient's loss of the analyst. Like the analytic work, the drama of termination is co-created and lived by both the treater and treated in intrapsychic as well as interpersonal space.

What happens when the patient exits the scene for the last time? Is it necessarily the last time? Is mourning the most apt metaphor with which to consider the process of termination? What changes occur in both the therapist and the analysand after the treatment is over? What remains of the analytic connection and the unique configuration of two people that has been profound, intense and hopefully mutagenic? Why are some terminations easier or harder for the analyst to endure than others? What constitutes a less than optimal or worse, a bad termination?

Of the many ironies we come to live with as psychoanalysts is that the intimate, genuine, authentic relationship we strive to create with our patients comes to an end. Especially in relatively successful treatments, but by no means limited to them, we come to know an enormous amount about the makeup of our patients, their strivings, their fears, their cherished successes and their humiliating failures, and their secrets, loves and hatreds.

Termination in psychoanalysis 151

And yet, the relationship ends relatively abruptly, and the person ventures back into his or her world, and then we know nothing. Even though we can spend weeks, months and even years preparing our patients for the end of treatment, when it arrives, the patient virtually evaporates, and we are left clueless about the continuing sagas of their lives. Like a death, we mourn them and they mourn us, but unlike a death, *both* parties undergo a mourning process, an impossibility with actual death, when mourning is limited to the person remaining alive. The nature, depth and length of mourning can be influenced by the nature, quality and affective tone of the relationship. Our affective responses toward our patients can achieve a full palate. At one time or another with all our patients and at different times with the same patient, we can fall in love, have sexual feelings, struggle with enormous rage or hate, admire, envy, be disgusted or proud, become frustrated or in awe, to name just a few of the possibilities. Then we have to say goodbye. Again, our responses to the therapy ending can be as varied and complex as our feelings evoked toward the patient during the therapy. I have found my feelings ranging from painful sadness and loss, to apathetic indifference, to good riddance! At times, particularly when experiencing sadness at the impending loss, I have felt it helpful to share some of my reactions with the patient. But I have no doubt it is also helpful for me as well. It is important to keep in mind that the processing the end of therapy, like the therapy itself, needs to be focused on the patient's needs, not our own, to avoid, as Fairbairn (1958) cautioned, exploitation of the patient in the service of our own needs. But I do maintain that some modicum of authentic expression of our struggle with separation at the finalizing of a therapy can be enormously helpful in normalizing the patient's struggle with these difficult feelings.

In any event, we more often than not are clueless to each other's lives once the relationship is severed. What becomes of the patient becomes, in our mind, a mixture of hope, concern, curiosity and perhaps fear for their future life. We work in a field with only a precious few indications of our efficacy. And these become even less following the departure of our patients. What becomes remembered, forgotten or distorted? How does the patient fare? How do we fare in their memory? Most of the time, we simply do not know. Like a death, the rest is silence. We need to be aware of our complex reactions to termination, continually monitoring our own as well as our patient's experience. We sometimes have a rarified glimpse into a patient's experience following termination, usually through reports by a third party. As I noted, occasionally, people return to treatment at some future date. We are then accorded a privileged opportunity to observe what has transpired since treatment ended. Has the change "stuck" or has the patient reverted to obsolete, less satisfying organizations of their psyche, ones that were neither adaptive nor beneficial to the cohesiveness and continuity of their self?

Just as the patient goes through a process of internalizing the ways of being with the analyst, the analyst goes through a similar process. The multiple ways in which the analyst and patient relate to one another are internalized and referred to at the onset of separation. If the analyst has been woven into the patient's ways of being, so has the patient's ways of being been similarly woven into the analyst. As Bass (2001) notes, "neither is the same again for having met the other in the way they did, and the trajectory of both lives will not be quite the same for the encounter" (p. 783). We do, as the analysis spins out its narrative, develop a set of intimate experiences that are unique to each patient–analyst dyad. Sometimes loving, sometimes not so loving, each patient can evoke within us just about any constellation of feelings that ultimately constitute extraordinarily intimate, authentic and meaningful relationships. Relationships whose self and other intersubjective patterns become to some extent a part of each of us.

The reactions of therapists to the loss of their patient at termination are also a multifaceted, multidetermined event. How does one begin to cast the end of a relationship that has endured months, years, even decades? My question for the purposes of this paper is not to tease apart the multiplicities of endings, but to provide questions about the fate of each of our participants as they return to life without the other.

On beyond death

The verb *to terminate*, taken out of the context of psychoanalysis, is typically associated with sinister motives and connotations: to be separated from a job, for example, or end a pregnancy, or, of course, worse, to die or kill. Similarly, the process of termination in psychoanalysis has been likened to a death. In its most classical sense, the death referred to is the death of the possibility of gratifying infantile wishes by one's parents in life, and in analysis by the transference figure of the analyst. Theoretically, to end neurotic hope would serve to free libidinal energy to be utilized for more adaptive purposes by the ego, with new and better objects. In the homeostatic balance of the psyche, the end of neurotic hope and dread would be replaced by a more realistic hope and dread. But first a mourning process would need to take place in order to release one's energy from neurotic aims with old objects and redirect it toward new, more satisfactory aims with new objects. The work of mourning has been described well by Freud (1917) in "Mourning and melancholia," and the work of mourning has traditionally been considered to be the work of termination. The predominant issues evoked during the analysis, particularly those of the transference neurosis, would be relived and reworked through one last time before the analyst and patient separate for a final time.

At some point during the history of analytic practice the convention changed. Although termination was still thought to represent a type of loss or death, it no longer was limited to the death of childhood wishes, but instead started to take on the meaning of the death of the analyst or the relationship with the analyst, both real and fantasized. Concepts of termination evolved, along with changes in the field of psychoanalysis, to derive less meaning rooted in drive psychology, and more meanings rooted in object relations. No longer did the end of an analysis evoke the relinquishing of drives, as much as it did the relinquishing of a relationship. Our primary need for relationship (Fairbairn, 1952), unmoored from its role in bringing about libidinal gratification, now became the focus of a treatment termination. Relational theory posits that the most influential ingredient in the bringing about of change is to be found in the analytic relationship (Fairbairn, 1958; Skolnick, 2006). It naturally follows that the relationship should take its rightful place at the center of the termination process.

Even in its simplest form, the mourning of a relationship during termination involves several different and overlapping mourning processes. First, the wished-for relationship with the analyst as a replacement for an earlier unsatisfactory relationship needs to be relinquished. Closely related is the need to mourn the fantasies toward the analyst, fantasies rooted largely in the patient's previous object relationships. But also to be mourned is the real relationship with the real analyst, the person who sits with his or her patient hour after hour, week after week, year after year, and attempts, from a continuous and benevolent vantage point, to help him untangle the strands of meaning in his life.

The picture has become even more complicated. From a relational perspective that is deconstructed out of the limitations of traditional transference and countertransference models, the analytic relationship becomes an ever-shifting, mutually contributed to and, more often than not, co-created series of interactions occurring between patient and analyst. As emphasized by both Bromberg (1998) and Davies (2005), the interactions among a multiplicity of both patient and analyst selves and self-states construct an endless array of old and new relationship configurations. Davies notes that when viewed from the vantage point of multiplicity, what is both renewed and relinquished during a termination process is not a singular patient–analyst configuration, but an array of self–other configurations that have come to the fore during the period of the analytic encounter. During the termination period, it is hoped that older, less beneficial ways of being will rear their heads and take their seat in the background while newer configurations of self and other will be reinforced in the foreground.

Also, as conception of the self has become increasingly contextualized, contemporary relational psychoanalysts have worked more and more from the vantage point of intersubjectivity, the interplay between the subjectivities of the analyst and the patient (Stolorow and Atwood, 1992). Ogden (1994) considers the unique interplay between each analyst–patient dyad an entity in itself, which he refers to as the analytic third. It is within the context of the third in which the therapeutic narrative is lived and created. This entity, the third, now also needs to be mourned at the end of psychoanalysis. More on this later.

We see then that the focus of termination changed from drives to objects, to multiplicities, to intersubjectivities. What has stayed constant throughout this perspectival shift is emphasis on the end of an analysis being likened to a death. As long as the end of a psychoanalysis meant the end of therapy with a particular analyst, it made sense to liken it to a death or loss. The finality of the treatment was considered necessary for the patient to face the relinquishing of either drive or object wishes. Analysts of many theoretical colors were advised to not leave an open door available. It is over when it is over, the clock has run out. Period.

An open door would short-circuit the finality of the old ways of being and leave open the hope for neurotic solutions to be realized. Anything less than a permanent separation with one's analyst at the end of treatment would both promote and signal incomplete work, or acting out.

But as with other shibboleths of classical theory, clinical experience has forced a reconsideration of the termination process so that it could no longer be contained solely within a death and mourning model. Irwin Hoffman

(1998) takes issue with the tendency to equate termination with death. Death, he argues, places a limit on any "chance to revise the meaning of our experience by reinterpreting earlier experiences in light of later ones" (p. 246). This is not necessarily the case with termination, especially when one's analyst is available for possible future contact. In this paper, I would like to further challenge the traditional linking of termination with death and mourning. Although like a death in important ways, there are dimensions of the termination experience that can only be explored through other models, including other models of time.

Priel (1997), drawing from advances in mother–infant research, has noted the close association of the concept and experience of time and early mother–infant configurations. Freud rooted the infant's growing understanding of time in the gap between stimulation and gratification – that is, in the workings of a solitary isolated mind. Priel states, however, that

> a different perspective on the sense and concept of time can be envisioned, not as pertaining to an isolated perceiving mind, but as a mutually construed organizational principle characteristic of mother–infant interactional patterns . . . The sense of time can be better understood as the unfolding of basic meanings related to identity and differentiation, continuity and change, in the context of infant caregiver interactional patterns.
>
> (p. 435)

Bollas (1989), also writing from a perspective that contextualizes the psychological conception of time, invokes Winnicott and makes a distinction between somatic time and object time. Somatic time is rooted in a timelessness, provided by the subject mother who, by accommodating to the infant's cycle of needs, protects the child from the ultimate demands of time. As the mother gradually fails the infant's omnipotent desires and becomes an object for the child, so too does she teach the child about object time, whereby the child gradually construes a realistic sense of time during the gap between the mother's absence and presence.

I think of somatic time and object time dialectically and in tension with each other. Termination, then, reckons with balancing both senses of time. That we need to end a psychoanalysis evokes issues of real, object time, clock-ticking time. A death–loss model of termination deals with the realities of object time, the clock running out of ticks.

When we leave our door open for future contact, we are evoking issues of maternal somatic time, which also continues to exist in the internal world of the adult. In this case, time does not become limited to the length of the episode of therapy. Instead, the possibility existing for future contact with an analyst can ease the stresses of the running out of object time. Like the workings of an hourglass, once the sand runs out, the hourglass can be flipped over, restarting the flow of time.

Gradually, throughout my career, I started responding to the end of the treatment more as a moment in somatic time by leaving open the possibility for future therapeutic contact. I did not neglect object time, in that the therapy would end and a termination date would be set and honored with a termination process. But not to overstate the obvious, unless one of the treatment pair has died, no one has actually died in real time, and that is a fact of the termination as well. This reality places an obvious but important limit on the death/mourning/grieving model of termination. To end a period of analytic work with the offer of an open door in the future takes the termination out of the realm of the finite. The message given is no longer,

> You must now learn to accept the limitations of our relationship because it is permanently finished. You will be able to have continued contact with me as I exist in your internal world, but you must relinquish all other wishes for it to be otherwise.

It has become rather,

> Our relationship is over for the time being and we will be separating. Yes, the therapy and termination process has involved the loss of pieces of yourself and pieces of us, but it has also provided new ways and possibilities of being – new ways of being that have been obtained partially through our relationship. The relationship is over for now, but do know that I am available for your use in the future.

This change in message pertaining to termination parallels a basic sea-change that has come about in the shift to a relational psychoanalysis. A one-person model asks the analysand to relinquish any attachments to the analyst rooted in the solipsism of one's closed internal world. The analyst's role has been essentially to evoke the past connections in the internal world, elucidate them and render them vestigial. The clock starts ticking from the moment the analysis begins. There will be a fixed amount of energy rearranged in a linear, fixed amount of time. There is plenty of time to explore, contemplate, act out, enact and identify with the analyst, but time is of the essence! It is over when it is over, and hopefully the analysand will hit the road moving forward by relinquishing old ways of being, with new more reality adapted ways of being firmly entrenched within the psyche to assure durability over time. The analysand must accept the limits of time, make those changes, relinquish hurtful, self-destructive connections, mourn their loss and move on.

As opposed to a closed system, energic model of psychoanalysis, which asks the patient to go back in time in order to move forward, a two-person relational model, even though not eschewing the past, invites the patient to connect in the present time in order to create an alternative narrative, and then move forward. The new narrative does not assume a fixed amount of energy or linear directionality. The treatment dyad is freer to move back and forth in time. Both older and newer ways of being and connecting are tried on, accepted or discarded. As I stated elsewhere (Skolnick, 2006), the hope is that the patient has, in the therapy, interacted with a good object in the form of the analyst and then carried the interactions into their lives following termination. It is assumed that the older maladaptive ways of being will not evaporate, but they will continue to live in tension with the newer ways of being. In that the older self states and self–other interactions are not necessarily given up, but rather added to, there is less emphasis on mourning a "dead" subjectively created analyst. The analyst, as new object, is allowed to survive. In that he or she survives, the analyst is available to interact with the patient at some time in the future. Future contacts with the analyst are not mourned, as they are in a classical model, but are welcomed as a possibility in a relational model.

Time after time: A clinical example

M, a bright, articulate and affable man in his thirties, was having a hard time wading through his ambivalence about getting married. He was in a relationship with a woman whom he loved and wanted to marry but remained inexplicitly stuck and unable to actually tie the knot. Our work together was extremely helpful in elucidating the source of his paralysis and enabled him to move ahead and, with lessened conflict, marry. His paralyzing conflicts had reliably surfaced at various times throughout his life, typically during periods of rites of passage. When confronted with transitions to new life stages, the primary issue evoked was one of separation from his alcoholic mother whom he wished to protect and cure. He had become her self-proclaimed caretaker from a very young age. His father, though well meaning, had in essence abandoned his wife by virtue of his high-powered job and frequent travel. He was rarely home to monitor her serious alcohol abuse, a task that fell largely into M's lap. In the world, M functioned as a well-integrated person, probably by virtue of his two considerably older brothers who raised him. But to his mother he was press-ganged into part object functioning. As he put it, he was a penis for her, virile, protective and a fount of strength. When approaching new episodes in life, episodes signaling increased autonomy and growth, his internalized abandoned and fragile mother would languish, if not die. I was for him a father who stuck around, protecting him from the burdens of caring for his mother and allowing him the freedom to leave her as he ventured forth into a successful life.

The termination process proceeded well. He was psychologically sophisticated and was able to revisit many corners of our work together. We traveled back and forth, reliving moments of our relationship including the good and idealized, as well as episodes of anger, competition and disappointment. But when the actual time came to say goodbye, as he was about to leave the room he informed me that he would be back to see me again when it was time to have children, referring to the next developmental bridge-crossing he was likely to face.

Sure enough, several years later, he contacted me for therapy because he and his wife were contemplating having children and he once again felt terrifically stuck. His issues were similar; his having a child would represent a further separation from and abandonment of his mother.

Therapy with M took place at a time in my career when I worked from a heightened conviction in a more traditional ego-psychological model of termination, one that likened it more exclusively to a death. Furthermore, death being final, my model of termination also included in it the supposition that a "proper" termination was one in which all childhood wishes were abandoned, the ego was strengthened, the superego was made more flexible and, voila! the work was complete. Should further treatment be required, it indicated that the first treatment, including the termination work, had been incomplete. From the moment M informed me, upon leaving, that he would see me again, I had doubted the efficacy of the first treatment. Had I failed to conduct a complete therapy? Had I missed some powerful dependency issues that needed further analysis? Had I not indeed been mourned (or mourn) like in a "proper" termination process so that the patient, or I, had been hanging on to ungratified wishes for need fulfillment?

During the second period of work with M, we went over much of the same territory as we had in the first. I was not hearing new issues and wondered what I was missing. The issues surrounding separation from his dysfunctional family resurfaced. The strengthening of his self and lessening of his guilt and shame were also revisited. I was not surprised then when, after a much shorter stay in therapy, he announced that he was ready to end treatment. He told me he felt he was indeed ready to start a family. About a year later, I received a birth announcement, followed by several more over the course of time. I now happily receive a Christmas picture every year of his burgeoning family, all of whom appear, at least in the picture, to be thriving.

My patient was wiser than I was. When M informed me at the end of our first course of work that he would be back, my fear of an incomplete analysis re-emerged, *theoretically*; he, by contrast, knew what he needed, *actually*. Today I no longer hold solely to a death model of termination. My relational sensibilities inform my approach to ending therapy. Termination is like a death, and can awaken issues of death and permanent loss, but it is not a death, either an actual one or of primitive drives and wishes. I prefer to regard it as one of many iterations of separation accompanied by a loss. It may or may not be a final separation. I always leave my door open at the end of treatment in the event that the patient might want to return at some future time for additional work. With many I emphasize that we all, being more human than not, can run into difficulty at any time in life, and that returning need not be considered a failure or defeat. In my experience, patients have returned for a number of reasons, some for another immersion in treatment, sometimes to pick up where they left off. Some whose growth after termination resulted in their increased awareness of issues they were not able to be aware of at the first termination. Others developed difficulties in reaction to a real-life trauma or difficulty. Some come for a session or two, frequently referring to such a return as a "tune-up." Some, like M, returned to be able to transition to another stage of life. To regard termination as a death would preclude allowing a patient to return. But aside from a real death, neither of us has actually died for the other, externally or internally. And of course, stuff happens.

I have since worked with a number of patients who have come, left and returned during the course of a therapy that spanned many years. Some might consider such treatments unsuccessful, or in Freud's word, interminable. As such, it might be posited that the internal economy of character structures remain unbalanced, or insufficiently treated. I prefer to regard such therapies as existing outside of a conventional time structure that we arbitrarily cast around a treatment. As such, it is not that each segment of therapy is incomplete, but our temporal definition of a course of therapy needs to be expanded. Rather than limiting therapy to a delineated period of objective time, might it be that the "perfect storm" that propels someone into treatment at any particular time involves a confluence of factors that includes a temporal context? The question we often ask, "Why now?" needs to be expanded into "Why now, and then?"

Consolidation

On more than one occasion, I noticed that a period away from treatment after termination had served to consolidate the gains of therapy for some patients. These patients appear to have shifted significantly in their psychological development during the period away from treatment. Integrations had been made, self-regulation was expanded, and reality testing existed more consistently. Their relationships could be seen to have provided more satisfaction, reflecting both growth and expansion of character adaptations. Potentials for change, hinted at but never realized during the therapy *per se*, blossomed and flourished when the patient was away from the therapeutic arena.

If we posit (Skolnick, 2006) that identifying with the analytic processes of the analyst in a therapeutic relationship is a powerful force contributing to therapeutic change, it would suggest that when identificatory processes are interfered with, change is harder to come by. A consistent factor in each of the cases where consolidation occurred after termination has been the presence of powerful annihilation fantasies and enormous destructive ideation. These forces seemed to derail adaptive processes and identifications in the presence of the analyst. Distance from the analyst appears to be the only way such identifications can occur safely. In the analyst's presence, the level of rage, envy and other equally destructive forces does not allow

Termination in psychoanalysis 161

internalizing interactions or the consolidation of these internalizations within one's own self–other object representations. A similar type of phenomena can be encountered in some patients who report a greater degree of closeness and ease with the therapeutic interaction during phone sessions. These patients have noted to me repeatedly that the distance provided by phone contact increases a feeling of safety and reduces anxiety. My sense is that non-phone, in-person sessions can rouse too many destructive forces that interfere with therapeutic internalizations.

Lenny, a middle-aged man with considerable difficulties in life, left a more than ten-year treatment following the death of his mother. Lenny led an exceptionally limited existence. Although talented at his craft, he obtained only very limited professional success. His immersion in his work was sporadic and with tentative engagement. He might spend several months focused and determined to achieve, followed by lengthy down times of little or no involvement, often sticking to a reverse sleep–wake cycle. He lived alone and rarely ventured out from what we came to call his cave, his safe retreat from the dangers and insults of the world at large. He was hampered by an unfortunate combination of perfectionistic rigidity, a severely compromised self-esteem and massive paranoid projections, so that the simplest of tasks, such as going to the store and buying a shirt, became fraught with fear, overly obsessive planning and paranoia.

Lenny suffered from enormous annihilation fantasies that dominated the transference and provided the most consistent and pervasive coloring to our relationship. In his mind I was perpetually attempting to destroy him, belittle him and abscond with his achievements. Whether I was affirming an accomplishment, being empathic for a difficult set of affects, or merely being supportive, he experienced me as demeaning or more typically, attempting to destroy him. He remained secretive with me and refused to reveal many of the details of his ongoing experience, again feeling that my destructive desires rendered him vulnerable. When his mother died, his inner world threatened to so thoroughly overwhelm him that he made a hasty departure from treatment, claiming that I no longer, if ever, provided help. He left precipitously, against my recommendations and allowing no termination process. To some extent, I was not surprised. Therapy with him had always been less than satisfying for both of us. Although he made some progress, it was anathema for him to let me in on it, and I typically had to glean his victories from indirect, unobtrusive hints he would sparingly throw my way.

He contacted me again after an approximately two-year hiatus when he was beset by powerful psychosomatic fears of dying. He had a litany of physical symptoms, all of which had proven negative by the medical consultations he frequently undertook. Yet he felt strongly that he was dying and that all his doctors either had been incompetent or were afraid to tell him the truth. I regarded his psychosomatic ideation as an extreme identification with his dead mother who had suffered a prolonged debilitating decline prior to her death.

Of note for this discussion, however, was that during his two years away from treatment, he appeared to have improved considerably. His career had progressed. He was working at it more consistently and with heightened perseverance. He had also been successfully taking control of his mother's estate. She had been a celebrity and left a complicated and extensive legacy in need of organization and legal protection. Lenny, who typically could quiver with trepidation at having to talk with a store clerk, was now taking meetings and holding his own with powerful agents and attorneys, demonstrating a sophistication that heretofore I had never witnessed.

It was startling to behold, and equally as puzzling to understand. Had he taken the therapeutic process (i.e., identifications) gathered during treatment into the world where they remained free to flourish and strengthen away from the analyst's perceived destructiveness? Perhaps the analyst's presence during treatment needed to be skirted so that changes could be made in an autonomous space, free from perceived threats by the analyst's expectations or his own projection of annihilation vulnerabilities?[2] What was truly remarkable was to witness the improvement he had made during time away from treatment as opposed to in it. One might claim that treatment had served destructive rather than beneficial purposes. Alternatively, given that the changes observed after termination were in the arenas worked on while in treatment, it would appear to indicate that interruptions were indeed necessary to further experience and consolidate gains aimed for in therapy.

I have observed similar improvement in other patients who have left and returned to therapy. I have become more sanguine with patients who announce their wish to leave therapy at inopportune times. Some do respond to my offer of an open door and return to continue to do the work at a later time. Of those who return, it is clear to me that many have continued to undertake the work of analysis away from our live interaction. If I may paraphrase Winnicott in saying that we often strive with our patients to help them achieve autonomy in the presence of another, perhaps for

Good, good-enough and bad terminations

The end of a psychoanalytic treatment can take many forms, both planned and unplanned. Freud (1937) mused about what actually constitutes the end of a psychoanalysis. He distinguished between the end of a treatment and a proper termination process, the former being a truncated therapy that has not worked through a termination process, *per se*. As we know from our work, the end of therapy can take an infinite number of forms, ranging from setting a planned end date that leaves time to process the ending, to the circumstance in which a patient exits without announcement and disappears without a trace.

When to end an analysis is the subject of much speculation. In its infancy, when analysis as a technique was nascent, its aim was to treat a certain set of neurotic symptoms so the ending was more or less dictated by the cessation of symptoms. The analysis of symptoms, through time, gave way to the analysis of character and character dysfunction. Once detached from symptom cessation *per se*, when to end the analytic endeavor entered into a far more nebulous region of uncertainty. Ferenczi (in Davies, 2005) was known to have written, "The proper ending of an analysis is when neither the physician nor the patient puts an end to it, but when it dies of exhaustion, so to speak" (p. 780). Writing much later, Levinson (1978) likened the decision to end a treatment with the aesthetic decision of an artist to declare that his or her work is complete. Overall, I tend to agree with Martin Bergmann (1997), that as a field, psychoanalysis has said little to adequately address this issue.

A discussion of when to end a therapy must include mention of the types of obstacles and pitfalls we run into that interfere with our clinical judgment about when to end a treatment. Extraneous issues to the criteria for terminating abound, such as the inherent conflict of interest between ending a therapy and the analyst's maintenance of income, or the reluctance of either party to end a mutually satisfying authentic attachment, just to name a few. Aside from the imperative that the analyst be vigilant about not privileging his or her own needs ahead of those of the patient, my bias is to try not to have a bias about timely endings of treatment.

Categorical recommendations frequently fail to recognize the uniqueness of each analytic dyad and likewise the unique circumstances and timing of each termination. The time for ending is best determined by a mutual exploration by each individual analytic pair. A comprehensive listing of the reasons for ending would take us way beyond the scope of this paper. The point I wish to stress here is that there is no easy set of criteria for ending.

Once we decide on ending, however, what makes the ending a good one? What are the qualities that distinguish a "good" or "good enough" termination from ones that go poorly? My contention is that a good termination is one that allows some dedicated period to process the multitude of meanings of the termination for both patient and analyst.

The scope of the termination process can cover an extremely broad universe of issues and experiences ranging from the specific ideographic events of the work together to more generic issues of separation and loss. It can be focused on what has been lost and what has been gained in the work, hopes for the future, as well as disappointments in the analysis. Surprises can arise, such as the appearance of completely new issues. Sometimes symptoms can arise, either a recrudescence of older ones or completely new ones. Schafer (2002) describes a defensive organization he calls the false depressive position, a pseudo-mature manner of coping with the stresses and strains of termination. He ascribes this stance to patients, but I believe an analyst needs to be on the watch for a similar defensive movement in him- or herself.

As with when to end an analysis, I recommend that there be no formulaic prescription as to the actual length of time set aside to complete the termination. The length of time can vary from dyad to dyad. I used to go by the rough estimate, supplied by precedent, which dictated about one month for each year in treatment. This at times had disastrous consequences. During one instance, the length of a successful treatment translated into such a prolonged and ultimately unproductive termination process, that we mutually decided to truncate the termination and be done with each other already. The needed work had been done early during the termination and it continuing was probably some expression of a lack of willingness for either of us to call it quits and say goodbye. For me personally, a prolonged termination is a signal of some difficulty one or both of us has with ending a productive relationship that has nonetheless run its course and is in need of ending. Likewise, I have found, at times, terminations of a relatively short duration to be profound, deeply authentic and mutually satisfying. As with the question of when to end a treatment, I have found there to be no categorical clues as to what might be a "correct" timely course to a termination process. We need to enter into each ending with a suspension of preconceived ideas about its proper length. That said, I find that "natural" ending points, such as a vacation or holiday, provide a reasonable, good-enough broad-stroke indicator of when to set a termination date, provided some period of time has been allotted to work through the termination.

To some extent, the end of the analytic relationship is present throughout the entire treatment,[3] but in my experience, once a final date is set, the termination process has begun. The content of future sessions will subsequently bring another filter, that of separation, always present but not always attended to, into the foreground of the analyst's listening process. Created "meaning" will now contain elements of the treatment ending and what that awakes in both the analyst and the patient.

Sometimes ending dates are forced upon a dyad by circumstances beyond either party's control, such as a business transfer or move. At such times, I would once again recommend that some period of time be spent defining a termination period so that some work be undertaken, even if by phone, and however truncated by time and distance constraints.

I have generally, but by no means exclusively, found that the quality of a termination process corresponds roughly to the quality of the therapy that has preceded it. With patients who have participated in a profound, genuine and multitextured experience with me, the process of ending the work similarly is as profound, genuine and multitextured, and will reflect the entire range of the distance traveled in the work. Older, less adaptive ways of engaging each other will arise as well as newer, more successful and expansive ways of being. The actual ending has typically been a mutually experienced bittersweet event in which profound feelings of sadness for the separation were expressed and hopeful expectations for the future were enjoyed. Such a termination usually gives way to a naturally occurring hearty hug before the final goodbye.

But this is not the case for all terminations. Treatments that have felt deficient in one way or another, I have found, typically end with a less than satisfying termination process. An ending with a patient who has been difficult to engage affectively will often reflect a similar disengagement. This can be the case regardless of the progress made or distance traveled in the work. Similarly, when the treatment has been unbalanced on some dimension, for example, with an excess of anger, grandiosity, dissatisfaction with the analyst or unanalyzed idealization, the ending will also feel similarly unbalanced. Again, the work may have produced mutually recognized gains but the ending can feel dull and flat, often with the nagging sensation that an essential piece has been and still is missing. Often, when such is the case, a mutual hug does not even enter into the range of possibilities for a final contact.

And some terminations can feel devastatingly empty, enraging or futile. In my experience these exits are rare. I recall the shock, anger and hopeless feelings that set in when a patient with whom I had been working intensively for several years disappeared suddenly from therapy, without a trace. He merely did not show for his next session. My calls and letters went unanswered. He took the end of treatment into his own omnipotent control, as if there had never been an "us." My best guess about such endings is that the patient, via a projective identification, has communicated to us a nonverbal understanding of an overwhelming and devastatingly futile object relationship they have experienced and is now ensconced with in their inner world, a relationship replete with hopelessness and feelings of annihilation. But that is just fancy conjecture, desperate clapping with one hand. We never truly know what has transpired.

Termination and the end of co-construction

For an endeavor that leaves no stone unturned in its quest to comprehend and construct meaning in human experience, psychoanalysis has been remarkably silent about the process of termination that continues after the analysis has ended. We rarely, if ever, study posttreatment phenomena and processes, behaviors, and continued construction of meanings after the analyst and patient have separated.

In this paper, I described and illustrated several circumstances when I caught a glimpse of the termination process that occurred following the cessation of therapy sessions. I would like to conclude by considering another aspect of the termination, the ending of co-construction.

The interactions between patient and analyst undergo a seismic shift following the last session in treatment. Although no longer are the two in actual proximity, they remain related to each other as a set of internalized identifications. As I noted, hopefully the ways of being of the analyst are internalized sufficiently by the patient to withstand the separation, as each analyst and patient continues in time without the other. Both Freud and Klein emphasized the importance to psychic equilibrium of maintaining internal object ties after a death, usually through identifications. In as much as terminations can resemble a death, at least for the current episode of therapy, it is similarly hoped that the relationship with the analyst will continue in some internalized form.

The internalizations, however, are subjected to the major currents in each person's character and may take on different shadings, meanings, forms, recollections and affective valence following the last session. Co-construction of memories, both actual and procedural, in both the analyst and the patient, comes to an end following the final session. What is remembered and maintained becomes subjected to the distortions and vagaries of memory, circumstance and time. Choices of what and how to remember the other become more and more affected by one-person internal operations.

We might find the diversions and back roads that shape treatment memories growing in disparate ways so that each person maintains recollections that have grown apart from, and gradually become less and less similar from, the other. When reconnecting with a patient after a period in which treatment has been in abeyance, I am struck by the number of times I have the jarring experience of coming across divergent memories. Usually I become aware of this phenomenon when a patient announces, "And I always have remember what you said . . . " or "And the most important thing you ever said was . . . " and then proceeds to recollect a quote of mine that not only am I fairly certain I have never said, but I am also of the firm conviction that those words, or anything similar to them, never would have crossed my lips.

We find that treatment memories are not encoded similarly, stored similarly or recalled in identical ways. In the context of termination, co-construction, it would appear to me, is ephemeral. It might exist for the moment during the treatment and contribute to the making of meaning, but does it continue over time? Ogden's third, the mingling of two subjectivities, can be viewed as a relatively brief phenomenon contextualized during the treatment but not afterwards. Like life in the primordial soup, it is the temporary dance created by two separate molecules, creating a higher-order system that rapidly disintegrates unless contact, now internal following termination, is maintained and repetition is allowed. As Hoffman (1998) so very well put it, "Although we cannot change any moment as it was experienced, we can make choices that affect the meaning to us of any particular moment as we think of it in retrospect" (p. 245).

I would add that co-construction cannot take place in retrospect. It becomes a victim of object time. The end of co-construction that comes with termination provides but yet another stress for both analyst and analysand as they part. Will the creation of meaning, so alive and vital during the intensity of their contact, be maintained? Will the illusion of their dance together survive the separation? And in what form will it survive? At the moment of departure, this question sits with the analytic pair as they move beyond the precipice into future time, and only time will tell.

Notes

1 A previous version of this paper appeared in Salberg, J. (2010). *Good Enough Terminations*. London: Routledge, published with permission by Taylor and Francis.
2 Although Bion's goal of the analyst freeing himself or herself from desire is a worthwhile and crucial goal, I believe the analyst's expectations are always present in some fashion, even if not explicitly or clearly stated or known consciously by the analyst.
3 Entire models of short-term therapy have been developed based on the inevitability of the final separation of therapist and patient. See Davanloo (1992) or Della Selva (1999) for discussions of short-term dynamic psychotherapy.

References

Bass, A. (2001). It takes one to know one: Or, whose unconscious is it anyway? *Psychoanalytic Dialogues*, 11: 683–703.
Bergmann, M.S. (1997). Termination: The Achilles heel of psychoanalytic technique. *Psychoanalytic Psychology*, 14: 163–174.
Bollas, C. (1989). *Forces of Destiny*. London: Free Association Books.
Bromberg, P. (1998). *Standing in the Spaces*. Hillsdale: Analytic Press.
Davanloo, H. (1992). *Short-Term Dynamic Psychotherapy*. New York: Aronson.
Davies, J.M. (2005). Transformations of desire and despair: Reflections on the termination process from a relational perspective. *Psychoanalytic Dialogues*, 15: 779–807.
Della Selva, P.M. (1999). *Intensive Short-Term Dynamic Psychotherapy: Theory and Technique*. London: Karnac.
Fairbairn, W.R.D. (1952). *Psychoanalytic Studies of the Personality*. London: Routledge and Kegan Paul.
Fairbairn, W.R.D. (1958). On the nature and aims of psycho-analytic treatment. *International Journal of Psychoanalysis*, 29: 374–385.

Freud, S. (1917). Mourning and melancholia. In J. Strachey (ed. and trans.), *The Standard Edition of the Complete Psychological Works of Sigmund Freud* (Vol. 14, pp. 239–258). London: Hogarth Press

Freud, S. (1937). Analysis terminable and interminable. In J. Strachey (ed. and trans.), *The Standard Edition of the Complete Psychological Works of Sigmund Freud* (Vol. 23, pp. 211–253). London: Hogarth Press.

Hoffman, I.Z. (1998). *Ritual and Spontaneity in the Psychoanalytic Process: A Dialectical-Constructivist View*. Hillsdale: Analytic Press.

Leupold-Lowenthal, H. (1988). Notes on Sigmund Freud's analysis terminable and interminable. *International Journal of Psycho-Analysis*, 69: 261–272.

Levinson, E.A. (1978). The aesthetics of termination. *Contemporary Psychoanalysis*, 12: 338–341.

Ogden, T. (1994). *Subjects of Analysis*. Northvale: Jason Aronson.

Priel, B. (1997). Time and self. *Psychoanalytic Dialogues*, 7: 431–451.

Schafer, R. (2002). Experiencing termination: Authentic and false depressive positions. *Psychoanalytic Psychology*, 19: 235–253.

Schlesinger, H.J. (2005). *Endings and Beginnings: On Terminating Psychotherapy and Psychoanalysis*. Hillsdale: Analytic Press.

Skolnick, N.J. (2006). What's a good object to do? *Psychoanalytic Dialogues*, 16: 1–29.

Stolorow, R.D. and Atwood, G.E. (1992). *Contexts of Being: The Intersubjective Foundations of Psychological Life*. Hillsdale: Analytic Press.

Chapter 7

Resilience across the lifespan

A confluence of narratives

Introduction

I was invited to present this paper on resilience in 2011 to the Austin Society for Psychoanalytic Psychology, Fall, 2011 Conference. In preparing the paper I discovered that resilience is typically studied from the perspective of general psychology and aside from a few miscellaneous papers (Anthony, 1987; Eisold, 2005; Fonagy, Steele, Steele and Higgitt, 1994) has hardly received attention from the psychoanalytic community, let alone those interested in relational psychoanalysis. Furthermore, the psychology literature has been primarily dedicated to the description of traits and characteristics of resilient people. While these are important descriptions, I agree with Stephen Seligman, who, in his most recent book, *Relationships in Development: Infancy, Intersubjectivity, and Attachment* (2018), makes a plea for a multidiscipline, multi-perspective approach to many of the issues we attempt to study only from a psychoanalytic perspective. A psychoanalytic approach can indeed add to an understanding of the unconscious motivations, unique experiences and psychodynamic genesis of resilience. It is but one ingredient, though that can be integrated or even synthesized with many – physiological, cultural, behavioral, gendered, historical and temporal, etc. – to create a fuller understanding of such a complicated phenomenon.

Many questions arise. What is resilience? How does it come about? Is it always a beneficial phenomenon, or does it coexist with the leading edge of what Winnicott (1960) refers to as the "false self," and I refer to as the "adaptive self"? Is it a one- or two-person phenomenon? The list is endless. Why limit its study to a single discipline? More and more, from my cursory survey of recent trends in scholarship and research, I find that there is an increased tolerance for cross-pollination with other disciplines, within and without of psychoanalysis. But that is a longer discussion and outside the purview of this book.

Resilience across the lifespan 171

From my clinical experience I've come to the somewhat surprising belief, for me, a relational psychoanalyst, that resilience is a character trait that does not fall solely within a two-person psychology, either in its development or functioning in an adult. Two of the patients I describe in this article were in possession of a fierce resilience that was somewhat inexplicable to me. I first speculated that their resilience was a variant of "false self" structures, born from interaction with narcissistically impaired mothers who were incapable of providing either sufficient or consistent emotional attunement. In both cases my patients developed as parentified children, unusually attentive to the needs of those around them. This somewhat textbook formulation appeased me for a while until it became too thin and formulaic. Both of my patients were too related and deeply connected to me in very real ways to merit being categorized as Winnicott's "false selves." Or perhaps they were variants of "false selves." When relating to someone I deem a "false self" I typically find myself bored, annoyed and fantasizing calling them out on their falseness with cries of, "Bullshit! Tell me what you are really feeling or thinking," or just, "Be real!" I never had that impulse with them. I always felt a partner in a genuine, give and take mutual relationship. Yes, they both suffered adversities growing up. One had a seriously alcoholic mother and the other, a popular, athletic and well-rounded student, was kicked out of his house at 17 years old for no readily discernible reason and forced to join the Marines.

More than most issues we attend to in therapy, I began to see the development of resilience as a feature of some people that challenges the predominant relational belief that our development is always ensconced in a two-person phenomenon. Resilience might indeed come about as a compensation for a lack of parental attunement, as Winnicott (1960) describes. Briefly, he holds that a parent, typically a narcissistically wounded parent, is emotionally unattuned to a child's needs and serves as a poor mirror to a child's experience. Winnicott claims this poor attunement forces the child to become prematurely attuned to the needs and desires of others, becoming in essence a parentified child. One of the frequent accompaniments of a parentified child is the imperative that the child be resilient, and take care of the parent.

But not all parentified children become caretakers. Both patients I refer to in my paper possessed a certain uncanny ability that to me transcended just being parentified. They both had a sense of time and timing that felt almost clairvoyant in their ability to be prescient to the inner workings of another's mind. I first became aware of this when, early in my work with one of them, he handed me a sketch of Winnicott's theory as it applied to him, replete with real, adaptive and false selves. Let me note here that when he handed me the sketch, I had only seen him for a one- or two-session consultation and had just begun taking a course on Winnicott. No doubt I might have transmitted to him, indirectly or unconsciously, some of my excitement about Winnicott's ideas. Still, his grasp of them way exceeded anyone I've ever labeled as being capable of performing a quick study. It was an uncanny experience. As I note in my paper, this occurred repeatedly until I felt it was an imperative I mention it to him. Undaunted, he told me this ability was like breathing to him. It had been operative, always, from as far as he could tell, forever. Perhaps it was a product of an inattentive and unattuned mother, but I began to experience it more as I do the gift of someone who possesses an extraordinary musical talent. Some innate relational skill, something one is born with that we do not entirely understand. And it was definitely a one-person phenomenon, not co-constructed. It appears to be some sense of time and timing that operates independently from development; It manifested as an exquisite sense of time that could anticipate another's organized experience with warp speed. I've yet to understand fully its mysterious phenomenology but it never felt performative, a feeling I frequently encounter in my relationship with someone who falls more neatly within the assemblage of a "false" self.

Soon after I set out to write this paper I realized that resilience was intimately connected with age and time, not only the resilience of the patient, but the resilience of the therapist as well. Furthermore, the resilience of each member of a dyad is influenced by the perceived resilience of the other.

As I have noted, in this paper I write about my experiences treating two people. One was a man about my age when I was in my early thirties, and the other was a man in his seventies I worked with when I was in my sixties. Obviously, there are an infinite number of age pairings between patients and therapists. In my analytic training, I learned that Freud (1915) considered transference to be timeless. So that when working with a patient older than myself, the transference is determined by the internal world of the patient and a 70-year-old man, let's say, can, internally, be six years old in the transference with a 30-year-old therapist. From my work with patients of different ages than me (either older or younger) I now conceptualize this issue of discrepant analyst/analysand ages somewhat differently and propose that transference and countertransference can both travel in time, both forward and backward. A therapist and patient of similar ages can appear as similar ages in the transference and countertransference. But they can also, in the same pairing of therapist and patient, be experienced as older and younger, or younger and older. Transference is not only timeless, but it can shift, via the operations of *Kairos*, in multiple directions, at different times in the same treatment. Relational theory has released us from the rather limited original theory about transference as representing only an attempt to realize an Oedipal transference neurosis. The combinations and permutations of analyst/ analysand pairings of ages, both internally derived (*Kairos*) and externally derived (*Chronos*) are infinite. It is up to the pair to figure out what assumptions or fantasies they are making about each other's age, the accompanying fantasies, and possible explanations. For example, I have experienced the older patient I described, who is exactly ten years older than me, at various times in the treatment, as my fantasized father, child, uncle or peer, existing across time frames past, present and future and with shifting affects – be it envy, admiration, love, annoyance and sorrow. Relational theory has freed transference from theoretically determined time shackles to move forward and backward in time with abandon. This obviously makes our intervening decisions more difficult, but infinitely more enriching when attempting to understand a patient's unique experience. The treatment situations also begin to resemble Melanie Klein's (1975a, 1975b) phantasmagorical conception of positions as rapidly shifting, as opposed to fixed developmental stages.

Another issue that arises in regard to time and resilience is that the meaning of the future for both the analyst and the patient takes on markedly different meanings. The prototypic analytic scenario has been to return to the past in order to decipher or re-decipher meaning in the present. When my patient and I, described in this paper, were approximately the same age, in our thirties, the futures we were imagining and dealing with in the present contained thematically approximately the same life issues. Our issues concerning resiliency were set against the expanding expectancies of establishing growing families, careers, and given our relatively similar class backgrounds, held similar fantasies about lifestyles, and expected satisfactions in upper-middle-class lives. Of course there were numerous individual differences, but the general trend was toward growth and expansion, and issues of resilience took a back seat as optimism about health, life expectancy and the lives of our families generally propelled us forward in life. The future, while containing uncertainties, looked promising and good. And if we had doubts, we could use therapy and new life experiences to minimize them and change what we needed to change.

Not so in my work as an aging analyst working with an even older and aging patient. We were, indelicately put, "over the hill," and the future, while still holding potential for growth, change and creativity, also had to contend with physical decline, retirement, loss and ultimately death. A different kind of resilience was indeed required for this stage of our lives. In the therapy situation, complications rapidly proliferated. Of course there were his issues about being in the thick of transitioning from old age to old, old age, commonly thought to begin in one's eighties. Retirement looms. His work sits, along with his family, at the epicenter of his self-definition. Co-mingled with aging landmarks are the deterioration of health, both his own and his close friends. One of his oldest childhood friends was descending into the abyss of dementia just as he (my patient) was struggling with the onset of an arrhythmia that caused him to collapse in front of an audience of several hundred. Then there was I, his analyst, traveling through space-time only about ten years shy of him. I felt I was witnessing a head-on collision with my own physical deterioration and ultimate fate, about ten years hence.

These existential anxieties, which I discuss in my paper on resilience, are categorically different than the usual anxieties evoked in the countertransference during a course of treatment. They are emotionally wrenching affects concerning deterioration and impending death and our defenses against these affects are expressed in powerful concordant or reciprocal (Racker, 1957) countertransference reactions. Witness my agitated attempt to deal with my countertransference evoked by my older patient. I hear a voice emanating from my own depths, "Grow up! Resolve your narcissistic issues!" "Didn't I do that already?" I protest. "Yeah, but as I tell my students, all our issues can surface throughout life." Yikes! It becomes an imperative for me to muster up my own resilience in order to face our mutual senses of mortality as we both career into our senior years, me old, he older. "I'm not ready for this, I protest. You need to shut up and buck up and be there for your patient," I lecture. And so forth until I settle into an empathic stance ready to hear and comprehend his experience.

He was eager to not only continue writing the narrative of his life, with its traumas, failures, victories and accomplishments, but he was also driven by an attempt to make sense, make new meaning, of how he was able to achieve as much as he did, and wind up where he was, including living in an urban aerie in some ways similar to but so different from the mountainous aeries of his youth in Wyoming. His fourth marriage was immensely satisfying (as he put it, "I finally got this relationship thing right") and his relationship with his children was solid and satisfying. His children forgave him his years lost to alcohol and looked to him now as the wise, loving center of the family. He had suffered profoundly at the rejection by his parents, and the ensuing effects that had on his sense of efficacy and self-esteem. It remained a mystery to him that he achieved such a high level of interpersonal and professional success.

I am attempting to get across to my readers a sampling of the deeply disturbing tasks of old age, the resilience it requires to negotiate them and the equally disturbing tasks of an aging analyst attempting to negotiate these existential issues with his or her patients while passing through the same temporal territory. Of course, it is an imperative that the unique histories and experiences of each participant are separated out and respected, with boundaries intact. After all, my history of growing up in New York City has virtually no resemblance to or overlaps with his experience of being raised on a ranch in Wyoming and then exiled to the Marines. But while our historical and other contextual issues diverge, the existential issues of age and aging are remarkably similar and have a profound effect on our relationship. I too was beginning to take stock of my life's narrative, pondering the choices I've made, the regrets, and the mysteries inherent in the shaping of a lifespan. A relational approach, as it becomes more and more detached from the positivistic certainties of a classical model of mind, development and therapeutic action, allows the relational analyst to explore analytic pairs of analyst and patient from an infinite number of shifting perspectives as the perceived roles of each member travel in age, time and place. These shifting perspectives are explored in the following paper on resilience

References

Anthony, E.J. (1987). Risk, vulnerability and resilience: An overview. In E.J. Anthony and B.J. Cohler (eds.), *The Invulnerable Child* (pp. 3–48). New York: Guilford Press.

Eisold, B. (2005). Notes on lifelong resilience: Perceptual factors implicit in the reation of a particular adaptive style. *Psychoanalytic Psychology*, 22: 411–425.

Fonagy, P., Steele, M., Steele, H. and Higgitt, A. (1994). The Emmanuel Miller lecture, 1992: The theory of practice of resilience. *Journal of Child Psychology and Psychiatry and Allied Disciplines*, 35: 231–257.

Freud, S. (1915). The unconscious. In J. Strachey (ed. and trans.), *The Standard Edition of the Complete Psychological Works of Sigmund Freud* (Vol. 14, pp. 159–217). London: Hogarth Press.

Klein, M. (1975a). *Love, Guilt and Reparation and Other Works, 1921–1945*. New York: Free Press.

Klein, M. (1975b). *Envy and Gratitude and Other Works, 1946–1963*. New York: Free Press

Racker, H. (1957). The meanings and uses of countertransference. *Psychoanalytic Quarterly*, 26(3): 303–357.

Seligman, S. (2018). *Relationships in Development: Infancy, Intersubjectivity, and Attachment*. New York: Routledge.

Winnicott, D.W. (1960). Ego distortion in terms of true and false self. In D.W. Winnicott, *The Maturational Processes and the Facilitating Environment* (pp. 140–153). NewYork: International Universities Press, 1965.

Chapter 7

Resilience across the lifespan
A confluence of narratives[1]
2011

Neil J. Skolnick

By all accounts my patient Ben should not have been functioning in life as well as he was. He was raised in a family with a powerful, prominent, but mostly absent father and a seriously alcoholic mother. His mother's alcohol abuse left her incapable of properly caring for a young child and when Ben was a toddler he was, on more than one occasion, found wandering the street outside his house in the upper-middle-class neighborhood where he lived. His mother was also unable to protect Ben from physical attacks from an out-of-control brother, several years older than him, attacks that left him hospitalized with broken limbs on several occasions. He did have two much older brothers who provided the closest semblance of parental care and guidance, though due to the great discrepancy in age, they were well out of the house by the time Ben turned eight. Ben excelled in school, graduated from an Ivy League college and was attempting to climb the ladder to establish himself in his chosen profession. His abusive brother, whom he described as a "red neck," went on to develop a serious dependence on drugs and alcohol and tripped through a series of revolving doors in and out of substance abuse rehab centers. When we started working, Ben was in his late twenties, his mother was seriously deteriorated and struggling with incontinence and the beginnings of dementia, his father remained ensconced in his work, his older brothers maintained families in distant states and he had no contact with his abusive brother. He entered treatment with two primary concerns: one was his indecision about asking his girlfriend of several years to marry him, and the other was his uncertainty about his ability to be successful at work. In other words, and for the purposes of this paper, he was smack in the middle of an identity crisis at a time when he was crossing the proverbial river into early adulthood.

I bring Ben up in this paper to illustrate the confluence of resiliency, developmental crisis and psychoanalytic process at this fraught juncture in a young man's life. How can we understand, from a psychoanalytic perspective, Ben's thriving against all odds? How does his resiliency manifest in the therapy and how is it addressed? How does it appear in the intersubjective space of our encounter? These are questions I would like to address.

With few exceptions (Anthony, 1987; Eisold, 2005; Fonagy et al., 1994), psychoanalysis has not paid much attention to issues of resilience. While it has been a mainstay of psychological and epidemiological studies, it has made scant appearance in the psychoanalytical archives. Furthermore, the resilience literature has been focused primarily on children. It represents, by and large, the contributions of psychology and epidemiology to identify factors that contribute to the ability of certain children to negotiate successfully ordinary developmental tasks in spite of all odds, in spite of cumulative adversity or trauma in their lives (Eisold, 2005; Masten et al., 1999; Werner and Smith, 1992).

An interesting attempt to relate resilience to psychoanalytic concepts comes from a study in which resilience was seen as one constitutional factor involved in whether or not someone was analyzable (Fajardo, 1991). For the purposes of that study, resilience was defined as:

> the capacity to regulate one's own states of experience, to maintain integrated states, and to recover from disruption. Resilience, so defined, is the ability to make use of the facilitating aspects of the environment and to withstand the disruptive aspects in order to maintain or to restore a cohesive state.
>
> (Fajardo, 1991, p. 108)

By and large, attempts to study resilience have historically focused on characteristic traits of resilient individuals. So, for example, Kumpfer (1999, in Clauss-Ehlers, Yang and Chen, 2006), in a comprehensive review of the resilience literature, organizes individual character traits that contribute to resilience into five major cluster variables: (1) spiritual or motivational characteristics, (2) cognitive competence, (3) behavioral and social competence, (4) emotional stability and emotional management and (5) physical well-being and physical competence. Such trait-based studies have shown that children who tend toward resiliency are likely to be independent, sociable, have an internal locus of control, be active and have a sense of agency (Kumpfer, 1999; Davis, 2001). This is but one of the many profiles developed to describe the characteristic traits of resilient children. Other accounts of factors contributing to resilience have located the lion's share of resilience in an individual's unique narrative, both actual and adopted, particularly as their narrative is situated in the context of meaningful relationships. As you might imagine, these latter, less specific or categorized factors, factors arising in context of relationships, come from psychoanalytic quarters, particularly relational psychoanalytic.

More recently, the resiliency literature has focused less on individual traits and more on process. The interaction between the individual and environmental factors is considered more important for predicting resilience than either factor alone. Many of these "process" studies have focused on identifying the circumstances, both individual and environmental, that create "protective factors" (Rutter, 1985), factors that foster the child's strength. "Protective factors" identified have included good intelligence, good communication and problem-solving skills, the capacity to engage others in relationships, the capacity for self-regulation in infancy, interpersonal awareness, the ability to plan, the determination to be different from abusive parents, and "ego restriction" or "overcontrol" (Eisold, 2005). Environmental factors that have been identified included factors such as available school, clergy, community and mental health supports (Werner, 1985; Rak and Peterson, 1996; Pianta and Walsh, 1998; Luthar, Doernberger and Zigler, 1993).

It was imminently clear to me that by many definitions, Ben was resilient. He had not only survived a childhood with extreme, traumatizing neglect and physical abuse, he had risen above his early environmental handicaps to thrive, both in school and socially. One could locate the causes for his resilience in the usual and fairly obvious places. He was intelligent, socially attractive and self-reflective. He was especially psychologically minded with his mentalizing abilities intact. He received some parenting from people other than his parents, most notably his older brothers, at least before they left home. In essence, he had a number of the "protective factors" noted by researchers.

But these more or less categorical features are never sufficient for a psychoanalyst, like myself, who is always concerned with the unique, inner regions of someone's psyche. In the quest to identify categories and traits, our psychometric measurement tools look to reduce error variance to negligible amounts. But as analysts our focus is typically away from the categorical and centered squarely on the error variance, those realms of character that hold individual meaning and uniqueness, those places ignored as noise by more standard pen and pencil statistical measures. Put another way, psychoanalysis concerns itself with the experience and dynamics of an inner world, a realm unique to each patient. And so it was with Ben that I discovered some remarkable regions of his inner world that contributed to his resilience. These were his unique narratives, narratives that were composed of inner object, and self and object interactions, that promoted his ability to endure under less than optimal circumstances.

It is my contention that exploration of inner world experience, both conscious and unconscious, adds greatly to our understanding of the intersubjective factors that contribute to one's resilience. Moreover, such explorations, of course, contribute immeasurably to the treatment process with resilient patients. But there is also a downside. As we shall see with Ben, resilient strength can arise from false self-configurations and this poses a dilemma for the analyst. Is resilience born of false-self threatened when it is analyzed?

Ben could be considered having been a parentified child. Lacking in any suitable, consistently attuned parental object, he became prematurely attentive to the demands and desires of others. In order to insure connection, he became highly attuned to their needs and wishes. This attunement contributed greatly to Ben's sociability, one cornerstone of his resilience. It manifested in the transference in a strikingly uncanny fashion. Not long after we started working, I realized that Ben was anticipating not only my every need, but also my thoughts and actions. More than once, in fact frequently, I would be internally pondering or synthesizing an interpretive remark when Ben would head me off at the pass by voicing the very remark I was concurrently thinking about. It was an experience that went beyond our just being on the same page, consciously or unconsciously. Phenomenologically it was as if he had snuck into my mind, excavated my thoughts and feelings, and presented them to me before I had the time to put them together myself. When I remarked on the experience to him, he casually responded, "Of course!" and that he had been doing this as far as he could tell his entire life; without effort, he would be two steps ahead of anyone with whom he was conversing. He noted that for him, to be interpersonally prescient was akin to breathing.

It was at this juncture that I ran headlong into the dilemma I described above. Ben was in possession of a premature and pervasive attunement to others. This was an attunement he probably developed early on to insure order and control of his self and object world while providing for the safety of his very being – both physical and emotional. In other words, he had developed what Winnicott would consider a protective, defensive false self. It was of a magnitude that exceeded the socially acceptable false self we all need to don in our public lives. It was compulsive and rigidly fixed. But it was also a bulwark of his resilience. It was an integral feature of his survival strategy. It enabled him to rise above the adversity that was his family and succeed in the separate regions outside his home. Do I analyze? Should I promote the chipping away at, and shedding of, this defensive false self in order to contact the defenseless, terrorized child on the other side? Or do I celebrate it as a strength of his resilient self? Do I go the either/or route, or the both/and path? This was over 20 years ago, before the flourishing of intersubjectivity theory and its distrust of binaries. I chose to both interpret and celebrate, enabling him to appreciate and deal with the tension between his creative and adaptive but compulsive accommodations to a dangerous world and the scared child within who might risk putting the accommodations aside.

As a side note, it was at around that time that I began to question the very notion of false self, with all the negative connotations it evoked. False is a powerfully bad word. False suggests lying, dishonesty, something regretful, something to be expunged. I came to prefer using "adaptive self" in place of Winnicott's false self. An adaptive self stands as a piece of jargon without the negative connotations of a false self. It also implies creativity, something to celebrate, not discard. And if false self contributes to resilience, why not call it adaptive and bring it on, at the same time work to soften its rigidity and compulsivity, freeing a person to explore new modes of being.

I also recognize that what we refer to as the false self can become rigid, automatic and very much feel disconnected from a sense of authenticity. I still think those less than optimal features can be worked with without the stigma of being called "false." Also, an adaptive self has been constructed to reliably shield the child from the intense pain of inadequate parenting that is stunted by the parents' narcissistic limitations. A narcissistic parent regards a child more by virtue of what the child can provide to fill the parent's self-object needs and precludes the parent from seeing who the child is – his or her individuality, needs, strengths and abilities. I strongly believe our attitude toward a patient that stems from a loving appreciation of the deprivation they have suffered and their creative ability to create a viable, albeit limited, self, will translate into more helpful interventions than those based on a consideration of the patient as being false.

There was another feature to Ben's resilience that we became aware of. This feature entailed a personal narrative rooted in an internalized and idealized part object. In one corner of his highly attuned self he felt compelled to take care of and protect all the members of his family, especially his mother and brother. He would take over paternal functions for the family during his father's frequent absences for work and likewise provide succor and nurturance when his mother was lost to alcohol. Ben informed me that he relished a secret fantasy that his entire self was a penis – erect, strong and providing. This appeared to represent an amalgam of maternal and paternal internalizations that remained idealized and ensconced as another cornerstone of his resilience. As with his extreme attunement to others, I chose to celebrate this region of grandiosity, while giving equal time to elucidating its limits. He was then able to integrate his image of himself as an omnipotent penis into a more balanced picture of himself that could be both resilient and vulnerable.

I was barely older than Ben when we first worked together and not much beyond the life-cycle concerns with which he wrestled. I could easily identify with the maturational tasks of his age – it was a time for starting families and establishing a vital role in the work world. It was a season for making major, life-determining decisions while establishing autonomy separate from childhood families. In short, Ben and I were both struggling with similar life and maturational issues. Though the form and content of our conflicts were different, I knew the outlines of the issues from a more immediate vantage point than had I been either much younger or older than him. This similarity surfaced in our interaction in a number of complicated ways. At times, he would compete with me, setting up an Oedipal arena in which he needed to insure the superiority of his prowess over mine. When he at times attacked my competence, he would evoke a similar competitive spot in me, which I needed to be acutely aware of so as not to enter the Oedipal arena with him. By not engaging in a competitive enactment, I provided a steady, strong and present object for him to identify with. I referred to such identifications in previous papers (Skolnick, 2006) as dynamic identifications. In brief, a dynamic identification refers to the internalization of an object relationship, not just the object. In this instance, it required an identification with a competent, competitive but not destructive or neglectful other and a self in relationship to this other.

He could also borrow my strength to fight off the demons that prevented his movement forward in his life. He could try on my own resiliency even as I admired and at times envied his. My resilience as I experienced it then was rooted in my optimism toward developmental and maturational leaps. It was also openly displayed as my wedding band. Knowing, and noting, that I was married increased his faith in his decision to marry his girlfriend. Briefly, his difficulty in tying the nuptial knot was coterminous with his difficulty in separating from his dysfunctional family. Partially, through his identification with me, he was able to make the leap into marriage.

My work with Ben highlighted, then, the relational confluence of two individuals, the patient and myself, the analyst, struggling with similar life stage issues. Ben's resilience, rooted partly in powerful idealized and idealizing identifications and partly in an adaptive self-structure, was engaged by the analyst in ways which strengthened the resilience and promoted an expanded, less rigid and more integrated self that, in turn, promoted an increase in autonomy that allowed a more complete separation from a dysfunctional family. Ben was able to marry and continue successfully in his career choice.

I will now shift gears and consider my work with an older person at a very different time in my career than when I worked with Ben.

A funny thing happened on the way to presenting this paper. I originally expressed an interest in presenting a paper not on resilience but on the treatment of older patients. But when Mary Moore (the head of the professional association in Austin) shared my idea with her colleagues, they all had a marked and most decidedly negative response, "Who would come to hear a paper on that?" Exactly my point! Her colleagues, without awareness, hit upon the reluctance of our profession to work with people of advanced age. The elderly are often relegated to a position of the "other," or the "not me," safely insulating psychoanalysts from the very human struggles, anxieties, fears and age-appropriate adjustments of a significant and growing portion of our population. How do we understand the almost kneejerk aversion to working with older people in analytic psychotherapy? What is getting stirred up in the therapist who sits across from an older person? What fears, anxieties and conflicts do we need to wrestle with? Why are we willing to explore our complicated, intense and often painful countertransference responses to younger patients, but shy away from them with older people? I do not mean to chide or excoriate practitioners for shunning work with the aged. We are after all more human than not. My purpose is to attempt to understand what underlies this reluctance in order to make what we have to offer available to a wider population and one that could so greatly benefit from in-depth exploration. My thesis is that working with older patients requires a certain degree of resilience in the analyst, particularly in those analysts who are aging (surprise, surprise!) themselves, that is not typically called forth in working with a younger population.

I look at this question as I turn to consider resilience in a different patient of mine, and my own therapeutic resilience when working with him. He is not a young man on the threshold of adulthood, but rather an accomplished man of 70+ years who is in the process of exiting middle age, exiting his career, a major component of his self-definition, and entering the ranks of the aged. And I am no longer an analyst in my early thirties. At 60+, I am only ten years shy of my "older" patient facing his older old age. I hope to accomplish two goals. One is, as with my younger patient Ben, to look again at a resilient patient from a psychoanalytic perspective and, two, to illustrate that the resilience of the analyst is challenged in ways that correspond to where the analyst might be situated in his or her own lifespan.

So there we were, my new patient Richard and I, sitting across from each other, intensely involved in the gathering of information about each other, both implicitly and explicitly, at the start of a course of therapy. A typical scene, the consultation was attendant with the usual issues and anxieties I experience when meeting a new patient for the first time. But there was something unusual happening that disturbed me in a way that was novel and profound. I became anxious about my age. I knew from the referral source that this was a man in his seventies. While I have worked with a number of older patients, I was not at all prepared for my reaction when I met *this* older patient. What occurred to me as we sat down was that the man was old, I mean really old, what some writing about therapy with the elderly would call approaching the older old as opposed to just old. But what precipitated my startled reaction was the realization that he was not that much older than me. I was sitting across from someone who provided a snapshot of me in just ten years hence. My experience was a markedly different countertransference reaction than I experienced in my past work with older patients. Typically, when working with an older patient in the past, I had been working with people who were old enough or almost old enough to be my parents. My struggle had been with countertransference issues that among others were encased in feelings about my aging parents. My own feelings about aging rarely, if ever, took center stage, at least not consciously. This time I was reacting to my own aging process as it was evoked by my somewhat older, older patient. I realized that I was identified with an old and aging patient and it precipitated a countertransference crisis of an entirely different order. The existential issues of aging flooded me full force, replete with unbearable affects associated with growing old, facing illness, loss, deterioration and dying.

These existential anxieties are categorically different than the usual anxieties evoked in the countertransference during a course of treatment – you know, the usual suspects – guilt, anger, rage, envy, greed, lust, shame, annihilation anxiety or swells of sadomasochism, to name several. In the course of our work we are called upon, on a daily basis, to experience, either in concordant or reciprocal (Racker, 1957) countertransference reactions, difficult emotionally wrenching affects and our defenses against these affects. By contrast, when we are called upon to experience the existential jolts of growing old and, dare I say it, death, we are out of the realm of internal fantasy and forced to confront the limits of time, actual reality in its starkest terms. Can there be a greater threat to our resilience as therapists? Unlike other professionals who work with older or terminally ill patients, we cannot comfortably objectify our patients, e.g., "otherizing" them thereby insuring a safe if not always comfortable distance from them and their issues. To do our work we need to crawl into their skin. In our efforts to be empathic to their plight we must try to comprehend their experience from the inside. And the inside landscapes of existential issues are bleak, heralding decline, illness, loss and death.

Contrast my initial session with Richard with a snapshot of my initial meeting recently with a much younger patient. This was not Ben, the previous patient I described who I worked with years ago. This was Sonny, a man in his late twenties, young enough to be my son. He entered treatment because of difficulties he was having controlling his anger with his girlfriend and with colleagues at work. He hoped to get married, have children and be successful at his chosen career in business, but was fearful that his impulsive expressions of angry outbursts would interfere. My initial response to Sonny was in the realm of avuncular, but did not stop there. While relishing the task of fostering this young man's rites of passage into adulthood, my feelings were soon complicated and compounded by that most evil of affects – envy. Damn, once again I had to wrestle with my own feelings of envy. After all, who at my age does not harbor some fantasies of being able to travel back in time, be a 20-something and do it all over again? Even were I to retake the same chosen paths, the opportunity to be in my twenties with my life stretched out in front of me presented an existential wish that clearly inhabits the realm of an older man's sport. Coming to terms with our limitations is a lifelong pursuit, requiring age-appropriate accommodations at all ages. Or to put it in more psychodynamic terms, I could look at the Oedipal conflict from both sides now. As has been noted (Davies, 2015) the Oedipal situation of the child does not exist in a vacuum. Instead, it is contextualized by the plight of the father who is preparing to leave the stage as the child is making his debut on the stage. The envy I experienced taxed my resilience in working with Sonny and required that I factor envious and competitive feelings out of the equation so that I could hear and work with his experience. But as challenging as feelings of envy may be, they do not compete with the utter narcissistic devastation that accompanies countertransference experiences of one's own mortality, the essence of the reaction I had to my older patient Richard.

So, it was comparatively easier to marginalize my bout of envy toward Sonny. With my avuncular feelings still intact, I could access my concordant identifications with Sonny's stage in life and the anxieties attendant to the coming of adult age in our society. The pressures of establishing an intimate relationship, separating sufficiently from our childhood objects in order to forge one's own path, achieving competence and success at work, these are the maturational issues within which we usually contextualize the experience of a person of Sonny's age. These are issues replete with mourning and loss of our childhood desires and can be accompanied by growth pains unrivaled to date. But again, difficult as that might be, my experience of breaking through a denial of death were of a different order of challenge.

As noted, when I worked with older patients in the past, I defensively lumped them squarely in the realm of "other." There was a convenient and comfortable discontinuity between them and myself. While I could be empathic with their dynamic and existential issues, I did not regard them as on a time continuum, or any continuum for that matter, with me. No, they were almost of a different species, the elderly, with no foreseeable connection to me or my stage of life. While I no longer had felt that they were not amenable to psychoanalytic exploration, as Freud taught us, I was nevertheless surprised and impressed when they could insightfully examine themselves, form transference relationships with me, and sound pretty much like my younger patients. I maintained a "some of my best patients are old" patronizing attitude toward them that I only recently, in retrospect, could grasp the nature of. But this time, with Richard, it was different and the difference lay in the reality that I was no longer a young therapist working with an older patient. The truth was I was an aging therapist working with an aging patient. I was in new territory.

Let me back up a bit. As most of you know, Freud (1905) was exceedingly pessimistic about the efficacy of the psychoanalytic process with the elderly. His sentiment was that middle- and old-age patients have developed rigidified character structures and defenses that preclude them from benefiting from the rigors of psychoanalytic treatment. In his words (Freud, 1905):

> The age of patients has this much importance in determining their fitness for psycho-analytic treatment . . . on the one hand, near or above the age of fifty the elasticity of the mental processes, on which the treatment depends, is as a rule lacking – old people are no longer educable – and on the other hand, the mass of material to be dealt with would prolong the duration of treatment indefinitely.
>
> (p. 264)

His sentiments had the unfortunate consequence of excluding older patients from the purview of psychoanalysis throughout most of the last century. A notable exception was Karl Abraham who as early as 1919 postulated that older patients should not be denied analytic treatment. Based upon his successful treatment of middle-aged patients he concluded that, "The age at which the neurosis breaks out is of greater importance for the success of psychoanalysis than the age at which treatment is begun" (Abraham, 1919). There has been a smattering of others who have advocated the efficacy of psychoanalysis with those over 40, but by and large, throughout much of the last century, psychoanalysts have shied away from plying their trade with older people. In a field where many practitioners of psychoanalysis continue their work well into old age, is it not somewhat hypocritical to aver that what we are called upon to do as analysts – that is, self-analyze – cannot be accomplished by our older patients? Is it not duplicitous to assume that the analyst could analyze his or her own rigid defensive structures while assuming older patients could not? And is it not disingenuous to deny an older patient a course of analysis because, as many have stated, they might die before the work is completed while many aging analysts seem to forget about their own impending death? So our objectifying the old is squarely rooted in realistic abject fear, as opposed to the irrational fear that can motivate our prejudices.

Other reasons have been used to rationalize not working intensively with older patients. We have been told they cannot withstand the pain of in-depth exploration, that is they would be lacking in resilience. Another excuse is that their lives have so little future, what benefits could come from a treatment, that, while having its eyes set on the past is also so future oriented in regard to goals and ambitions?

More recently there have been a number of reports of successful treatments of older patients, well into their nineties. As Frieda Plotkin (2000) points out, these treatments tend to follow two divergent thoughts regarding work with the elderly. Some (Fenichel, 1945) caution against in-depth exploration and advise a more supportive treatment, while others (Segal, 1958; King, 1980) promote more insight-oriented approaches (Hoffman, 1998).

In my practice, I have noticed a gradual shift in the age of my patients. They are most definitely graying. Whereas in the past, my patients' average age ranged approximately from 20 to 40, with an occasional older patient, more recently that average age has shifted. I am now seeing many more people in their forties, fifties and sixties, with a number well into their seventies. Why this is not completely clear to me. Certainly, it is partly due to the aging of patients I have treated for a long time, either continuously or more frequently, in episodic contacts. As one woman in her sixties whom I have treated on and off since her thirties reminded me during our last termination, "I know what to expect from you. After all, we grew up together." But I also seem to be getting more and more referrals of older patients, I suppose because people assume that an older therapist would be more attuned to the issues of aging. And besides, younger therapists are, as I have noted, reluctant to work with aging patients.

The graying of my practice has come with unexpected benefits. I have found that the urgency of limited and accelerating time has, contrary to conventional psychoanalytic wisdom, not been accompanied by an increased rigidity, but instead has fostered a delightful suppleness of character that is matched only by the increased motivation to do the work. By and large, my experience has been that these people are serious. They do not want to waste time and prefer to get right down into the mud and confront issues that previously might have given them pause. Many figure that this is their last opportunity to do this kind of exploration and they do not want to squander it. Of course, not all enter treatment this way and indeed there are those whose character dysfunctions have become more entrenched, making the work as difficult as it is challenging. But I have been pleasantly surprised by the eagerness of many to wade into deep waters with dispatch.

But the graying of my patients has also surprised me with unexpected stress that challenges my resilience in new and daunting ways. Being a graying analyst places my work with older patients in a very different context than when I was younger. I sometimes feel bombarded by the daily parade of existential dilemmas that I can no longer deny or distance myself from as I could when younger. Day after day, hour after hour, I am privy to issues of career endings, declining health, imminent death and serial losses. In order to remain in empathic step with my patients it is necessary that I wrestle with these issues myself, without denial. The issues are no longer academic or in the realm of inner fantasy. It is not enough to be empathic with a patient's feelings about the approach of the end of life. I must realize that the chances that I might die before the patient have greatly increased since earlier in my career. Which one of us might be struck by a debilitating or deteriorating illness? How do I envision retirement now that it is closer than ever? No wonder Mary Moore's good colleagues eschewed a paper about working with the elderly! Who would want to listen to this? But these issues have become a daily part of my career at this stage of the game. A stage when I am an aging therapist working with aging patients. And let me assure you, it involves summoning resilience as never before. Battles with diminishing time, the limits of time are no longer in the realm of the safely theoretical; they are rooted in the real.

Back to Richard, my 70+ year old patient. Richard entered treatment at the suggestion of his wife who complained he was not able to express his feelings with her and had withdrawn from her generally. He concurred and stated he had a lifetime of difficulty expressing himself in intimate relationships. He had been in therapy earlier in his life, valued the process and wanted to undergo a course now to tackle this issue at this advanced time in his life, not only in order to finish incomplete business, but to obtain optimal satisfaction from life during his remaining years.

As with young Ben, it became clear to me that Richard was a remarkably resilient man. He grew up in a family on the west coast with three sisters, one who committed suicide about ten years ago. His mother was a constricted, paranoid and extremely religious woman who incessantly preached that we were put on this earth to suffer. Her religiosity was rooted in a strong vein of projection and paranoia. She began to have enormous difficulty with Richard when he entered adolescence. He was a top student, athletic and popular. He and his friends engaged in the usual teenage shenanigans, but nothing illegal or outrageous. As he has noted on more than one occasion, he wasn't a bad kid at all. Regardless, her pervasive paranoia led her to accuse him of continuous transgressions, imagining that he was involved in "unholy," aka sexual, "activities." Ironically, she did not include in the unholy column her daily requests that he come in and talk with her while she was submerged naked in her bath with nothing but a small washcloth floating on the surface of the water to cover her nudity.

When he turned 17, his mother, with his father's passive complicity, threw him out of the house. He left, never to return. He proceeded to lie about his age, joined the navy and at 17 found himself stationed in a foreign country alone, confused and utterly dejected. With grit and determination, he made it through his stint in the armed forces. As he put it stoically, he was a tough kid so he just toughed it out. The mantra of his being a tough kid was one he subsequently carried with him throughout much of his life and evoked in times of difficulty. I have no doubt that his narrative of his being a tough kid provided one of the backbones of his resiliency. Moreover, his family shielded his mother's pathology and, because of the size of his father's local factory, held a prominent position in their small community. Here we come up against another paradox about resiliency. On the one hand, his identification with his family's prominence added to his personal sense of resiliency. But it also meant that he was alone in acknowledging his mother's pathology. To the community she was a pillar; to him she remained an unstable, dangerous and abandoning person. He was utterly alone with his trauma. Only later, as adults, did he and one sister commiserate about the truth of their mother's pathology and the disastrous effects it had on their family.

Richard's resilience was inconsistent, evident at some times in his life, and not at others. He managed to put himself through college, married three times and fathered six children (both natural and adopted) with his second wife. When his children were young, he resorted to excessive alcohol abuse and continued to do so until he was 50, when he entered rehab and became sober, which he has remained since. On becoming sober, he became severely depressed and entered insight-oriented therapy. Remarkably, throughout all, he established and maintained an enormously successful career in New York City politics and is still called upon today to advise city leaders in high-profile issues. Ironically, history repeats itself as he, like his parents, has become a prominent member in the town he now lives, shielding his alcoholism and depression from public view.

The dynamic sources of Richard's resiliency were not easy to locate. He did have one sturdy older cousin whom he remembers fondly and with whom he seems to have identified. Time spent with his cousin, a professor in a nearby college, was always cherished, as he seemed the only person to recognize and affirm his strengths. He credits his cousin with providing love and guidance when it was lacking from his parents. This idealized cousin remains one of the cornerstones of his resilience. He also has one surviving sister, living close by in New York, with whom he has been increasingly able to express his feelings about being abandoned and who has provided confirmation of the trauma that occurred (for her as well) when he was cast out of his house. She assures him that it was traumatic, not just for him, but for his sisters as well. Contrary to his wives' complaints about him playing a victim, he long ago forgave both his parents. What he is still angry about is that aside from his sister, and now me, no one has allowed him to express his pain about being evicted from the family at 17 and left to fend on his own. An attendant feature to his being abandoned by his family at 17 was that he had grown up fully expecting to take over his family's large lucrative business. When kicked out, his vision of his future was obliterated. The safe anchor it provided evaporated and he was left in a world without a foreseeable future. He was robbed of a future world to inhabit.

As with Ben, while his defensive style added to his resilience it at the same time precluded a more satisfying connection to others in his life. For Richard, it was life saving for him to maintain a carefully guarded distance from both men and women. His tough, stoic, strong, hyper-independent, "Marlboro Man," somewhat intimidating veneer, while socially and professionally attractive, kept him from a more flexible affective life while it at the same time fueled his resiliency. Likewise, his controlled and controlling stance with others has always kept him in a one-up winner's position but constricted in his relationships. As with Ben, in treatment I have both confronted and celebrated his resilient features. They have provided for his survival while robbing him of fuller satisfying relationships with others.

Richard is grateful for the opportunity to express his feelings and conflicts in therapy with me. Ironically, in his line of work as a political advisor he is often called upon to assess the feelings and experience of others in order to assist with implementing political policy decisions. He is a master at reading the mood of others in ways that promote resolution in delicate political situations. But, as he notes, he feels unable to express his own feelings, moods and desires in his intimate relationships. What we have discovered is that it is not so much that he has difficulty expressing intimate feelings as much as he has chosen to express them to women who refuse to hear him. To be sure, his wives, like his mother, have been highly reactive and angry women who would chastise him for any attempt on his part to make reference to his traumatic past. They would accuse him of playing the victim and exhort him to buck up. The result is that he has never told his story, even in prior therapies, for fear of being accused as weak. Now, approaching his twilight years, he desperately wants to express himself before it is too late. We have created a safe place for him to do that and he is grateful.

Since my writing the first draft of this paper, Richard has met and married a woman who is more than willing to hear and be empathic to the traumas in his life. She has proven to be a wonderful partner. As he says, "I finally, in my seventies, got this marriage thing right." As I put it, casting a jaundiced eye at Freud's warnings about the limited potential for change in late life, our patients can most definitely aspire to and achieve life-altering change throughout the lifespan.

A major influence on his resilience had been his relationship with his children. The family constellation is a complex one with four natural children (all boys) and two adopted children (one boy and one girl) of a different race. His son has had difficulty with his own addiction to drugs, but appears to be functioning well at present. A further complication was the tragic death, several years ago, of one of his sons from a rare degenerative disease. His steadfastness with his children as a father has been a source of great pride to him. He shoulders great guilt for the years when he was drinking and was much less available to them. He is concerned that he is not as close to them as he would like to be. He has made it known that he wants to compensate for the years he was lost to alcohol. As treatment progressed his relationships with his children become closer and increasingly intimate. He is perched firmly as the patriarch of the family.

Our relationship has manifold facets. In the transference I am alternately his passive father, idealized cousin savior, and his son with whom he can feel paternalistic. Apparently, my perception of his process of aging being one step ahead of mine is matched by his perceiving me as one step behind him. He will frequently, when talking about his declining health, point out to me that I'll experience similar difficulty in due time. To my narcissistic horror, I cannot only relegate his medical forecasts for me as transferential hostility, but must acknowledge their possibility as imminently possible if not probable. While I considered his predictions to be a manifestation of his envy at my younger age, I have come to realize that they also fall in the realm of avuncular as well as commiseration rather than conveyers of resentful envious put-downs.

This is one juncture where my own resilience as an analyst is sorely tested. As I noted, not only with Richard, but also with most of my elderly patients, I am confronted with what feels like a daily bombardment of 'Chronos', of real time mortal, life-ending realities. My own omnipotent, narcissistic illusions of living forever are repeatedly called out on the carpet, and ruthlessly squelched. Issues of loss, both of others as well as my own capacities, hover in the room like unwanted visitors outstaying their welcome. The possibility of illness in all its possible incarnations looms like the wild strands of Medusa's hair. In order to maintain a concordant, empathic response with my patient I am forced to experience my own demise in an experience-near fashion that is distinctly more stressful than when I was younger and could more easily deny or avoid any personal threat from the ravages of time. And then I need to recover, to right myself and maintain a calm therapeutic stance. And this occurs several times a day. Again, we are all asked to confront our own anxiety ridden conflicts during the course of our work. It's a necessity if we are to do this work properly.

Internally, Richard maintains a steadfast identification with his passive father that informs his self-perception despite his career success. It's an identification he also brings to his relationship with each of his rather strident, insecure wives. This identification does not appear to have contributed to his resiliency, except perhaps through a powerful counter identification, a commitment he adheres to in order to de-identify with his father. He is aware that his decision to adopt disadvantaged children was an attempt to undo the abandonment these children experienced from their own parents, thereby undoing the abandonment he suffered from his.

On another note, when considering both young Ben and old Richard's resiliency, it also has become evident to me that for the most part they both function in the depressive position. The organization of their self and objects are both complicated but integrated. Their internal worlds may split into part object functioning, but the tension between their paranoid/schizoid and their depressive position organizations lean heavily in the direction of depressive position, integrated whole self and object representations. In thinking about Ben and Richard and other resilient patients I have worked with, I would tentatively though heuristically conjecture that resiliency requires the ability to achieve depressive level functioning. This would also suggest that someone in their lives provided a good enough object experience even when it was lacking from their parents. This idea meshes well with the literature on resiliency that often attributes a child's resiliency to exposure to someone other than their parents who has taken an active interest in their well-being.

I hoped to have demonstrated that a psychoanalytic understanding of both Ben and Richard provides a useful addition to a traditional trait-based classification of resiliency. Both patients possess some of the aforementioned classic characteristic traits of resilient people; they are intelligent, attractive, active with a sense of agency, and able to self-reflect.

A psychoanalytic exploration goes beyond a trait based understanding of their resiliency. We can discover aspects of each that adds to an ideographic understanding of their unique inner lives and allow me to be more empathic with their experience. Ben's idealized image of himself as a strong, providing penis and likewise Richard's identification with an idealized cousin contributed to their fortitude. These internal objects were the stars of the individual narratives that fostered their resilience. Richard's narrative was of a strong, silent tough guy while for Ben it was of a strong nurturing provider. These narratives of resilience, however, contradicted our psychoanalytic conceptions of well-being in that they were comprised of a measure of rigidified adaptive (what Winnicott called "false") self. I found myself balancing on a tightrope attempting to both celebrate and challenge their fortitude. The trick was to find a way to help them understand the adaptations they creatively adopted in order to survive and allow them to put some of those more rigid adaptations aside while still maintaining their integrity and fortitude.

As for my resiliency in working with an older population, the stress of the countertransference does not, of course, approach traumatic proportions like the traumas suffered by my patients. But significant and profound issues of aging, bordering on the traumatic, are evoked and must be tolerated. I have learned a great deal from working with people who's advanced age led Freud to conclude they were not suitable for psychoanalysis and now find the work deeply rewarding. And lo and behold, my older patients are beginning to look a lot younger to me every day.

Note

1 A previous version of this paper was presented at Austin Society for Psychoanalytic Psychology Fall, 2011 Conference.

References

Abraham, K. (1919). The applicability of psycho-analytic treatment to patients at an advanced age. In *Selected Papers* (pp. 312–317). New York: Basic Books, 1953.

Anthony, E.J. (1987). Risk, vulnerability and resilience: An overview. In E.J. Anthony and B.J. Cohler (eds.), *The Invulnerable Child* (pp. 3–48). New York: Guilford Press.

Clauss-Ehlers, C.S., Yang, Y.T. and Chen, W.J. (2006). Resilience from childhood stressors: The role of cultural resilience, ethnic identity, and gender identity. *Journal of Infant, Child and Adolescent Psychotherapy*, 5: 124–138.

Davies, J.M. (2015). From Oedipal complex to Oedipal complexity: Reconfiguring (pardon the expression) the negative Oedipus complex and the disowned erotics of disowned sexualities. *Psychoanalytic Dialogues*, 25: 265–283.

Davis, N.J. (2001). Resilience in childhood and adolescence. Presented at Media conference at George Washington University, Washington, DC.

Eisold, B. (2005). Notes on lifelong resilience: Perceptual factors implicit in the reaction of a particular adaptive style. *Psychoanalytic Psychology*, 22: 411–425.

Fajardo, B. (1991). Analyzability and resilience in development. *The Annual of Psychoanalysis*, 19: 107–126.

Fenichel, O. (1945). *The Psychoanalytic Theory of Neurosis*. New York: Norton.

Fonagy, P., Steele, M., Steele, H. and Higgitt, A. (1994). The Emmanuel Miller lecture, 1992: The theory of practice of resilience. *Journal of Child Psychology and Psychiatry and Allied Disciplines*, 35: 231–257.

Freud, S. (1905). On psycho-therapy. In J. Strachey (ed. and trans.), *The Standard Edition of the Complete Psychological Works of Sigmund Freud* (Vol. 7, pp. 257–268). London: Hogarth Press.

King, P. (1980). The life cycle as indicated by the nature of the transference in the psychoanalysis of the middle-aged and elderly. *International Journal of Psychoanalysis*, 61: 153–160.

Kumpfer, K.L. (1999). Factors and processes contributing to resilience: The resilience framework. In M.D. Glantz and J.L. Johnson (eds.), *Resilience and Development: Positive Life Adaptations* (pp. 179–224). New York: Kluwer Academic/Plenum.

Luthar, S.S., Doernberger, C.H. and Zigler, E. (1993). Resilience is not a unidimensional construct: Insights from a perspective study of inner city adolescents. *Dev. Psychopathol.*, 5: 703–717.

Masten, A.S., Hubbard, J.J., Gest, S.D., Tellegen, A., Garmezy, N. and Ramirez, M. (1999). Competence in the context of adversity: Pathways to resilience and maladaptation from childhood to late adolescence. *Development and Psychopathology*, 11: 145–169.

Pianta, R.C. and Walsh, D.J. (1998). Applying the construct of resilience in schools: Cautions from a developmental systems perspective. *School Psychol. Rev.*, 27: 407–417.

Plotkin, F. (2000). Treatment of the older adult: The impact on the psychoanalyst. *Journal of the American Psychoanalytic Association*, 48: 1591–1616.

Racker, H. (1957). The meanings and uses of countertransference. *Psychoanalytic Quarterly*, 26(3): 303–357.

Rak, C.F. and Peterson, L.E. (1996). Promoting resilience in at-risk children. *Journal of Counseling and Development*, 74(4): 368–373.

Rutter, M. (1985). Resilience in the face of adversity: Protective factors and resistance to disorder. *British Journal of Psychiatry*, 147: 598–611.

Segal, H. (1958). Fear of death: Notes on the analysis of an old man. *International Journal of Psychoanalysis*, 39: 178–181.

Skolnick, N. (2006). What's a good object to do? *Psychoanalytic Dialogues*, 16: 1–27.

Werner, E.E. (1985). Stress and protective factors ni children's lives. In A.R. Nicol (ed.), *Longitudinal Studies in Child Psychology and Psychiatry* (pp. 335–355). New York: Wiley.

Werner, E.E. and Smith, R.S. (1992). *Overcoming the Odds: High Risk Children from Birth to Adulthood*. Ithaca: Cornell University Press.

Chapter 8

Rethinking the use of the couch

A relational perspective[1]

Introduction

A number of years ago, as I was teaching the first class of my semester-long course on Fairbairn, a course I had been teaching at the NYU Postdoctoral Program in Psychoanalysis and Psychoanalytic Psychotherapy for many years, I remarked that I was no longer using the couch for all my patients undergoing a psychoanalysis. Two students decided to drop the course on the spot. When questioned they, with visible anger, told me that if I didn't use the couch, I was not conducting a psychoanalysis and they had no interest in taking a class that was not about psychoanalysis. I was somewhat taken aback because the NYU Postdoctoral Program was, and still is, ensconced in an academic setting, not a freestanding institute. As such, students typically expected that the courses were taught in a non-doctrinaire, academic style where questioning and healthy skepticism was the rule rather than the exception. Nonetheless, these two disgruntled candidates were unimpressed and decided to go search for a course in real psychoanalysis, not fake psychoanalysis. And of course they were not alone. How often have we heard criticism of theory or technique that strays from Freud's opus, and is, with intent to shame, held up as not psychoanalysis? At best, the critics might concede it is a watered-down version of psychoanalysis sometimes referred to as "supportive" and appropriate for patients not "healthy" enough to endure the rigors of a "real" psychoanalysis. Be it off the couch, of lesser frequency, or with an analyst who actually talks to his/her patients, sometimes even self-revealing, these "parameters" (Eissler, 1953), as they used to be called, were added on if the patient was deemed in some fashion unable to undergo a "real" psychoanalysis.

This strict "constitution-like" adherence to Freud's text, despite the fact that Freud himself strayed from it, became a powerful disincentive for others to modify, reject or creatively expand psychoanalytic theory or technique. As we know from history, many early acolytes (i.e., Jung, Ferenczi) were actually thrown out of the club should they publicly repudiate his ideas. This situation continues into the present. After spending countless hours of study and supervised clinical work, let alone enormous sums of money, to be allowed into the psychoanalytic "club," many analysts are afraid of being labeled something less than a *real* psychoanalyst should they stray from a strict doctrinaire orientation. After working countless hours with countless patients from a psychoanalytic orientation, I find it difficult to understand how any psychoanalyst can adhere to a strict reading of Freud. Considering the uniqueness of each patient, their unique histories, their unique developmental trajectories, their unique responses to analysis and their unique outcomes in therapy, etc., it amazes me that clinicians would adhere to a singular emphasis on "correct" psychoanalytic technique, rather than an emphasis on tailoring their technique to the unique situation and needs of each patient. As Fairbairn (1958) said in his most well-known paper on technique:

> In general I cannot help feeling that any tendency to adhere with pronounced validity to the details of the classic psychoanalytic technique, as standardized by Freud more than a half century ago, is liable to defensive exploitation, however unconscious this may be, in the interests of the analyst and at the expense of the patient, and certainly any tendency to treat the classic technique as sacrosanct raises the suspicion that an element of such a defensive exploitation is at work.
>
> (p. 81)

Once unmoored from classical psychoanalytic drive theory and technique, and its more contemporary variants such as ego psychology, a refreshing breeze propelled me toward reconsidering some of the standard bearers of a classical approach from a range of relational perspectives. I employ the plural – *perspectives* – because just as there is no singular object relations theory, or self psychology theory, so too is there no one, unified relational psychoanalytic theory. As I have noted repeatedly throughout the chapters of this book, I tend to envision relational psychoanalysis as a theoretical tent casting its umbral shadow over those theorists (psychoanalytic and others) who do not regard Freud's metapsychological drives as the building blocks of character, development, pathology and treatment. These schools would include interpersonal, object relations, self psychology, aspects of Kleinian and contemporary Kleinian theory, infant researchers, and more recently Bionian theory and field theory.

In the present chapter I reconsider the use of the couch in psychoanalysis, perhaps the most iconic representation of the entire endeavor. I review the history of its use from Freud's initial declaration of preferring it because he tired of people staring at him all day, every day, to his bestowing it with necessary status, to variations in recommendations for its use. I consider criticisms of its use from conservative to radical. I consider why some analysts still prefer to use the couch. Ultimately, I conclude that while using the couch has its merits for some patients, it should by no means be considered as a necessary and imperative requirement for a treatment to be labeled a psychoanalysis. I also encourage analysts to use the couch for at least some period during all psychoanalyses.

Issues of time can also can intersect with the use of the couch, and their interaction can play a crucial role in many of the standard bearers of psychoanalytic technique. These rituals are typically the concerns of *Chronos, objective tick-tock* time, such as the length of a session or the length of a 'complete' treatment. How long should a termination process take? Should a segment of termination be conducted off the couch? Cancellation issues can be vexing and they typically are interwoven with time considerations. Tradition dictates the ubiquitous "24-hour" rule, that a patient must cancel a session no less than 24 hours before the session or be charged for it. In my practice, I long ago shed the 24-hour rule for a more flexible, "for the occasion" rule. This rule requires that patients need to notify me of a cancellation with enough advanced time *for the particular occasion*. For example, if the boss sends the patient for a meeting in Boston less than a day before the session, I do not hold the patient responsible.[2] Related are issues of lateness (analyst and patient) or earliness (patient). Needless to say, for an analyst, these issues can attract infinite meanings, such as sexual or aggressive or monetary. Then there are issues of power, oppositional tendencies, or obsequious obeisance to rules. The temporal issues are endless. And these are just the objective, tick-tock *chronos* issues.

Subjective issues of time, or *Kairos*, set the context for so much that arises in an analysis. As I have noted a number of times throughout this book, past, present and future dance in fantastical ways across a patient's

200 Neil J. Skolnick

narrative field, creating new meanings, new memories or distortions of old ones, space for growth, confusions, or new certainties and new questions. Regressions and progressions are charted in time. *Après coups* and *nachträglichkeit* are powerful subjective phenomena whose trickery can render older memories and meanings either expanded or vestigial. Time is ever-present in the psychoanalytic process, prompting Meissner (2007) to claim that time should be considered of the essence of the entire endeavor:

> Time is of the essence in psychoanalysis. It is of the essence both in terms of external time parameters within which the analytic process is conducted and in terms of the intrapsychic subjective processes of time experience that govern our attitudes toward, use of, and experience of the time phenomenon . . . Analyst and patient engage each other in a parallel flow of time experience on multiple levels, both verbal and linguistic and nonverbal and paralinguistic (in Stern, 2004).
>
> (p. 59)

Given that time is free to travel backwards and forwards during a psychoanalytic session, one would imagine that the couch is particularly suited to foster time's subjective peripatetic tendencies. Freedom from the analyst's eye contact could promote both a focus inward and also an unmooring of the analysand from the clock. Indeed I have found that to be the case with many patients, but definitely not with all. First, I have noticed that a number of patients feel perfectly free to wander in time and space while sitting up and facing me. Conversely, I've worked with a number of people who become, at times, intolerably anxious when on the couch and cling to concrete indices of time. ("What time is it?" "How much longer do I have?" "I think I'll sit up for the last few minutes.") Regardless of the source of the anxiety, they are unable to loosen the moorings of time while on the couch. As I say in my ensuing paper about the use of the couch, an analyst needs to feel free to put patients on the couch and take them off, depending on the experience of their patients at differing points of time in the work. In essence, I argue for a measure of flexibility when using the couch, or not. Each patient is unique in their relationship to the couch, as is each analyst, and each analyst/patient pairing. Furthermore, each patient, analyst and pairing are unique in their relationship to the couch at different points in time. In concluding this brief introduction on a relational consideration of the couch ceremonial, I maintain that as we shift to a relational model of psychoanalysis it would be beneficial to take this opportunity to re-examine a number of our technical assumptions. Moreover, I am suggesting that we formulate newer models of technique at the nexus of relational theories, temporal issues and technical concerns.

Notes

1 This paper was originally published in *Contemporary Psychoanalysis* (2015), 51: 624–628.
2 Actually, my cancellation policy is more complicated. I bill for all sessions, attended or not, with some exceptions. If the cancellation is in good faith, as in *for the occasion*, I do bill but offer a makeup (not charged). If I perceive the patient has just blown off the session, for no good reason, I bill and do not offer a makeup. Whereas if there is a death or serious illness I do not bill. And so forth and so on. In my experience, there is no one-size-fits-all cancellation policy. My policy tends to be almost tailor-made for the individual patient. I try to balance my need for income with fairness and respect for the patient's circumstances.

References

Eissler, K.R. (1953). The effect of the structure of the ego on psychoanalytic technique. *Journal of the American Psychoanalytic Association*, 1: 104–143.
Fairbairn, W.R.D. (1958). On the nature and aims of psychoanalytic treatment. *International Journal of Psycho-Analysis*, 39: 374–385.
Meissner, W.W. (2007). *Time, Self, and Psychoanalysis*. New York: Jason Aronson.
Stern, D.N. (2004). *The Present Moment in Psychotherapy and in Everyday Life*. New York: Norton.

Chapter 8

Rethinking the use of the couch
A relational perspective[1]
2015

Neil J. Skolnick

Introduction

A number of years ago, during the course of a long and relatively successful analysis with an attractive, intelligent and narcissistically scarred 30-something married woman,[2] talk about sex pervaded the treatment room. Yet, despite my best efforts, analytic sex never happened. Neither verbal nor physiological passion was aroused in either of us toward the other and the transference–countertransference arena remained a virtual sexual wasteland. Given the combined heritage of a sexually abusive cousin, a sexually abused and deadened mother, and a brother who was inappropriately seductive if not actually abusive, we addressed sexuality from many corners of this woman's inner and outer world. As with many adults who had been sexually abused, she infused the majority of her relationships with sexually tinged behavior and affects meant to define, control and ensure relatedness. It remained an ongoing source of puzzlement to me that the transference–countertransference interaction itself was devoid of sexual charge. A year or so into the treatment, she engaged in a long and sexually torrid affair with a man that was secreted from her husband and discussed freely with me.

Although I made a number of attempts to elicit whether she experienced sexual feelings toward me, she could not locate them. Either they did not exist, or perhaps they did, but she was reluctant to express them. Being transference-savvy herself (she did not work in the field, but rather she was a systems analyst and had experience with prior therapy), she was puzzled by this. She could intellectually acknowledge that her affair might involve some transference implications (e.g., "acting out"), but could not locate transference in her affects, thoughts, dreams, wishes or fantasies pertaining to me.

Analytically humbled, I became resigned to the possibility that we might never understand, never consummate, this transference–countertransference piece, and relegated it to one of the unknowable regions of my work with her. After all, hadn't she made considerable progress in the analysis? Hadn't she become unstuck in love and work" Maybe a "good-brother" transference was all she really needed anyway.

And then she sat up. Toward the winding down of the analysis, when the frequency[3] of the sessions was reduced, she requested increased face-to-face contact with me. We both agreed, upon exploration, that the impending termination had awakened a need to have more visual contact with me.[4]

And we were both equally surprised by the consequences. First, I saw her eyes; eyes that were striking, stunning, engaging, seductive, compelling and overpowering. Years of quick greetings and swift goodbyes had accorded our eyes the most fleeting of contact, as the couch was hastily settled into or rapidly departed. Likewise, she now had access to my eyes – eyes that could be available to her as the leading edge of a new object relationship. A new mode of relating, a seeming portal to as yet unknown self and other psychic states and organizations, was opened to both of us.

And sure enough, when she sat up, full-blown transferential sex made its long awaited debut in our analytic space. Both of us experienced sexual charge. For her as I now discovered, sex – visually and viscerally – was control and control was sex. In as much as my eyes could appear loving or assaulting, the imperative for her became to ensure safety, via control by eye contact, and especially sexual control. We came to understand that in her efforts to tolerate a pervasive series of overly stimulating, overly seductive and actually abusive encounters with her brother and her cousin, she had internalized a set of self and object relationships that demanded that she ensure sexual seduction as the currency of any and all relationships. Without sexual contact, either actual or symbolic, relationships (including with me in the transference) remained for her vaguely unreal, without vitality and hopelessly ephemeral. Tremendous wells of shame also became available for our analytic inspection. Following these paths of shame led us to as yet unrecovered memories of her brother being present when her cousin abused her, and ultimately to actual abuse by her brother himself.

We began to understand that her sexual trauma had also been enacted in her family symbolically by means of a puzzling and paradoxical ritual that was established to concurrently display and deny the sexual transgression that had occurred. At family celebrations, she would don her sexiest, most slinky and vampish dresses and rush to dance with her brother, usually at the enthusiastic insistence of her relatives who came to expect and delight in their "performance." They would eat up the dance floor, garnering the gaping stares and cheers of the guests. They were, in essence, publicly displaying their sexual ritual for all to witness and at the same time they were inducing in the spectators a massive, externalized dissociation of their incestuous enactment. Instead of horror, they created spectacle. She and her brother exercised absolute control as they focused all eyes on them, while remaining totally unaware and dissociated from the incestuous replay of their display. They danced on and on, in a continuous frenzy of look but don't look, see but don't see, the horrific truth of their denied incest.

Moreover, her ongoing progress in therapy became exemplified by her evolving attitude toward this ritual. At the outset of treatment she proudly pronounced what a fabulous pair she and her brother made, dazzling friends and relatives with their dance performance. Much later in treatment, when dissociative processes were significantly lessened, she experienced overwhelming shame and humiliation at the image of the two of them "doing it" on the dance floor. We came to understand that these public displays were desperate attempts to reveal what was known, what could be seen, but could never be spoken. So the couch, in effect, proved to be iatrogenic, preventing (or perhaps buttressing her own dissociative defenses against) the sexual enactment with me, the acknowledgment of which turned out to be crucial for her growth.

It does not require much of a leap to understand the inadequacy of the couch – and its forced exclusion of eye contact – to access the experience of sexual abuse. As pointed out by a number of my patients who suffered sexual abuse, eye contact is a crucial and neglected aspect of the phenomenology of the immediate abusive encounter and its aftermath. As a witness to their trauma, I began to imagine myself into the experience of a child meeting the eyes of the sexual tormenter, especially if that abuser was a family member. What is seen during those moments of intense familiarity, unspeakable arousal and intense abusive betrayal? The previous psychic organizations the child has constructed with a cherished love object are traumatically challenged as they are forced to confront a Bosch-like visualization of hell (Gibson, 1973). Love and hate, rage and excitement, betrayal and romance, existence and nonexistence vie for psychic space, just as the familiar meanings and scenarios of occupying psychic space are shattered by the impact of a vertiginous tornado. And the next day, the family sits down together, as usual, for breakfast. Where do their eyes land, and what might they be announcing, denying or both? The ultimate trauma for my patient was the impossible pairing of affirmation and annihilation, experienced in the contact with her brother's eyes during the actual abusive episode.

When my patient sat up, a crucial and yet unknown set of self and other organizations became available for our analytic examination. We spoke about the effects on each other of our mutual eye contact when sitting face to face. We discovered that, prior to sitting up, eye contact had been scrupulously avoided and – for her – eye contact had always been a crucial component of her interpersonal regulatory adaptation. She was an attractive woman, but it was primarily with her eyes that she captured, controlled and transformed the other. Deprived (or perhaps avoidant) of this opportunity with me by virtue of her being on the couch, this particular and pervasive dynamic never became manifest in the transference–countertransference relationship. Being characteristically compliant, she remained on the couch throughout most of the treatment. Toward the end of work together, she was able to muster the assertiveness to ask to sit up, a need she had felt previously but had been reluctant to ask for because it might go against "correct" analytic technique.[5]

I later realized that I had been colluding with her avoidance of eye contact with me. I often felt a strange visual sensation when she came into the office and our eyes met for a millisecond before she assumed her usual position on the couch. But I was at a loss to verbalize the experience. It was only when we were sitting face to face that the experience became available to conscious thought and thus could be verbalized. I came to realize that the discomfort I had been feeling during our brief visual contact was composed of powerful opposing forces to look and not look, to sexually desire, and to be overcome with massive shame and humiliation.

We learned of an overpowering and lopsided tension between her desire and her dread of seducing me, as well as her complementary desire and dread of being seduced by me. One experiential pole had required seduction by either of us to ensure and control my love and connection. For her, seduction would have vitalized our relationship, giving it a three-dimensional texture and charge. It was a paradox that she was terrified that were she to achieve seductive success, she would relinquish total control, act inappropriately and overwhelm me with powerful, uncontrollable, overstimulating lust (the lust she identified with and internalized from actual sexually abu-sive encounters). She feared ultimately being reduced to an unbearable smoldering heap of humiliation and shame. As you might imagine, shame and humiliation intruded massively into many corners of her experience. The sexually charged Scylla and Charybdis of seducing or being seduced conspired to keep our relationship avoidant and devoid of sexual desires or fantasies. Having no eye contact, maintained by virtue of her being on the couch, ensured safety at the expense of a fully vitalized connection. This changed radically when she sat up.

I contend that by shifting from the couch to an upright position both of us engaged a fundamental and visually mediated psychic organization of her relational self. Additional organizations of self and other became fully available to the therapy only after she sat up, allowing her eyes, my eyes and our eyes to enter the room. Our therapeutic relationship entered new experiential realms. I felt the enormous power of her seduction and the power of her eye contact, and a full palette of sexual feelings toward her awoke in me, along with accompanying guilt, shame and fear. As with other analysts working with adults who had been abused, I began to experience multiple shifting countertransferential states inherent to the abusive situation (Davies and Frawley, 1994): the seductive abuser, the abused, the indifferent mother, the caring bystander and the neglectful bystander, to mention a few. As these roles made their presence in the here-and-now of the transference–countertransference interaction, we were able to examine them in experience-near, safe ways. Although the analysis had already freed her to embrace and experience pleasure in expanded areas of her life, these accomplishments became even more pronounced with a reduction of her shameful, guilt-ridden sexuality, sexuality that pervasively blanketed her experiences within familial, professional and community relationships.

Would this pivotal piece of analysis have eventually surfaced had she remained on the couch? Would this have been a complete analysis had she never sat up? Should she have sat up earlier? For the entire treatment? Should all analyses be conducted in both modes? Were the gains she had made in treatment prior to sitting up substantial enough or were they just a prologue to the changes she made when sitting up? This clinical experi-ence, along with others, led me to reconsider, from a relational perspective, yet another psychoanalytic shibboleth: our tenacious hold on the definitive pairing of psychoanalysis with the required use of the couch.[6]

With the advent of relational models of psychoanalysis, and the concomitant emphasis on intersubjectivity (Skolnick and Warshaw, 1992), it was inevitable that many of our clinical and technical recommendations, conventions and assumptions would reverberate with the rippling tides of theoretical change and beg reconsideration. Both Bass (2007) and Davies (1994), among others, have written about their experiences with injecting increased flexibility into the frame of the treatment situation. It is not surprising that some of our more cherished and timeworn technical customs have lagged behind recently emerging (and at times, momentous) theoretical revisions. Outfitted by the weighty trappings of our professional heritage, we conservatively cling to precedence. Precedence masquerading as validity gives us the permission (and comfort) to hold onto unquestioned standard-bearers, despite dramatic new theory that loosens our conventional clinical assumptions and casts us into uncharted technical waters. There are many reasons for psychoanalysts of all colors and stripes to maintain conventional techniques and act as if these are sacrosanct, even as we explore and embrace new theory. A number of hypotheses have been proposed for our continued insistence on the use of the couch to define a psychoanalysis. These will become clearer as I discuss the historical rationales for, and criticisms of, its use.

The couch in psychoanalytic heritage

In my experience, no holdover of Freudian technique has been subjected to less questioning than the use of the couch in psychoanalysis.[7] There have always been distant rumblings (Fairbairn, 1958; Fenichel, 1941), but how many of those rumblings have actually trickled down to clinical practice? One of the more scathing criticisms of the couch was put forth by Robertiello (1967):

> It is pretty well accepted that it is the therapist's personal impact much more than his theoretical frame of reference that produces change. And, of course, on this score the use of the couch and the classical technique keeps this at an absolute minimum. It is really quite an anomaly that therapists have been going out of their way for the past 60 years to minimize their most effective tool . . . It [the couch] is truly a ridiculous anachronism . . . it is an interesting museum piece and something amusing like a chastity belt or a washboard.
>
> (p. 69)

Other criticisms have come from leaders of the interpersonal school. Neither Sullivan nor Fromm used the couch (Schachter and Kachele, 2010). Ben Wolstein (personal communication, c. 1986), a former supervisor of mine and venerable senior analyst steeped in Sullivan's interpersonal tradition, admitted once that he really could not defend the use of the couch for an interpersonal analysis. Nonetheless he used it, and planned to use it always, because, he stated, in so many words, it's part of our professional tradition and wardrobe, and besides, we just do. In several informal surveys I conducted among analysts of differing theoretical backgrounds I found that in general less than one-third of their patients were treated with psychoanalysis on the couch. The consensus of another group of analysts whom I encountered at a series of meetings in Vienna was that the only patients they placed on the couch were analysts-in-training. Edgar Levenson (as reported in Schachter and Kachele, 2010) claimed that none of the candidates in training with him at the William Alanson White Institute use the couch.

Thus, despite the occasionally voiced criticism, Moraitis (1995, p. 275), issue editor of an issue of *Psychoanalytic Inquiry* devoted entirely to the use of the couch, noted that the couch technique is the "least controversial issue in psychoanalysis." It is interesting that a 2008 pilot questionnaire of graduates of the White Institute found that "77% of the recent graduate respondents had used the couch either all the time or frequently throughout their own training analyses" (Schachter and Kachele, 2010). Not of inconsequential importance, the couch has become almost synonymous with psychoanalysis; its use heralded with pride and accomplishment; its essence held up as our very trademark and logo. Its iconic status is well-founded.

No historical retrospective on the couch would be complete without consideration of Freud's original recommendation for its use. This recommendation appeared in Freud's (1913/1955), "On beginning the treatment," and is worth repeating:

> Before I wind up these remarks on beginning analytic treatment, I must say a word about a certain ceremonial which concerns the position in which the treatment is carried out. I hold to the plan of getting the patient to lie on a sofa while I sit behind him out of his sight. This arrangement has a historical basis; it is the remnant of the hypnotic method out of which psycho-analysis was evolved. But it deserves to

be maintained for many reasons. The first is a personal motive, but one which others may share with me. I cannot put up with being stared at by other people for eight hours a day (or more).

(pp. 133–134)

In the same paper, Freud then de-emphasizes his personal motive for recommending a horizontal position and elevates it to a technical imperative:

I insist on this procedure . . . for its purpose and result are to prevent the transference from mingling with the patient's associations imperceptibly, to isolate the transference and to allow it to come forward in due course sharply defined as a resistance. I know that many analysts work in a different way, but I do not know whether this deviation is due more to a craving for doing things differently or to some advantage which they find they gain by it.

(p. 134)

Others have speculated that there might have been other motives that propelled Freud to place his patients on the couch. Schachter and Kachele (2010), noting the difficulty Freud had with criticisms from his colleagues, speculate that by placing patients on the couch, Freud was protecting himself from his patients' disagreements and criticisms.

Nonetheless, as noted by many (Fairbairn, 1958; Gedo, 1995; Jacobson, 1995), the couch, for Freud, evolved from a holdover of hypnotic procedure to a personal preference in order not to be stared at, to ultimately a procedural imperative necessary for the isolation of the transference resistance. Perhaps his not-so-subtle insinuation that the non-use of the couch represented oppositional tendencies on the part of the offending analyst contributed to the couch procedure, in fairly rapid order, assuming its time-honored position as one of the preeminent fixtures of psychoanalytic treatment. Moraitis (1995) pithily states, "generally speaking there seems to be an implicit consensus among psychoanalysts that using the couch in psychoanalytic treatment constitutes the sine qua non of the whole enterprise" (p. 275).

In addition to Freud's original rationale, other justifications for using the couch have been proposed. Its use has been most frequently thought to increase free association, which in and of itself is thought to be therapeutic. Many feel that free association leads to an expression of a patient's conflicts and inhibitions and ultimately to understanding and interpretation (Schachter and Kachele, 2010). Aside from the consensus that there is no consensus as to what free association actually is and who is capable of producing free associations, it has been noted by several analysts that it does not necessarily lead to therapeutic gain (Bordin, 1966; Schachter and Kachele, 2010).

Other analysts may feel that the couch increases the focus on interior states. There are analysts who claim that patients lying on the couch are less defensive and less inhibited than those in a sitting up position. Closely related are analysts, especially those with a Winnicottian bent, who hold that the couch offers a comfortable, warm holding environment, allowing for the provision of maternal ministrations.

In addition, there are the hosts of unstated reasons that people employ the couch. These have more to do with feelings of professional allegiances and efficacy. Using the couch is thought of as doing "real" analysis, probing the deepest strata of a patient's personal experience. Often when an analyst notes that his or her patient is on the couch, he is not only announcing that a "real" psychoanalysis is taking place, but also averring, with a degree of professional esteem and pride, that he or she is a "real" analyst and not conducting a merely supportive psychoanalytic psychotherapy.

I propose that with the shift to an emphasis on relational models, the historical rationales for the mandatory use of the couch have been stretched to their theoretical limits. If one maintains an allegiance to a strictly one-person model, one in which transference is shaped entirely out of the patient's internal world and projected onto the analyst, who only promotes, isolates and interprets it, then the use of the couch – for the most part – remains indisputable. If one adheres to a model of psychoanalysis that holds that psychic truth is uncovered by the analyst and the treatment method aims at revealing a positivistic truth of the dynamic unconscious, then the use of the couch makes continued sense. However, if psychoanalysis is ensconced in a hermeneutic scientific paradigm (Gill, 1983; Hoffman, 1998), where a relativistic truth is mutually constructed from a set of meanings created by both analyst and analysand in intersubjective space, then it becomes increasingly difficult to justify the use of the couch as the sine qua non of the process.

As noted, Freud's (1913/1955) decision to put his patients in a horizontal position was dictated largely out of a personal preference. One has to admire his candor when stating he simply did not like being looked at hour after hour, day after day. While having personal preferences in doing the work we do makes enormous sense to me, no one technique should be reified. Relational analysts from many theoretical camps have noted that personal preference and style infuse much of our work, whether consciously deliberate or not (Aron, 1996). Numerous hints about our inner and outer lives abound. We all exhibit place variations in decor, comfort, distance, lighting, seating arrangements and so forth that are both an expression of careful clinical thought but also include a large measure of personal preference, style and issues unique to our own characters. What, when and how we intervene are signposts to our inner worlds. Thus, Freud's dictum that the couch is necessary to isolate the transference is rendered almost nonsensical in a relational world in which virtually no psychological event, internal or external, is understood apart from its context.

If we assume psychoanalysis to be a process that attempts to explore and expand the ever-increasing complexities, paradoxes and dialectic tensions of our patients' social and private selves; if we assume it attempts to co-create a reality in which two are primarily devoted to exploring the subjective realities of one (patient); if we assume that we as analysts are devoted to understanding and fleshing out our patients' experiences and needs – to then assume that only one physical, logistical positioning of patient and doctor can accomplish all of the above can be likened to assuming that one can understand and fully appreciate a complex sculpture by looking at it from only one vantage point. That we have deified Freud's recommendation and not allowed for serious experimentation and critical discussion is, unfortunately, one example, of many in our profession, in which precedence can become not only a substitute for validation but, also, virtual tyranny.

Fairbairn (1958), in his now classic article on psychoanalytic technique, states that psychoanalysis is first and foremost a form of therapy, and that:

> The body of theory subsequently elaborated to explain the phenomena elicited in the psychoanalytic situation has, of course, been found to have explanatory value . . . but this does not affect the fact that psychoanalytic technique remains bound up with the psychoanalytic situation in a therapeutic setting. In light of the historical origin of psychoanalysis, it thus becomes a question whether the classic restrictions of the psychoanalytic situation are not in some measure arbitrary.
>
> (p. 80)

He continues by stating that many of the classic restrictions, including – but not limited to – the use of the couch, might indeed serve more to cater to the analyst's own interests, than to the interests of the patient or the therapy. Rooting the mutagenic effects of psychoanalysis first and foremost in the relationship between the patient and analyst, he boldly claims both participants have needs in the situation that must be acknowledged. He makes the pronouncement, unusual for its time, that:

> In general, I cannot help feeling that any tendency to adhere with pronounced rigidity to the details of the classic psychoanalytic technique, as standardized by Freud more than a half century ago, is liable to defensive exploitation, however unconscious this may be, in the interests of the analyst and at the expense of the patient; and certainly any tendency to treat the classic technique as sacrosanct raises the suspicion that an element of such a defensive exploitation is at work.
>
> (p. 81)

In the same spirit, Goldberger (1995) and, more recently, Hirsch (2008), make the well-taken point that the couch can serve the dual purpose of providing a defensive function for both the analyst as well as the patient. From personal experience, I tend to agree. I had become aware, on more than one occasion, that my continued use of the couch appeared to be doing more good for me than for my patient. So it is that I have, with preconscious relief, colluded with a number of patients who, in their characterological efforts to be good, delightful or entertaining, have lulled me into a comfortable and welcomed complacency, even as they continued obediently and productively free-associating on the couch. When awakening from these pleasant and, at times, seductively timeless interludes, it ultimately became a clinical imperative for me to recognize my contribution. By having the patient sit up, transference–countertransference stalemates became alive in affectively charged and highly effective moments (as in the stunning shift when my patient and I had access to each other's eyes). These moments can be profoundly disquieting for both analyst and patient. As noted by the contemporary Kleinian, Irma Pick (1985), analyst disturbance, signaling a profound resonance to a patient's internal object world, is a prerequisite for some of our most exciting and fruitful therapeutic interactions. My contention is that to engage alternate modes of relating (e.g., visual, nonverbal, intersubjective) can be crucial in accessing profound internal dynamic and motivational patterns. These alternate modes can be precluded by the traditional supine position. With the patient I described, sexuality was organized into and experienced through powerful, interpersonal visual cues: cues denied by the use of the couch, yet necessary for a more thorough understanding of her psychic organization and experience. If visual channels of organization are not available because of the use of the couch, what other channels might we be missing? Auditory? Kinesthetic? Positional choice? At one time, Fairbairn (1958) advocated that the patient and analyst sit in chairs near but not directly facing each other, so that the patient could choose when to establish eye contact or not.

Was this not foreshadowing some of Beebe and Lachmann's work (1992) on mother and infant influence on mutual eye contact? Do we want to limit these other modes of relating – as in the classical proscription – or let them flourish, helping us to achieve a greater understanding of a wide range of a patient's idiographic ways of being in the world?

There is increasing evidence from developmental psychoanalysis and the neurosciences that supports the argument for the existence of an "intersubjective motivational system" basic to human functioning (e.g., Emde, 1988; Seligman, 2009; Stern, 1985; Trevarthen, 1993; Tomasello, 1999). Fundamental to the idea of an intersubjective motivational nexus is the existence of mirror neurons. Although research into mirror neurons is still in its infancy, there has been extraordinary evidence stemming from the discovery of mirror neurons that substantiates their role in mediating and enabling intersubjective experience. In brief, intersubjective identification is thought to include domains of action, sensations, affect and emotion that are mediated at the level of mirror neurons in the brain (Gallese, 2009). Mirror neurons are premotor neurons that fire when an action is executed and when it is observed being performed by someone else (Gallese, 2009). The same neurons that are triggered in action are triggered by the observation of that action. Furthermore, it has been demonstrated (Gallese, 2009) that mirror neurons do not merely fire at the visualization of an action, but can fire in ways that represent knowledge of the meaning or intention of the action. If mirror neurons play a role in mediating intersubjective experience, the question follows as to how much valuable psychoanalytic understanding has been limited by limiting visual contact of patient and analyst when using the couch?

Another frequently stated rationale for the use of the couch is to avoid mutual influence. The set-up is thought to prevent the analyst's facial expressions from influencing the patient's associations. Likewise, the reduction in interactional pressures is thought to free the analyst to be more reflective and more able to achieve an ideal analyzing state. Gedo (1995), in particular, notes that by having one's face shielded, the analyst is allowed to respond to the material without constraint, becoming readily aware of the affective aspects of that response. In face-to-face contact, he claims we are more guarded and lose some of our emotional responsiveness. This rationale, it appears to me, has its origins in the conception of the analytic situation as a specialized medical setting, akin to the surgical operating room. Both the analyst and patient are thought to suspend their beliefs in the totality of the human interactional aspects of the situation. Freud promoted this curious form of dissociation when he related to his patients as people outside of the consultation room, feeding them meals and lending them money. These interactions were then relegated to some split-off place, seemingly not affecting the interaction between him and his patients when they were back in the consulting room, in their prescribed places.

We can be grateful that psychoanalysts of all persuasions have noted, and respected, the enormously complicated two-way direction of influence and interaction that occurs between patient and analyst. Patients can be as aware of our states, internal and external, from a fleeting glance as they enter the office, or from the squeak of our chair, as they can by faceto-face contact. Likewise, countertransferential pressures from the couch (i.e., peculiar postures or nonverbal communications) can rattle our "ideal states" as much as eye contact. More to the point, relational analysts, as previously stated, have become less interested in limiting these mutual influences and more interested in using them as the foundation of our clinical data.

Turning from clinical to theoretical rationales for placing patients on the couch, the procedure is thought to put the analysand in an infantile position, promoting a regression. This rationale has received support from a wide spectrum of theoretical orientations. Be it the regression aimed at the development and isolation of the transference neurosis promoted by the classical analyst, or the regression promoted by the object relational analyst geared toward the stripping away of layers of false selves in order to return to the point of interrupted provisions of developmental requisites; the classical self psychologist's goal of resurfacing archaic self-object needs buried within aborted self development; or the contemporary self psychologist's goal of evoking archaic self/self-object constellations: all look to the couch to promote the process.

Newer conceptualizations of regression are emerging that challenge traditional notions. These arise from a number of sources: mother–infant research (Stern, 1985; Beebe and Lachmann, 1992), advances in intersubjectivity theory (Ogden, 1986; Benjamin, 1992; Lichtenberg, 1995; Lichtenberg, Lachmann and Fosshage, 1992) and a reemergence of focus on dissociative and self-state processes (Davies, 1996, 1998; Bromberg, 1996). Ogden (1986, 1989) challenges traditional conceptions of regression in ways that particularly impel a rethinking of the use of the couch. He has provided us with a compelling perspective on the Kleinian concept of "positions" that highlights nonlinear conceptualizations of development and psychic organization. In brief, he defines developmental positions as dialectic generative organizations of experience that both define and negate each other. Instead of existing in stepwise sequence, these developmental positions are posited to exist dialectically, in constant tension with each other, generating experience, both internal and external, throughout life. Functioning in one mode of organizing experience – paranoid/schizoid or depressive – is not thought to be a regression from the other.

To conduct an analysis from a perspective that poses nonlinear, dialectically opposed states of organization involves not a privileging of earlier and/or deeper stages of development (as in a regression), but instead, engaging and disengaging with shifting organizations of experience, constantly defining and negating each other as they struggle for optimal balance. Experience in any position that becomes too rigidified contributes to pathological imbalance. Regression is no longer, therefore, conceived of as linear or unidirectional in such a schema. The patient can be thought to be freer to move in more complicated sequences of experience, either this way or that,[8] circulating among depressive, paranoid/schizoid and autistic/ contiguous organizations. This conceptualization of regression, with its emphasis on lateral, as opposed to vertical movement, renders the model of a linear regression to earlier states, upon which justification for the couch is often predicated, anachronistically limiting.

Lichtenberg et al. (1992) and others (Fosshage, 1992), have presented a strong argument for a reconceptualization of psychoanalytic technique based on the interaction of five basic motivational systems. These systems work in infinite forms of harmony or competing discord as they attempt to steer a well-balanced (or not), cohesive (or not), modulated (or not), flexible (or not) path for the self through life. In their technical vision the analyst is freer and has more flexibility to empathically travel throughout a patient's motivational landscape. Although they do not specifically refer to the use of the couch, it appears self-evident to me that the limiting interaction to the supine position can likewise limit access to the experiential matrices rooted in five shifting motivational systems.

Conservative and radical critiques of the couch technique

Although, as a rule, analysts have been fairly reluctant to give up the couch as a necessary, if not defining feature, of an analysis, there have been rumblings, both recent and past, challenging its use as mandatory. These shifting tides have come in various and ranging forms. For the purposes of explication, I have grouped the correctives proposed into conservative and more radical categories.

Considering the conservative proposals first, these analysts work from the vantage point that the use of the couch is the baseline procedure, and non-use is a deviation from the correct technique. Those working from this perspective typically consider a patient's request to sit up to be the manifestation of a resistance, which calls for insight or interpretation (Gedo, 1995). Another version of this point of view is one that views the couch as baseline, but with patients demonstrating a so-called legitimate need to sit up, usually rooted in severe pathology (Wolf, 1995) or in an ego deficit (Gedo, 1995). In these cases, the request is granted, not necessarily interpreted, and the treatment continues but is considered decidedly "less than" a real analysis, which may or may not continue at some point with the patient back on the couch. In both models, emphasis is on something awry or amiss in the patient, with no consideration of any analyst variables, therefore remaining internally consistent with an exclusively one-person model of therapeutic interaction.

A less conservative approach is one that attempts to describe diagnostic distinctions between those who might better be treated on or off the couch. Lichtenberg (1995), in a particularly candid and refreshing consideration of his own experiences on and off the couch, considers work off the couch to be a psychoanalysis, but makes clear diagnostic distinctions between those patients who might benefit from this type of analysis. In general, the "sicker" the patient, defined by compromised ego functioning or earlier developmental disruption, the more the analysis might need to be conducted sitting up. According to him, these patients might need to work on issues of attachment or communication better served by faceto-face contact. He, like others who take this approach, still maintains the couch as treatment of choice for most patients, except those requiring such a deviation. Another version of this approach considers work off the couch a prerequisite to work on the couch for "sicker" patients who need this deviation.[9] Blatt (1992) finds some evidence that patients with anaclitic psychopathology evidence greater therapeutic gains in working on the couch, whereas patients exhibiting introjective psychopathology evidence the opposite, that is, improving less when using the couch. Of course, many – if not most – patients present with an admixture of anaclitic and introjective concerns.

Shifting to a consideration of more radical proposals for change we find those who no longer consider the couch to be the sine qua non of a psychoanalysis. Fenichel, as early as 1941, was one of the first proponents of this when he wrote that the definition of an analysis should not be based on technique, nor on external measures, but rather on the management of resistance and transference thereby locating the definition of analysis in the nature and goals of the process, separating it from the analyst's behavior or patient's posture. Lichtenberg (1995) sounds a modern version of Fenichel's (1941) prescription when he claims that the couch is neither a trick nor a magical device, but merely a tool and not the defining feature of an analysis. These authors note that for a subset of patients, such as those with excessive shame, or the overly compliant or submissive, the couch can impede an analysis, therefore we need to be elastic in the application of technical rules. Although not considering the couch as the sine qua non of the process, these authors retain the sentiment that treatment on the couch is the first order of business. Although deviations are considered as acceptable procedure, i.e., legal, if we may, they remain as alterations to standard procedure.

Which brings me to the most radical of proposed changes: that is, one that no longer considers the couch to be necessary for an analysis. Jacobson (1995) acknowledges that having a patient sit up calls on the analyst to make a distinction between patients for whom the couch is no longer productive and patients for whom requests to sit up require interpretation, and that the decision is neither simple nor straightforward, often representing a complex mixture of motives. He notes, and I agree, "I don't believe the problem is solved, however, by simply assuming that the couch posture is the baseline that must be unvaryingly maintained" (p. 310).

An implication of this model of complexity would be that a poor fit to the couch does not necessarily represent primitive psychopathology or unsuitability to a psychoanalysis and also that some severely impaired patients can work productively on the couch. Likewise, a "healthier," but compliant, patient on the couch can present as much difficulty analytically as a more dysfunctional patient who might be thought of as needing to sit up.

Schachter and Kachele (2010), after reviewing the research on the effect of the couch on free association and treatment outcome, conclude that there is no empirical evidence for placing all patients on the couch. They recommend that the selection of a position for the patient requires careful, empathic, flexible clinical judgment by the analyst, including consideration of the analyst's own theory, as well as of the patient's personality characteristics and diagnosis.

In sum, a sampling of traditional rationales for the couch procedure has been presented. To this has been added some of the correctives, both conservative and radical, that are proposed by contemporary theorists. If we increasingly become convinced of the relational, intersubjective and contextual nature of the human situation; if we believe more in the evidence from attachment, mother–infant and psychoneurological research in the interactive nature of growth and motivational systems; we can no longer defend the necessary use of the couch. Given the emergence of profoundly different models of regression, psychic organization, development and psychopathology that have arisen from relational paradigmatic shifts, it is but a small step to envision psychoanalysis off the couch as accessing multiple dimensions and organizations of a patient and analyst's interaction, all of which may contribute to psychoanalytic insight and therapeutic gain.

It would be tempting at this point to take these considerations a step further and present an argument for an even more radical approach to using the couch, that is, not to use it at all. We could cast the couch into the wastebasket of quaint anachronistic psychotherapeutic tools, where it could take its rightful place next to the orgone box and phrenology. At one time, I did consider being a proponent of such a position. Instead, my clinical experiences have led me to conclude that the couch can provide one means, though not necessarily the only or best means, to access relational configurations. In several instances, I have found that moving someone *onto* the couch has promoted a psychoanalytic inquiry. I think of two cases.

In both, an ongoing treatment off the couch, although successful in many respects, was not allowing us to access powerful affects that would have advanced the work. One patient was dealing with traumatic preverbal experiences of sexual abuse and the other was dealing with an early experience of the loss of his mother when he was ten years old. Both treatments appeared to have stalled when attempting to access a more complete experience of these early traumas. In both, I was frustrated that this was occurring and took a "let's see what happens on the couch" approach. And the move actually potentiated a vitalized experience of early affects. It is not clear to me why this happened. Although there are numerous possibilities within a relational paradigm why this might have occurred, including, but not limited, to the possibility that the couch reduced the interference of direct eye contact (and its draw toward here and now interactions) to the converse possibility that being on the couch resembled and accessed the self and other interactions occurring at the time of the trauma. What has become clear is that, as I mentioned, there are numerous portals to unconscious experience and we should not limit ourselves to any rigid adherence to a categorical "standardized" technique.

As noted, a relational approach challenges us to consider the transference–countertransference matrix as a complex, often co-constructed, intrapsychic, interpersonal and intersubjective event (Benjamin, 1992; Ghent, 1989; Gill, 1983). Accepting that the analytic relationship is as much a product of the interaction between two subjective worlds as it is the overt manifestation of the separate intrapsychic worlds of each, forces us to reconsider one of the primary rationales for utilizing the couch, that of isolating the transference in its purest – that is, one-person – form. If we no longer view the transference as solely a projection of the patient's internal dynamic structure, and no longer view the countertransference as the reaction of the analyst's unanalyzed internal structure to the transference, then it makes little sense to view either as separate. The transference–countertransference matrix can no longer be considered a static entity to be isolated and held up for inspection, but rather a dynamic, vital, ever-evolving, ever-shifting temporal process contributed to by both parties. In that case, to speak of the couch as isolating the transference is patently absurd.

If, indeed, both the analyst and analysand are contributing to some construction of a narrative truth that emerges in their relationship, then to tie each into prescribed limited and limiting positions does not allow for the complete interaction of their colliding worlds. Finally, if the structural issues of deeper versus surface, or the temporal issues of earlier versus later, are no longer considered crucial to an exploration of the totality of the patient's shifting experience, then the use of the couch to promote a linear regression no longer makes sense as a necessary component of the process.

I think of a woman I treated in a traditional analysis on the couch for approximately seven years. When it ended, I had the nagging feeling that a piece of this woman's experience, namely her pervasive hostility, had not been sufficiently analyzed. My suspicions were supported when, upon termination, she presented me with a gift of a cartoon she had drawn of a laboratory rat(!) laying on an analyst's couch. Fortunately, the treatment resumed after a hiatus of several years. By this time, I had been experimenting with working with patients both on and off the couch, so I recommended sitting up. On the couch, this woman had been depressed, tearful and compliant much of the time. Although I felt and made reference to her hostility, it never directly surfaced in our discussions, except in the most intellectual of forms. When sitting up, the patient became significantly less compliant and began to express a side of herself that had remained asleep on the couch. To my surprise and delight, she possessed a delightful, sophisticated and thoroughly engaging sense of humor that was previously unknown to me. We experienced and discussed her humor from many vantage points, including its major role in the expression of her hostility, which also began to surface more directly in the sessions. Her humor, although at times functioning as a defense, also was embraced as an important and self-maintaining strength of her personality. Had I not seen her face-to-face, would I have ever experienced this facet to her character? Did the first course of analysis free up this facet of her personal idiom, to be revealed only later in the second course?

When she sat up we spoke about the change it engendered in her. She had been raised in a military family (her brother was a high-ranking officer) where strict obedience to authority was the order of the day. She transferred this submissive attitude toward authority to the couch where, she stated, she felt she was expected to obediently comply with the task at hand: serious free association. This submissive attitude did not leave room for humor, let alone any expression of aggression, as that might signal disrespect for the rules and regulations of authority. By contrast, we also learned that she cherished her time off the military base, where she felt significantly freer to express a more spontaneous and less constricted, "duty bound" military-base seriousness. When her humor surfaced, it greatly enhanced my understanding of her psychic equilibrium, particularly as it was closely linked with the accessing, expressing and understanding of her hostility. On the "regulation" couch we approximated the relationship of a rigid officer and his daughter. Off the couch, we were off base (double entendre intended). And it did give me great pause as I wondered what else I might have been missing with all my patients when I confined them to a single posture thought to evoke the entirety of their internal and external experience.

If we view psychoanalysis as a process ultimately aimed at freeing a patient from the constrictions of their past embedded in a closed world of pathological adaptations, then to impose a posture in which the patient remains subordinate and infantilized, if not immobilized, runs the risk, for some, of creating the same situation that got them into difficulty in the first place, at best, or re-traumatizing them at worst. Goldberger (1995) tells of a patient who sat up in order to feel that she indeed did own her treatment. If we maintain that the relationship with the analyst accounts in large measure for therapeutic change (Fairbairn, 1958), then to create this relationship by forcing one of its participants to lay on a Procrustean couch can be seen as impeding the flourishing of the richness and complexity of the relationship.

The patient–analyst relationship is a special, stylized relationship that requires a complicated and well-rehearsed, but flexible, frame. The analytic frame ensures, among other provisions, a safe holding environment (Winnicott, 1951) in which both patient and analyst may feel safe to play with illusory and transitional space. My point is that to accomplish this freedom, we need to be aware of the limitations and constrictions an insistence on the couch might impose. Although part of my conviction in this regard has been dictated by my relational sensibilities and my increasing conviction in a constructivist theoretical approach (Hoffman, 1998), the lion's share of the switch in my technique was propelled by my clinical work in which I began seeing more and more patients off the couch. I became increasingly impressed by the range and depth of the analytic work that could be accomplished without the couch. It increasingly felt to me that the couch was not only impeding the work at times, but that it was instrumental in inducing an artificiality to the clinical situation that detracted from a mutual, genuine contact with my patients, both conscious and unconscious. I can say that since moving my patients off and on the couch, the work feels richer, more multidimensional, and I seriously wonder how much I actually missed by years of confining patients to the couch.

A final note: I have often been asked if I could suggest specific recommendations for when to shift a patient on or off the couch. From my experience, I have adamantly become opposed to any categorical rule in this regard. I consider accessing the uniqueness of each individual to be a major goal of a successful treatment. In brief, the uniqueness of a person perpetually shifts, from self-state to self-state, contextually as well as temporally. I have been impressed with both the depth of exploration some patients can achieve when sitting up as well as the strength of avoidance and denial that can occur on the couch. Consider my patient who grew up an officer's daughter. If one holds up the use of the couch as a pathway to deeper and freer exploration, it would have been counterintuitive and possibly absurd to expect that, with her, the use of the couch would have resulted in – as it did – a more rigid authority-based transference configuration. Her characterological rigidity actually decreased when sat up and we accessed additional self-other templates, developed when apart from her brother and the context of his military environment.

Notes

1 This paper was originally published in *Contemporary Psychoanalysis* (2015), 51, 624–648, published with permissions by Taylor and Francis.
2 All identifying information about the patients mentioned in this article has been disguised.
3 Although frequency of sessions is typically wedded to the use of the couch in distinguishing a psychoanalysis from other psychodynamic therapies, I chose to limit the focus of this article to the couch procedure only.
4 I have observed that abused patients frequently request increased eye contact, especially toward the end of treatment. My understanding is that the impending separation evokes a need to actually see me seeing them. When staring into the eyes of their abusers they had suffered the unbearable experience of the annihilation of their self. They were invisible in the eyes of the other. To see the analyst seeing them can affirm and strengthen their newly acquired sense of self.
5 As noted previously, she had prior treatment, one time per week, sitting up. She was a savvy New Yorker with many friends in psychoanalysis, which she understood was typically (and correctly!) conducted on the couch.
6 Several informal surveys I conducted revealed that although analysts of all theoretical orientations still advocate the use of the couch, in actuality, a sizable majority of treatments (at all frequencies) are conducted off the couch.

Rethinking the use of the couch 223

7 Although it has received scrutiny, in my opinion, the questioning of the use of the couch has not been challenged nearly as much as other standard bearers of "real" psychoanalysis, such as frequency for example.

8 I purposely use "this way or that" instead of "forward or back" in order to de-stigmatize "back" from its connotation of more pathological. "Back," as in experience that is paranoid/schizoid (Klein), archaic (Kohut), or regressed (Freud), can be a source of enormous creativity and use in evolving newer, expanded ways of being in the world.

9 The arguments that insist on limiting the label "psychoanalysis" exclusively for treatments using the couch are often bolstered by a hidden but powerful motivation to justify the tremendous commitment in time, money and sweat undertaken in psychoanalytic training. The intensive and extensive training, as the rationale goes, is to obtain expertise in a special rarefied form of treatment that is diluted if one considers off the couch treatment under the same umbrella. Use of off the couch treatment also threatens exclusion from the elite club of psychoanalysts.

References

Aron, L. (1996). *A Meeting of Minds: Mutuality in Psychoanalysis*. Hillsdale: Analytic Press.

Bass, A. (2007). When the frame doesn't fit the picture. *Psychoanalytic Dialogues*, 17: 1–27.

Beebe, B. and Lachmann, F. (1992). The contribution of mother–infant mutual influence to the origins of self- and object representations. In N.J. Skolnick and S.C. Warshaw (eds.), *Relational Perspectives in Psychoanalysis* (pp. 83–117). Hillsdale: Analytic Press.

Benjamin, J. (1992). Recognition and destruction: An outline of intersubjectivity. In N.J. Skolnick and S.C. Warshaw (eds.), *Relational Perspectives in Psychoanalysis* (pp. 43–60). Hillsdale: Analytic Press.

Blatt, S.J. (1992). The differential effect of psychotherapy and psychoanalysis on anaclitic and introjective patients: The Menninger psychotherapy research project revisited. *Journal of the American Psychoanalytic Association*, 40: 691–724.

Bordin, E.S. (1966). Free association: An experimental analogue of the psycho analytic situation. In L. Gottschalk and A. Auerbach (eds.), *Methods of Research in Psychotherapy* (pp. 189–208). New York: Appleton-Century-Crofts.

Bromberg, P. (1996). Standing in the spaces: The multiplicity of self and the psychoanalytic relationship. *Contemporary Psychoanalysis*, 32: 509–537.

Davies, J.M. (1994). Love in the afternoon: A relational consideration of desire and dread in the countertransference. *Psychoanalytic Dialogues*, 4: 153–170.

Davies, J.M. (1996). Dissociation, repression and reality testing in the counter-transference: The controversy over memory and false memory in the

224 Neil J. Skolnick

psychoanalytic treatment of adult survivors of childhood sexual abuse. *Psychoanalytic Dialogues*, 6: 189–218.

Davies, J.M. (1998). Repression and dissociation – Freud and Janet: Fairbairn's new model of unconscious process. In N.J. Skolnick and D.E. Scharff (eds.), *Fairbairn: Then and Now* (pp. 53–70). Hillsdale: Analytic Press.

Davies, J.M. and Frawley, M.G. (1994). *Treating the Adult Survivor of Childhood Sexual Abuse*. New York: Basic Books.

Emde, R.N. (1988). Development terminable and interminable: Innate and motivational factors from infancy. *International Journal of Psycho-Analysis*, 69: 23–42.

Fairbairn, W.R.D. (1958). On the nature and aims of psychoanalytic treatment. *International Journal of Psycho-Analysis*, 39: 374–385.

Fenichel, O. (1941). Problems of psychoanalytic technique. *Psychoanalytic Quarterly*, 8: 303–324.

Fosshage, J. (1992). Self psychology: The self and its vicissitudes within a relational matrix. In N.J. Skolnick and S.C. Warshaw (eds.), *Relational Perspectives in Psychoanalysis* (pp. 21–42). Hillsdale: Analytic Press.

Freud, S. (1955). On beginning the treatment (further recommendations on the technique of psycho-analysis I). In J. Strachey (ed.), *The Standard Edition of the Complete Psychological Works of Sigmund Freud* (Vol. 12, pp. 121–144). London: Hogarth Press (original work published 1913).

Gallese, V. (2009). Mirror neurons, embodied simulation, and the neural basis of social identification. *Psychoanalytic Dialogues*, 19: 519–536.

Gedo, J.E. (1995). Channels of communication and the analytic setup. *Psychoanalytic Inquiry* 15: 294–304.

Ghent, E. (1989). Credo: The dialectics of one person and two person psychologies. *Contemporary Psychoanalysis*, 25: 169–211.

Gibson, W.S. (1973). *Hieronymus Bosch*. New York: Thames & Hudson.

Gill, M. (1983). The point of view of psychoanalysis: Energy discharge or person? *Psychoanalysis & Contemporary Thought*, 6: 523–552.

Goldberger, M. (1995). The couch as defense and as potential for enactment. *Psychoanalytic Quarterly*, 64: 23–42.

Hirsch, I. (2008). *Coasting in the Countertransference*. Hillsdale: Analytic Press.

Hoffman, I.Z. (1998). *Ritual and Spontaneity in the Psychoanalytic Process*. Hillsdale: Analytic Press.

Jacobson, J.G. (1995). The analytic couch: Facilitator or sine qua non? *Psychoanalytic Inquiry*, 15: 304–314.

Lichtenberg, J.D. (1995). Forty-five years of psychoanalytic experiences on, behind, and without the couch. *Psychoanalytic Inquiry*, 15: 275–280.

Lichtenberg, J.D., Lachmann, F.M., and Fosshage, J.L. (1992). *Self and Motivational Systems*. Hillsdale: Analytic Press.

Moraitis, G. (1995). Prologue: The relevance of the couch in contemporary psychoanalysis. *Psychoanalytic Inquiry*, 15: 275–280.

Ogden, T. (1986). *The Matrix of the Mind· Object Relations and the Psychoanalytic Dialogue*. Northvale: Jason Aronson.

Ogden, T. (1989). *The Primitive Edge of Experience*. Northvale: Jason Aronson.

Pick, I.B. (1985). Working through in the counter-transference. In E.B. Spillius (ed.), *Melanie Klein Today* (Vol. 51, pp. 34–47). New York: Routledge.

Robertiello, R.C. (1967). Two views on the use of the couch: The couch. *Psychoanalytic Review*, 54A: 69–71.

Schachter, J. and Kachele, H. (2010). The couch in psychoanalysis. *Contemporary Psychoanalysis*, 46: 439–459.

Seligman, S. (2009). Anchoring intersubjective models in recent advances in developmental psychology, cognitive neuroscience, and parenting studies: Introduction to papers by Trevarthen, Gallese, and Ammaniti & Trentini. *Psychoanalytic Dialogues*, 19: 503–506.

Skolnick, N.J. and Warshaw, S.C. (1992). *Relational Perspectives in Psychoanalysis*. Hillsdale: Analytic Press.

Stern, D. (1985). *The Interpersonal World of the Infant*. New York: Basic Books.

Tomasello, M. (1999). *The Cultural Origins of Human Cognition*. Cambridge, MA: Harvard University Press.

Trevarthen, C. (1993). The self born in intersubjectivity: An infant communicating. In U. Neisser (ed.), *The Perceived Self: Ecological and Interpersonal Sources of Self-Knowledge* (pp. 121–173). New York: Cambridge University Press.

Winnicott, D.W. (1951). *Collected Papers: Through Paediatrics to Psychoanalysis*. London: Tavistock.

Wolf, E.S. (1995). Brief notes on using the couch. *Psychoanalytic Inquiry*, 15: 314–324.

Chapter 9

Relational psychoanalysis
An assessment at this time

Neil J. Skolnick

This chapter presents a critique of relational psychoanalysis at this juncture in time, when it has established itself as a major force in psychoanalytic theorizing and practice, and is currently traveling through its middle age. No longer a neophyte seeking to establish its validity amongst the more established psychoanalytic schools, it has yet to consolidate its mature identification. Will it rise to the gravitas of classical psychoanalysis, or recede into an historical footnote?

There have been a growing number of critiques of relational psychoanalytic perspectives to date. Reaching its middle age allows us to consider its usefulness from a more mature, time-tested vantage point, both as a theory and as a treatment modality. Not wanting to be repetitive with much that has already been written, I provide several of my own criticisms, that range from more or less major criticisms to minor pet peeves. Of importance, I reiterate what Susan Warshaw and I maintained in the introduction to our 1992 compendium of relational authors, *Relational Perspectives in Psychoanalysis*. Written to commemorate the inauguration of the relational training track at the NYU postdoctoral program, we noted that there was no one integrated relational theory. Relational psychoanalysts hale from many diverse camps, from object relational, self-psychological, interpersonal, intersubjective, infant research, field theory, neurobiological approaches, neo-Kleinian schools, and others. All share the perspective that the basic building blocks of human development, character formation, motivations and psychopathology are rooted in human relational configurations rather than the psychosexual drives of classical psychoanalysis. The situation remains somewhat the same today. While relational psychoanalysts have more clearly delineated some of the important similarities and differences amongst the different schools, each offering a relational perspective, both theoretically and clinically, we have yet to produce a unified relational theory. While that was arguably the hope back then, a more unified theory has not materialized. That's not necessarily a bad thing. It is what it is, a group of diverse psychoanalytic approaches that have rejected Freud's metapsychological drives as the ultimate explanatory bottom line in human development, motivation and psychopathology, and replaced them with the primary importance of the establishment and maintenance of satisfying human relationships. Drives remain as important variables, but are thought to be shaped by relational configurations and relegated to secondary importance.

I have divided my assessment of current relational theory and practice into a few sections below. Some of my criticisms fall under big "C" Criticisms and some small "c" criticisms, which are probably better thought of as pet peeves. Some apply to psychoanalysis as a whole, and some are more directed to relational psychoanalysis. Many excellent critiques have been written and in particular, have appeared recently in the two edited volumes by Aron, Grand and Slochower (2018a, 2018b). In the interest of not wanting to be repetitive with what has been written, I have tried to focus on issues that have not been previously mentioned.

A plea for a measure of less hubris

This criticism is not directed solely toward relational psychoanalysts but rather toward all of us who do this fascinating though endlessly impossible work.

A good number of years after I completed my own analysis, my aunt, my father's sister, died. When rifling through her papers we discovered my grandfather's naturalization papers. Listed on it were his children – my father, my aunt, my uncle – and Gertrude. Who the hell was Gertrude? We all chimed in at once. Turns out Gertrude was another child of my grandfather's, born of a previous marriage, prior to his marriage to my grandmother. His first wife (Gertrude's mother) had died. So Gertrude was my father's half-sister. Well? So what happened to Gertrude? Our curiosity could not be contained. Turns out she was ejected from the family, my father, with only disgust in his voice, informed us. "Why?" we of course demanded to know. He could only respond sullenly and tersely, "She wasn't good enough for the family," and that was the last we ever heard from my father about Gertrude. He refused to say more. He took the secret of Gertrude to his grave. There being no other living relative who could inform us, we were left to our own unsuccessful internet searches and finally just to our speculations and fantasies. We figured she must have had an out of wedlock child, and left it at that.

But the discovery fell on my ears and soul with a thunderous resonance. When my father was about 8–10 years or so, his older sister, Gertrude, a teenager (we figured), was thrown out of the house and family, never to be heard of again. While my analysis, completed about 30 years ago, was successful on many fronts, there was a question that it never answered, and now it turns out, never could have been answered in analysis because I did not know what I did not know. My father, a reasonable, hardworking and in many ways unpsychologically-minded father of the 1950s, periodically, during my growing up, would disown my sister or me because we, in his mind, had done something unspeakably bad. For example, when my wife and I sent out birth announcements for our first child the announcement read, "Neil Skolnick and Karen Goldberg are thrilled to announce the birth of their daughter . . . " to which he responded after several months sulking in our presence (sulking and not talking to us being his usual announcement of imminent disownment), "People are going to think you are not married." This, despite the fact we had only sent it to their friends who had been to our wedding. So for years I added this periodic disowning to the list of my grievances against my father.

But the knowledge of Gertrude changed all that. I now, many years after my analysis ended, appreciated that my father was traumatized as a latency age young boy. He lost his sister to some unspeakable, shameful sin. Latency age boys, fresh out of their Oedipal[1] resolutions, are often hyper-concerned with absolute rules that govern right and wrong in the world, as is often manifested, for example, in their encyclopedic memory of the rules of baseball. My father, like a good latency age boy, reasoned that if you do not adhere to an absolute right, you are unworthy of continued love and deserve to be abandoned, just as his sister was. Years of my resentment toward my father slowly melted away as I began to experience compassion for his plight in a universe that had been interrupted by a trauma that stamped in a hyper-rigid conception of morality that he, averse to self-exploration, held until his death. We never talked about Gertrude; his shame precluded that. My own sadness was overwhelming, but as is often the case with sadness, it proved less imprisoning than the restraining iron bars of resentment. And it led to a continuous diminution in my own sense of worthlessness and shame, which had been significantly reduced in my previous "concluded" analysis, but never to this extent.

I bring up the story of Gertrude in an attempt to make a plea for a measure of humility as we attempt to assess not only relational theory, but also any set of theories, models or paradigms that guide us in the study and practice of psychoanalysis. We practice an odd, mostly unstated, version of grandiosity to assume that our particular theory of choice will successfully uncover, integrate, explain and synthesize the information we gather about a person, and point us toward successful resolutions in their therapy. There's so much we do not know, or will ever know, or is kept private by the patient, or been lost to a secret, or has been forgotten or distorted, or as the existence of my phantom Aunt Gertrude so vividly demonstrated – we do not even know that we do not know. To me this further lends support to what Guntrip (1975) in his landmark paper, "My experience of analysis with Fairbairn and Winnicott," sagaciously stated, "Theory does not seem to me to be the major concern. It is a useful servant but a bad master liable to produce orthodox defenders of every variety of the faith" (p. 145).

I maintain that relational theories have provided an important correction to the drive based psychoanalytic canon for two reasons in particular. From its inception at the end of the twentieth century, relational psychoanalysis hit the ground running. After years of adhering to a psychoanalytic theory and technique based on a platform rooted in a quasi-biological, metapsychological theory of drives, psychoanalysts of all stripes, or "immigrants," as they were labeled by Jodie Davies (personal communication, c. 1992), flocked to an increased acceptance of a model or paradigm (Skolnick and Warshaw, 1992) of a psychoanalytic science based on human connections, rather than quasi-biological explanations. This shift, in my mind was fueled partially by an increased acceptance of post-modern sensibilities, such as relative truths, as opposed to absolute truths, as well as the experience-near language used by many relational thinkers who eschew an overuse of psychoanalytic jargon. Experience-near language presented a refreshing antidote to the (often) obscuring language of metapsychology.[2] More on this later in this chapter.

I'd like to stress that there was not then, nor is there today, only one unified relational theory. Instead there are a number of theories embracing a relational perspective. I pretty much hold to the same definition of what comprises a relational theory as I did when Susan Warshaw and I wrote, in 1992, in the introduction to our edited volume, *Relational Perspectives in Psychoanalysis*:

As psychoanalysis prepares to enter its second century, a number of prominent scholars have noted the fundamental conceptual shifts that have occurred within the discipline, shifts that many believe present major challenges to the classical metapsychology (see, e.g., Gedo, 1979; Eagle, 1984; Greenberg and Mitchell, 1983; Mitchell, 1988). There is increasing focus on, and acceptance of, the primacy of relationships with others in the development of the personality, with major ramifications for conceptions of psychic structure, theories of motivation and pathogenesis, and clinical technique.

(p. xxiii)

I still agree with what we said then, but would like to note several problems that have arisen by virtue of shifting to a relational sensibility. First and foremost there is a tendency, wish or hope that by focusing on all brands of theory that do not maintain the drives as the ultimate bottom line explanations, that we will ultimately come up with a unified relational theory of human functioning. I emphatically maintain that the puzzle is too vast, too complicated and contains too many uncertain moving parts operating in too many uncertain contexts for such a unifying theory to be viable.[3]

Another problem that has arisen within the relational world has been a tendency, misguided I hold, by different relational camps, to define the construct "relational" according to the narrow perspective of their own camp. Instead of viewing relational as a large tent encompassing a number of theoretical approaches with a relational cast, some approaches have been considered by their adherents to be the sole rightful proprietor of the relational imprimatur. So it has come to pass that some consider relational to mean object relational, others consider it to encompass only intersubjective theory, others field theory, and so forth and so on. This has been but one problem that arose when we abandoned the large tent approach to embracing multiple theories.

When looking to define relational by elevating a single theoretical camp, i.e. intersubjectivity, to encompass the entire endeavor, we run the risk of creating a Rashomon on steroids. Which one of the multiple particular theoretical paradigms do we choose, and how will that in any way create a more useful understanding? I continue to maintain that relational theory is still a work in progress and that it has room for plurality, a number of differing approaches included under its umbrella. They can usefully be seen as existing in tensions with each other, but none can be held up as the predominant identifying essence of the entire relational project.

Here is Emmanuel Ghent writing in the Foreword to the same 1992 volume edited by Susan Warshaw and myself:

> I believe "relational analysis" represents a step in the direction of moving beyond the idiosyncratic languages and conceptions that parented it- an effort to push past the political polemics that separated the speakers of these dialects from one another and an effort to explore the commonalities and the divergencies in the theoretical grouping that came, respectively, to be called interpersonal theory, British object relations theory, self-psychology, and what I would refer to as advanced ego psychology.
>
> (p. xx)

Today, I would add to Ghent's list of camps embracing a relational perspective infant observation research, developmental psychoanalysis, neo-Bionian theory, field theory and some contemporary Kleinian approaches.

I turn now to additional criticisms of the relational project. I present them in no particular order and, again, they could be considered small "c" criticisms as opposed to large "C" critiques of the entire endeavor. Even better, I grouchily refer to them as my "pet peeve pleas."

A plea for a measure of less co-construction

Almost synonymous with a relational approach and seen ubiquitously throughout the relational literature is the assumption that all human thought and affect, conscious and unconscious, and behavior, are co-created. While there are many who write about the universality of co-creation, I find Ogden (1994) to be one of the clearest proponents of this sentiment. Co-creation is an idea that attempts to refute a one-person psychology when attempting to understand all of human development, psychological structure and interpersonal and intersubjective relations. In essence it adheres to the idea that no human thought, action or creative endeavor can exist outside the context within which it occurs.

This idea becomes more complicated in that it is sometimes not clear whether an author is referring to the current context in which something occurs or the developmental origin of the particular something being observed. The roots of co-construction can be located in some versions of Sullivanian Interpersonal psychoanalysis and have found a comfortable home in post-modern philosophy. I have always taken issue with the assumption of the ubiquity of co-construction, especially when considering the clinical situation in which the observation occurs. When analyzing any moment in a psychoanalytic session, the genesis of that moment might lie with the patient, or with the analyst, or it might be co-created by both. Acknowledging that it is rarely clear from whom any interactive moment arises is an imperative I believe we all need to entertain, accept and live with.

I would also add that if we take the confluence of psychoanalysis and temporality seriously, the situation becomes infinitely more complicated. If any moment in the dialogue between a patient and analyst can be considered a melding of past, present and/or future, the context of the dialogue not only is set by the two participants in the treatment space, but now includes the interaction of each participant, potentially operating in three tenses of temporality with the other participant functioning in their three tenses. Given that each participant is possibly functioning in more than one tense at the same time (e.g., past and future) the permutations and combinations of analyst, patient, and temporal tenses of past, present and future creates a virtually unknowable and frankly absurd context for their interactions.

Obviously, I am creating this exercise in absurdity (and overly concrete obsessiveness!) to make a point that to conceive of all clinical interaction as co-constructed is resorting to a limited, most likely unknowable, proposition. As limited as if we would be viewing it all as determined solely by one participant, as in a one-person psychology. In the time-unhinged space of subjectivity and intersubjectivity there's room for a spectrum of influencing factors operating in an untold number of temporal directions. We must rely on our knowledge of the patient, ourselves and circumstances of each to make our best clinical judgment to determine, in the words of Edgar Levinson, "What's going on around here?" Sometimes moments are co-created, and sometimes they are not.

Moreover, at the risk of sounding overly concrete again, we need to also acknowledge that the psychoanalytic situation presents us with two conscious minds interacting with two unconscious minds. In addition, these four minds, two conscious and two unconscious, are interacting at both a singular moment in time and at the same time, at an infinite number of moments in time for each participant, both conscious or unconscious, any of which could include a multitude of other participants. Yikes! It is virtually impossible to track or know which, what, where, when or who. To declare that all is co-created is a monumental assumption that disregards the multitude of alternatives, including, at the minimum, what we are observing might arise from only the analyst or only the patient. No wonder there is an excess of uncertainty in our work. We typically accept the uncertainty and deal the best we can. But we also need to accept the sources of all the error variance in the system and not just assume all is co-created.

Obviously, we cannot be expected to parse out all the participants in any interaction. We can hardly be expected to know whom we are dealing with at any moment in time. But I think we can initially reduce the possibilities to a manageable choice by considering that what we might be experiencing at any moment could be influenced more by you, or me, or the both of us. And the choices are not necessarily mutually exclusive, but sometimes they are. For example and hypothetically, a patient starts a session talking about an incident from the night before. We are attempting to listen on the many levels, dimensions and registers we typically listen, but our thoughts keep returning to the actual medical diagnosis hanging in the balance of a diagnostic test just performed on a close relative, the results of which will be unknown for at least a week. Can we say the distraction will affect our listening? Probably. Can we say our being distracted is influenced by the issue the patient is talking about? Maybe. Those who adhere to the conceit that all is co-created might assume that the form of our distraction is related to the incident the patient has brought up. I strongly take issue with this assumption. I think our distraction in such a situation belongs solely to ourselves and has not been co-created. As the session continues there is the possibility that where the patient continues might be influenced by our being distracted, and then the situation can be considered co-created. And so forth and so on we need to be prepared for an oscillation in the genesis of a session swinging back and forth between a one- and two-person event, but not just assume all is co-created.

On a larger philosophical stage the concept of co-construction arises out of the post-modern turn and appears to wreak destruction on old-fashioned notions born of the Enlightenment, such as individual free will, individuality and, in the words of contemporary post-modern critic, Jon Mills (2017):

What we see in abundant today in the analytic literature are constant references to relatedness in lieu of intrapsychic life, and emphasis on intersubjectivity over internality, constructivism versus discovery, context and perspective rather than universal proclamations, contingencies contra absolutes, skepticism over certainty, consensus—not truth—and conscious experience over the primacy of unconscious mentation.

(p. 314)

I do take issue with Mills' sweeping criticisms of post-modern sensibilities. I would prefer to compare modern and post-modern ideas dialectically, but I do think he states a healthy corrective against the occasional tyranny of the post-modern certainty about co-construction at the expense of alternate sensibilities in relational theorizing.

An interesting corrective to the co-construction issue has been provided by the Boston Change Process Study Group (BCPSG) (2010). Stating that, "The word *construction* implies a directed process in which preformed elements are brought together according to an *a priori* plan," they argue for substituting co-*created* for co-*construction*, because when the process of co-*creativity* is at play, the elements are brought together more or less spontaneously without prior plan or design. This allows for a degree of uncertainty and unpredictability, which more closely matches the therapeutic situation, "as the therapist and patient attempt to mutually apprehend and align their emerging intentions and initiatives in the service of a sustained shared direction in the interaction" (p. 103)

Thankfully, they add, "Parenthetically it must be mentioned that not every direction that could be co-created would be healing or constructive for the patient." I would like to underline this last statement. Just because our theories make logical sense, just because they demonstrate a degree of internal reliability, even validity, does not mean they have clinical efficacy. Not only do we often forget this, when we stand on soapboxes singing the praises of the particular theory to which we are wedded, it fosters our grandiosity, preventing us from admitting to mistakes and failures. It can also lead to biased clinical reports, tweaked to conform to substantiation of our favorite theories. We may do this for personal gratification or to please political alliances, both in the service of career advancement, rather than patient care.

A plea for a measure (literally) of validity

It is well recognized that psychoanalysis falls at the crossroads of many disciplines and is not just a purely empirical scientific pursuit. It overlaps realms of study including, but not limited to: philosophy, social and natural sciences, art, anthropology, gender studies, and developmental and child psychology. All of the above have made useful contributions to a psychoanalytic discipline. As such the construct of "validity" has peppered our papers in a number of different ways. I am not insistent on psychoanalysts providing more validity for our constructs, many of which cannot be held up as scientifically valid (I dare anyone to provide data attempting to validate such concepts as the anti-libidinal ego, or even just "ego" for that matter).

However, when we do attempt to refer to the scientific validity of any of our constructs, we often do it in a sloppy, meaningless manner. This criticism is most likely a holdover born from my experience in conducting basic science research and working from a scientific empirical model that puts a great emphasis on the importance of the demonstrated validity of our concepts and constructs. Scientific validity in such a pursuit refers to the empirical demonstration that the construct we are attempting to validate exists in objective reality and has a relationship resembling other similar constructs (convergent validity) and is different from constructs purporting to measure a different construct (discriminate validity). Let's say we were attempting to develop a paper and pencil scale to measure one's proclivity to the affect shame. At the same time we are developing the scale, we also would be providing validity for the construct of "proclivity to shame." We would want to provide convergent validity with other measures of shame, e.g., self-report measures. Self-report measures of shame would need to demonstrate a moderate to high correlation with our new pencil and paper measure of "proclivity to shame." Conversely, we would want to demonstrate what shame is not. We would want to demonstrate low or no correlations with, let's say, measures of embarrassment or guilt. This would be a measure of discriminate validity. This might be a simple review for many who have studied validity in test construction, but not necessarily familiar to those from other disciplines who become psychoanalysts.

So what's the point? Our psychoanalytic literature is filled with examples of precedence masquerading as validity. Just because a construct, e.g., "the third," has a long, proud history of being used, it does not necessarily mean that it has acquired the status of scientific validity. I have no difficulty with employing constructs which do not exhibit scientific validity, like the "third," which can be endlessly useful in describing our experiences, the experiences of our patients, and the interactions between us (i.e., Benjamin, 2004; Ogden, 1994). But my beef is with those who speak of such constructs as *scientifically* valid because of the frequency with which we speak of them, their precedence in the literature, perhaps. They have never been subjected to the required scientific tests of convergent and divergent validity. Many of our psychoanalytic constructs hold prominent places in our theories, such as projective identification, enactments, internal saboteurs, etc., which is fine with me, but we cannot refer to them as scientifically valid. Many of these proposed constructs I use freely in my work and my writing. But without rigorous testing they cannot be considered either empirically valid, or not. Therefore we need to be humble when criticizing others who use these constructs as well as those who do not.

I need to stress that I have no trouble working with variables that are not scientifically valid. In our work, as I have noted, we appeal to a number of rigorous disciplines, including philosophy, art, history, chaos theory, etc. that either are not concerned with the issue of scientific validity, or they adhere to alternate models of science, such as hermeneutics. They all can enrich the texture and depth of our work. My objection is when the concept of validity is incorrectly invoked to either prove the truth of one's convictions or damn the convictions of those from another psychoanalytic camp. We need to accept that our constructs, and theirs, are *both not scientifically valid*, but they can be theoretically and clinically useful. Therefore, we cannot base our criticisms of constructs from other schools of psychoanalysis on their lack of validity. That's not a valid criticism! We might not believe in them, but that says nothing about validity – just belief. Projective identification is often spoken of by some schools contemptuously as not a valid construct, and by other schools as valid because of its ubiquitous usage. Neither side is correct.

A plea for a measure of lucidity

Q: What do you get if you cross a member of the Mafia with a Postmodernist?

A: An offer you can't understand.

This joke pokes good-humored fun at the style of writing adopted by many who write from a post-modern perspective. It can equally be applied to some of the excessive jargon employed across all models of psychoanalysis. But being allied with the relational school, I'd like to focus on the tendency of some relational analysts to employ a postmodern turn in their writing style.

Part of the problem, for me, is that those purporting to write from a post-modernist style are confusing post-modern principles with a style of writing that aims to obscure rather than elucidate. Relational psychoanalysis and post-modernism make good intellectual partners. Relational sensitivities borrow a number of tenets from post-modernism, including, though not limited to:

1. There is no objective reality or truth. Rather, truths are relative and constructed. They reside in the individual interpretations of reality. Therefore, universal truths and categories are not particularly valid and are subjected to intense skepticism.
2. The skepticism extends to the universal validity of hierarchies, binaries, categories and stable identities.
3. There is no such thing as human nature. Instead, all human behavior and psychology are socially determined and constructed.
4. Language does not refer to a reality outside itself.

It is the last tenet listed above, that language does not refer to a reality outside itself, that I have the most trouble with when relational authors write from a post-modern perspective. They will often attempt to present their ideas by constructing a language which obscures conventional meanings and deconstructs formal rules of language. I understand the advantages of postmodern *theory* to tear down encrusted meanings, linkages, attitudes and beliefs and make space for new constructions, arrangements and orderings of beliefs, attitudes, even truths.

But I think it is a mistake for relational psychoanalysts to overuse this style of writing. In that it can serve to obscure rather than elucidate clearly what an author is attempting to say, it can be overly confusing to a reader not schooled in the principles of post-modernism. This would include most psychoanalysts from other orientations and probably a fair number of relational psychoanalysts as well. It would also include members of allied professions and disciplines (e.g., medicine, nursing) as well as the general public. The consequence of this would mean that we would have a hard time raising interest in others about what we are about and what we try to accomplish. If we are attempting to reach out to a wider and wider audience who could potentially benefit from our craft, it does not serve our purposes to represent our discipline in cumbersome, difficult to comprehend, obscuring language that has undertones of elitism, if not intellectual discrimination. If we want to keep psychoanalysis alive as a viable alternative for people in need of relief from their pain, suffering and self-defeating patterns, we need to be clear, and write clearly, about what we do.

A look toward the future

Relational psychoanalysis continues to be massively popular as a theoretical and clinical orientation within psychoanalytic communities. Witness the large number of psychologists holding memberships in divisions and sections of the American Psychological Association concerned with relational perspectives, as well as the large national and international membership of the International Association for Relational Psychoanalysis and Psychotherapy (IARPP).

However if an informal survey of my colleagues provides any indication, relational psychoanalysis as a discipline has reached a plateau. Relational journals such as *Psychoanalytic Dialogues: The International Journal of Relational Perspectives* continue to be very well subscribed. Field theory has provided a welcomed new turn, and many are flocking to the ideas of Bion in a revival of interest in the advances he contributed to Kleinian theory.

But I do hear increasing grumbles about the lack of much new being said and the sentiment that relational articles are becoming strikingly similar, offering little in terms of an advance of ideas or material. I think I am safe in making the prediction that relational psychoanalysis is here to stay for the foreseeable future, but I do think it is in need of an infusion of new ideas and energy to keep it vital and groundbreaking. I list, for the reader's perusal and criticisms, several suggestions for future direction:

1   We need to promote younger members in our ranks and not discriminate or exclude them. We need to celebrate their creativity, no matter how far afield it might seem. When I was in training it was a common complaint that our senior analysts were fond of eating their young.

They would at times harshly criticize aspiring analysts, if not totally block their promotions within the field. Sometimes, of course, this represented an appropriate competitive weeding out process, but quite frequently it had more sinister motives, particularly in the realm of envy, as younger analysts were moving toward center stage while envious more senior analysts were moving off the stage. Envy sometimes operates in the eye of the beholder and its perception an expression of the anxieties and insecurities of aspiring professionals. But we also know that envy for youth can be a very real phenomena, impeding their promotions and advancements. We need to be mindful of not repeating the mistakes of the envious.

2 We need to include more peripheral disciplines under the relational tent, rather than treating them as the hated "other." We could revive interest in theories long ago scorned. Maybe Carl Rogers, or Franz Alexander or Fritz Pearls might have something to say to relational theory when resurrected in today's relational context. Jean-Baptiste Lamarck, long discredited in the field of genetics, is being revisited seriously by the field of epigenetics, as it attempts to define mechanisms involved in the transmission of environmental events occurring in one generation that affect the genetic expression of traits in the next.

Resurrecting discredited or out of fashion theories to advance relational theory today would provide an apt exercise in temporal time travel as we venture to the past in order to advance into the future.

3 Our understanding of the links between the study of evolution and development has undergone an interesting about face over the course of the last century. Once thought to be closely linked, biologists, including Charles Darwin, were quite interested in developmental phenomena and consequently became highly influential to Freud as he formulated his foundational thinking about psychoanalysis. This was a short lived collaboration as biological constructs of evolution and development veered apart from each other and, not inconsequently, further afield from psychoanalysis (Hofer, 2014). But as Hofer points out in the same (2014) seminal article, exciting new recent discoveries have promoted a rapprochement between the long diverging studies of development and evolutionary biology in the creation of a new field familiarly referred to as "evo-devo." Furthermore, and pertinent to my argument, this new alliance has returned biological ideas closer to those of psychoanalysis, particularly regarding the role of early

parent–infant interactions in influencing child development. Beebe (2014), in a commentary on Hofer's work, declares that:

> Myron Hofer's integration of research and theory into a synthesized view of evolution and development is a powerful and elegant achievement. He argues that the epigenetic revolution provides a way to integrate evolution and development, which were considered separate processes for most of the twentieth century. Moreover, Hofer argues that our understanding of the effects of early experience gleaned through animal models provides a new, rich biological underpinning to the psychoanalytic theory of the effects of early experience – a way to re-integrate biology and psychoanalysis
>
> (p. 23)

After a century in which psychoanalysis and biology largely ignored each other, the advances in evo-devo research have brought about radical change, especially with the advent of the burgeoning study of epigenetics, which has marked implications for the understanding of the connections between the biological and the psychoanalytic. At the center of this revolution has been the discovery of the role of a number of processes at the molecular/genetic level in which the expression of an organism's genetic make-up can be influenced by environmental changes and regulatory manipulations that effect the development of the individuals. Not only have animal model studies demonstrated that early changes in mother–infant interaction can have marked effects on an animal's development that persist into adulthood, but the effects can persist into future generations (Skolnick, Ackerman, Hofer and Weiner, 1980). The mechanisms for the persistence of the environmentally induced developmental changes appear to operate at the molecular/genetic level and have striking effects on the *expression* of the genetic material, not the genetic material itself. As Hofer (2014) puts it:

> our new knowledge of the nature and role of genes, and of the *many novel mechanisms for their regulation during development* has restored our understanding of biology to a position much more supportive of Freud's formulation of psychoanalytic theory than at any time since the end of the nineteenth century.
>
> (p.13; italics mine)

Eric Kandel (2012), the Nobel prize winning psychoanalyst has been promoting the integration of psychoanalytic research with the advances of the evo-devo based research, especially at the level of molecular neuroscience. My knowledge of these findings is rudimentary, but it seems to me that it is just a short theoretical and epistemological leap to subjecting ideas garnered from relational psychoanalysis to the principles of mind being discovered and plotted by findings at the molecular level of evo-devo research. In looking toward the future of Relational Psychoanalysis, this suggests to me that we need to put dedicated efforts toward substantiating relational principles with evidence from neuropsychological research.

Temporally, I have moved far afield from neuropsychology in my career, where I have invested my passion, interest and efforts toward becoming the best practitioner, teacher and supervisor of psychoanalysis that I could become. While I have tossed an occasional glance toward the neuropsychology world, I have not invested myself in it as I had earlier in my career. However, as I write this I am not unaware that through a measure of irony and a temporal trick of time, my interests have travelled full circle! I find myself at this juncture in time promoting the new fertile field of neuropsychology in which I recommend that in order to keep relational psychoanalysis vital it is an imperative to explore the links between relational psychoanalysis and biology, links that I explored almost 40 years ago.

Notes

1 While I do put stake in the existence of a set of Oedipal conflicts, I do not regard its genesis as a sexual inevitability, the resolution of which results in "normal" sexuality. I consider it a construction occurring as the child attempts to work out its own multiple, and sometimes competing identifications – physical, sexual, gender and otherwise, as it first notices and then gets entwined in, the complicated and competing engagements with both parents.
2 While many who write from a post-modern perspective use obscuring language, post-modernist philosophy itself does not dictate the necessity of using language that obscures.
3 See an interesting conversation between A. Bass and A. Harris in Aron, Grand and Slochower (2018b).

References

Aron, L., Grand, S. and Slochower, J. (2018a). *De-idealizing Relational Theory: A Critique from Within*. New York and London: Routledge.

Aron, L., Grand, S. and Slochower, J. (2018b). *Decentering Relational Theory: A Comparative Critique*. New York and London: Routledge.

Beebe, B. (2014). Myron Hofer's synthesis of evolution and development: A commentary. *Neuropsychoanalysis*, 16(1): 23–28.

Benjamin, J. (2004). Beyond doer and done to: An intersubjective view of thirdness. *Psychoanalytic Quarterly*, LXXIII: 5–46.

Boston Change Process Study Group (2009). The "something more" than interpretation revisited: sloppiness and co-creativity in the psychoanalytic encounter. revisited: sloppiness and co-creativity in the psychoanalytic encounter. *Journal of the American Psychoanalytic Association*, 53(3): 693–729.

Boston Change Process Study Group (2010). *Change in Psychotherapy: A Unifying Paradigm*. New York: Norton.

Eagle, M. (1984). *Recent Developments in Psychoanalysis*. New York: McGraw-Hill.

Gedo, J. (1979). *Beyond Interpretation*. New York: International Universities Press.

Greenberg, J. and Mitchell, S.A. (1983). *Object Relations in Psychoanalytic Theory*. Cambridge, MA: Harvard University Press.

Guntrip, H. (1975). My experience of analysis with Fairbairn and Winnicott. *International Review of Psycho-Analysis*, 2: 145–156.

Hofer, M.A. (2014). The emerging synthesis of development and evolution: A new biology for psychoanalysis. *Neuropsychoanalysis*, 16: 3–22.

Kandel, E.R. (2012). Biology and the future of psychoanalysis: A new intellectual framework for psychiatry revisited. *Psychoanalytic Review*, 99: 607–644.

Mills, J. (2017). Challenging relational psychoanalysis: A critique of postmodernism and analyst self-disclosure. *Psychoanalytic Perspectives*, 14: 313–335.

Mitchell, S.A. (1988). *Relational Concepts in Psychoanalysis*. Cambridge, MA: Harvard University Press.

Ogden, T.H. (1994). The analytic third: Working with intersubjective clinical facts. *International Journal of Psycho-Analysis*, 72: 593–605.

Skolnick, N.J. and Warshaw, S.C. (1992). *Relational Perspectives in Psychoanalysis*. New Jersey: The Analytic Press.

Skolnick, N.J., Ackerman, S.H., Hofer, M.A. and Weiner, H. (1980). Vertical transmission of acquired ulcer susceptibility in the rat. *Science*, 208: 1161–1163.

Index

Abraham, Karl 187
abuse 26, 35, 73–75, 133, 177, 179, 202–205
acquired characteristics, inheritance of 5, 47, 239–240; ulcer susceptibility in rats 40–43, 49–54
adaptive self 181–182
afterwardness 15
age/aging 26–27, 172–175, 183–189, 193, 195
ambivalence 86, 87–88, 99–100, 104, 105, 106, 107, 108; and bad objects 122; and depressive position 88–89, 90, 104; and splitting 105–106
analyst disturbance 212
analyst/patient relationship: age and aging 172–173, 183–193, 195; good object and dynamic identification 124, 126–134, 182–183; sexuality 134, 202–206; uniqueness of 147–148, 152; withheld secrets 64–65, 68–69; *see also* termination of therapy; transference/countertransference
analytic third 127, 154, 167
annihilation anxiety 24–25, 86, 87, 90, 106, 137, 139
après coup 13, 15, 116, 200
Aristotle 9
arrow of time 10, 19
attunement 125, 127, 136–140; and parentified children 171, 180
avant-coup 15–16

bad objects 94–95, 96, 97–98, 106, 107–108, 122, 123, 126; idealized and exciting 101, 106, 122, 123

Baranger M. and Baranger, W. 14
Bass, Anthony 4, 152, 207
Beebe, Beatrice 4, 240
biology, psychoanalysis and 239–241
Bion, W. 134, 147, 238
Birksted-Breen, Dana 11, 15, 116
Blatt, S.J. 217
body ego 20–21
Bollas, C. 16, 147, 155
Boston Change Process Study Group 113, 234
Bromberg, P. 4, 154

cancellations, patient 199
central ego 85, 96, 98, 102–103, 106, 107, 123
change processes 113–117
children: acquisition of a sense of time 20–22, 23–24, 89–90; modulation of moods 36–37; object relations theories 85–90, 92–109, 122–125; oral stage 104–108; and parental love 125, 135, 137; resilience in 171, 178–179, 181, 194; and secrets 63–64, 66–67, 73–75; trauma 96, 228
Chronos 12–13, 23–27, 143, 144, 146, 199
clinical examples of: annihilation fantasies 161–162; disappearing patients 166; dynamic identification 129–134; empathic attunement 35–37, 138–140; lack of parental love 136; paranoid-schizoid states 34–37; refusal to acknowledge time constraints 25–28; resilience 171–175, 177–178, 179–181, 182–186, 188–195; returning patients

30–34, 162; secrets and secrecy 70–72, 75–76, 77–81; sexual transference/countertransference 202–206; stalking behaviour 30–31, 78–79, 80
co-creation theory 231–234
conflict, adaptive development and 89, 107–108
consistency of caregiving 23–24, 26
continuity of shared memory 28–29
cortisol 43
couch technique 7, 199; critiques of 207–208, 210–213, 216–222; defensive function 212; extent of use 208; Freud 208–209, 210–211; justifications for 208–211, 213–215; and patient needs 200, 212, 216–222; in psychoanalytic heritage 207–216; radical approaches to 217–218; and regression 214–215; and relational model 210–211, 214, 218, 219, 221; and "sicker" patients 216–217, 218; and time 200; and transference/countertransference 203–206, 209, 211, 212, 219; and visual contact 200, 203, 204, 205, 206, 209, 212–214, 217, 219
countertransference *see* transference/countertransference

Darwin, Charles 5, 41–42, 239
Davies, Jody Messler 4, 6, 57, 154, 207
death: fear and denial of 26–27, 174, 185, 188, 193; Freud and Klein on 166–167; as metaphor for termination 17, 143–144, 151, 152–153, 154–155, 156, 158–160, 166–167
death instinct 86, 92, 107, 114, 144
defense mechanisms 95, 122, 123; splitting 85–87, 88, 90, 98, 105–107
depressive positions 86–89, 90, 100, 104, 107, 194; false (Schafer) 164
determinism 144
disease susceptibility, acquired 40–43, 41–43, 49–54
disorders of temporality 15
doubt 122, 123; *see also* ambivalence
dread 60
dreaming 13–14

drive theory 2, 8, 58, 113–114, 115, 145, 198–199, 226–227
dynamic identification 125–134, 182–183
dynamic structure 125–126

early maternal separation in rats 5, 40–43, 49–54
ego and superego 11–12, 20–21, 85, 96, 98, 102–103, 106, 107, 123, 126
Einstein, Albert 10, 12–13
elderly patients 174–175, 183–189, 192–193, 195
empathic attunement 125, 127, 136–140; and parentified children 171, 181
environmental effects on gene expression 5, 40–43, 47, 239–240; see also epigenetic phenomena
envy 186, 193, 239
epigenetic phenomena 5, 40–43, 47, 239–240
eternity 145–146
Europa Europa (film) 67–68
evo-devo research 239–241
evolutionary biology 5, 41–43, 47, 239–240
exciting objects 101, 106, 122, 123
experience-near language 229
eye contact 200, 203, 204–205, 206, 209, 212–214, 217, 219

Fairbairn, W.R.D. 84–85; divergences with Klein 92–95; on doctrinaire orientation 147, 198, 211–212; dynamic structure 125–126; on the id 92; infantile dependence period 104–105, 106; on loving relationships 125, 135, 137; object relations theory 74, 85–90, 94–99, 100–109, 121–125; redefinition of Freudian concepts 58; on the therapeutic relationship 124; use of jargon 58, 85
false memories 29–30
false self 171, 172, 181–182
fantasy 3
Fenichel, O. 217
Ferenczi, Sándor 163
Field Theory 14
Fonagy, P. 15
fragmentation 145–146

Index

frames of time 23–27
free association 209–210, 218
Freud, Sigmund: body ego 20; couch technique 208–209, 210–211; death and mourning 153, 166–167; and doctrinaire orientation 197–198; drive theory 58, 114, 198–199; elderly patients 187; evolutionary biology 239; love and sex 134–135; secrets 61, 68–69; termination of therapy 149–150, 163; time 11, 13, 155
Fromm, Erich 208
future time 12, 15–16, 60

Ghent, Emmanuel 4, 231
Goldberger, M. 212, 221
good objects 85, 87–88, 95–98, 107–108; clinical evidence of repression 99–109; defined 121–122; *vs.* idealized and exciting objects 123; origins of 122–123; and the therapeutic relationship 124–129
Green, Andre 11
Greenberg 45, 46–47, 57
Greenson, R. 69, 112
Gross, A. 62
Guntrip, H. 229

Hartocollis, P. 21
hate 36, 104, 108
Hawking, Stephen 10
Hirsch, I. 212
Hofer, Myron A. 239–240
Hoffman, Eva 9, 19
Hoffman, Irwin 154–155, 167
hope 60, 90

id 92
idealized objects 122, 123
idealizing transference 34–35, 134
identification, dynamic 125–134, 182–183
incest 203–205
infantile dependence period 104–105, 106; *see also* oral stage
intimacy: and secret-keeping 67–68; taboo on 135

Jacobson, J.G. 217–218
James, William 21
jargon 58, 85, 229, 236–238

Kachele, H. 209, 218
Kairos 11, 13, 23, 24, 28–33, 144, 173, 199–200; eternity and fragmentation 145–146
Kandel, Eric 241
Khan, M.M.R. 63–64
Klein, Melanie: on death and mourning 166–167; depressive position 12, 86–89, 90, 100, 104, 107, 109, 194; divergences with Fairbairn 92–95, 107–108, 122–123; good objects 107–108, 122–123; love and sex 134–135; paranoid/schizoid position 12, 34–37, 86, 125, 137–140, 215
Kuhn, Thomas 45–47
Kumpfer, K.L. 178

Lamarck, Jean-Baptiste 41–42, 239
language: obscuring 229, 236–238; shift in theoretical terminology 58, 115, 118
latency age 228
lateness 24–26, 199
Levenson, Edgar 208
Lichtenberg, J.D. 215, 216–217
life instinct 86, 122, 144
linear and non-linear time 10, 12–13, 15, 23–25, 116; and termination of therapy 144–145, 157
Loewald, Hans 11–12, 144–146
love 134–136; and ambivalence 87–88, 104
Lyons-Ruth, K. 113, 114

Margolis, G.J. 62
maternal separation in rats 5, 40–43, 49–54
Meares, R. 64
measurement of time 13
Meissner, William 9–10, 20, 200
memories: recovered 99–101, 203; and retrospect 15, 29–33, 146, 167–168
Mills, Jon 233–234
Mitchell, S. 12, 45, 46–47, 57, 95, 108, 134
Modell, A.H. 13
moment in time, elusiveness of 57–58, 116
Moraitis, G. 208, 209
mother-infant interactions 15, 16–17, 20–22, 23–24, 96, 155, 213, 240
movement, time and 9–10, 21

246 Index

nachträglichkeit 13, 15, 31–32, 146, 200
narcissism 24–25, 181
neuroscience 213, 241
neuroses 63

object relating (Winnicott) 24
object *vs.* somatic time 16–17, 155–156
Oedipal conflict 186
Ogden, T.H.: ambivalence and splitting 87, 88; analytic third 127, 154, 167; co-creation theory 231; dreaming 14; internalization of object relationships 96–97; on Klein's psychic positions 12, 137–138, 215
oral stage 104–108

paranoid/schizoid position 34–37, 86, 125, 137–140, 215
parentified children 171, 180
Parsons, M. 14, 15–16
passion 102–103
past time: as deterministic 144
phone therapy sessions 161
Piaget, Jean 20
Pick, Irma 212
Plotkin, Frieda 188
post-modernism 237
present time, elusiveness of 57–58, 116
Priel, B. 22, 155
psychoanalysis: doctrinaire orientation 197–198, 211–212; multi-disciplinary 235, 239–241
punctuality 24–26, 199

rage 138–140
regression 214–215
relational psychoanalysis 2–4, 57, 229–231; and classical techniques 118, 206–207, 210–211; and co-construction 231–234; criticisms of 226–238; defined 229–230; and drive theory 2, 8, 58, 113–114, 115, 226–227, 229; future of 238–241; plurality of approaches 7–8, 57, 198–199, 226–227, 229–231; scientific validity 235–236; theoretical jargon 58, 115, 118, 229, 236–238

relative time 12–13
relative *vs.* absolute truth 2, 16, 45–47, 119, 229, 237; *see also* doubt
repetition compulsion 114
repression 85, 88, 95; of good objects 85, 98, 101–103, 106, 108–109; and secret-keeping 62–63
resilience: and age/aging 172–175, 188–189, 193, 195; defined 178; and depressive position 194; and dynamic identification 182–183; and false self 171–172, 180–182; individual and environmental factors 170, 172, 178–179, 194; and inner world experience 179–180; in parentified children 171, 180
retrospect *see nachträglichkeit*
Robertiello, R.C. 207
Rubens, R.L. 96, 98, 102–103

Schachter, J. 209, 218
Schafer, R. 164
science, philosophy of 44–47
scientific validity 235–236
secrets 6, 59–61, 64–65; announced but withheld 68–72; ego psychology 62–63; Khan 63–64; meant to be shared 64, 65–68; object relations perspective 63–64; relational perspective 64–65, 81–82; secrecy as a character style 75–81; shameful 72–75, 203–204, 228
self-hatred 73–75
self, sense of time and 20–24, 155
Seligman, Stephen 11, 14, 22, 170
sense of time: development of 20–24, 155; disordered 15, 24–26, 34–37; *see also* eternity; fragmentation
sexual abuse 35, 73, 202–205, 219
sexual drive 134–135
sexual seduction 203, 205–206
shameful secrets 72–75, 203–204, 228
somatic *vs.* object time 16–17, 155–156
spatial perception, time and 21
splitting 85–87, 88, 90, 98, 105–107, 122, 123
Stern, D. 13, 15
subjective time *see Kairos;* somatic *vs.* object time

Sullivan, Harry Stack 208
Sulzberger, C.F. 62
superego 12
Suttie, Ian 135

technique, issues in 118–120, 207, 215–216; *see also* couch technique
temporal disorders 15
termination of therapy: and co-construction 166–168; and consolidation 160–163; death and mourning metaphor 17, 143–144, 151, 152–153, 154–155, 156, 158–160, 166–167; Freud 143, 149–150, 163, 166–167; and linear *vs.* non-linear time 143–146, 155; and relational model 17–19, 143, 150, 156–157; return of patients after 17–18, 28–33, 146, 154, 156, 157–160, 162; successful and unsuccessful 149–150, 163–166
time 9–10; being on time 24–26; *Chronos vs. Kairos* 11, 12–13, 23–33, 143, 144, 146, 173, 199–200; developing a sense of 20–24, 155; elusiveness of 57–58, 116; eternity and fragmentation 145–146; linear *vs.* non-linear 10, 12–13, 19–20, 23, 116; and paranoid/schizoid states 34–37;

and psychic structures 11–12; somatic *vs.* object 16–17, 155–156
time frames 23–27
timelessness 13, 14–17, 35–37, 155, 172–173
transference/countertransference: and age 172–174, 184–187, 193, 195; and couch technique 203–206, 209, 211, 212, 219; sexual 202–206; shift to relational perspectives 112–113
transitional phenomena 66, 77
trauma: cross-generational effects of 43; and hope 90; and parental responsiveness 95, 96; and perception of time 15, 35; and secrets 64, 73–74, 228; sexual 35, 202–205, 219; and successful analyses 150; and use of couch technique 219
truth, relative *vs.* absolute 16, 45–47, 119, 229, 237; *see also* doubt

unconscious good objects 96–109; clinical evidence for 99–104
unconscious past 144

Warshaw, Susan 4, 7, 57, 226, 229–230
Winnicott, D.W. 14, 16–17, 23–24, 58, 66, 94, 171
Wolstein, Ben 208